To Ardelle Striker
in appreciation for her encouragement and friendship

ROMANTIC STAGES

ROMANTIC STAGES

Set and Costume Design in Victorian England

by ALICIA FINKEL

McFarland & Company, Inc., Publishers
Jefferson, North Carolina, and London

British Library Cataloguing-in-Publication data are available

Library of Congress Cataloguing-in-Publication Data

Finkel, Alicia, 1934–
    Romantic stages : see and costume design in Victorian England / by
Alicia Finkel.
        p.   cm.
    Includes bibliographical references and index.
    ISBN 0-7864-0234-2 (lib. bdg. : 50# alk. paper) ∞
    1. Theaters—Great Britain—Stage-setting and scenery—
History—19th century.   2. Costume—Great Britain—History—19th
century.   3. Set designers—Great Britain.   4. Costume designers—
Great Britain.   5. Romanticism.   I. Title.
PN2087.G7F56   1996
792'.025'094109034—dc20   96-639
                                                                                    CIP

Manufactured in the United States of America

McFarlrand & Company, Inc., Publishers
  Box 611, Jefferson, North Carolina 28640

Contents

Preface

THE PURPOSE OF THIS BOOK, which was originally planned as a chronological study of set and costume design in the Victorian era, is to demonstrate the pervasive influence of the Romantic movement well beyond the 1830s, the decade when most scholars consider it to have become extinct. While doing research, I discovered to my profound fascination that virtually every aspect of theatrical production from the mid–nineteenth century to the beginning of World War I had been touched by the same aesthetic concerns associated with Romanticism, particularly those in the realm of the visual arts.

By focusing on the work of some of the most notable Victorian and Edwardian actor-managers, and the designers with whom they collaborated in a series of productions, I hope to evoke for the reader that romantic mood which, like a golden thread, may be followed through their theatrical endeavors.

This book is also a personal search for the origins of the art of stage design as a profession, and a long overdue homage to the pioneers in set and costume design from the perspective of a practicing designer.

My debt to the work of other historians, of both the nineteenth and twentieth centuries, is incalculable. Their detailed investigations of particular subjects—art, theatre, social history—made it possible for me to discover and trace the relationship between Romanticism and the theatre. Both the specialist and the general reader may find further topics of interest by consulting the books and articles cited in the notes.

Research for this book was made possible by two grants from the National Endowment for the Humanities: "Travel to Collections" in 1985, and "Summer Stipend" in 1986, as well as several grants from the University of Connecticut Research Foundation between 1983 and 1994. I am extremely grateful to those institutions for their support.

It is a pleasure to thank members of libraries and museums that assisted me on this project: Christopher Robinson, keeper of the University of Bristol Theatre Collection; Isobel Sinden of the Victoria and Albert Museum Picture Library; Allison Derrett, assistant registrar of the Royal Archives at

Windsor Castle; Claire Hudson, head of Library and Information Services, and Andrew Kirk, curatorial assistant, at the Theatre Museum; Christopher Webster of the copyrights office at the Tate Gallery; Dr. Jeanne T. Newlin, curator of the Harvard Theatre Collection; and the staffs of the British Library and the Colindale Newspaper Library.

I am particularly grateful to Mr. Teddy Craig for his hospitality the two lovely afternoons I spent with him at his house in Aylesbury in the spring and summer of 1986, talking about his grandparents, Ellen Terry and Edward William Godwin; for showing me some of his illustrious family's heirlooms; and for reading a draft of my article on his grandfather. I would also like to thank Miss Sybil Rosenfeld for making time in her busy schedule to grant me an interview and generously providing me with a copy of her article on Alma Tadema's designs for *Coriolanus*.

For permission to quote from copyrighted material, I must thank the following publishers: Greenwood Publishing Group, for quotations from *Personal Reminiscences of Henry Irving*, by Bram Stoker; John Murray Publishers, for quotations from *The Gothic Revival*, by Sir Kenneth Clark; Little, Brown and Company, for quotations from *Classic, Romantic and Modern*, by Jacques Barzun; and Random House, for quotations from *The Social History of Art*, by Arnold Hauser. I also thank Russell Jackson, editor, for allowing me to use excerpts from several articles published in *Theatre Notebook*.

I am most in debt to Dr. Ardelle Striker, who, long before I ever considered writing anything, much less a book, encouraged me to try and continued to lend her help and advice with great patience through the years. I appreciate the helpful comments of all my friends and colleagues who read the manuscript at different stages of development, among them professors Gary English, Jerry Krasser, and the late Valerie Schor.

Last but not least, I am grateful to Jack Nardi and Jim Fulton for having convinced me that the fact I was writing a book on a nineteenth century subject did not mean I had to do it by candlelight with a quill in my hand, and that perhaps it would be a good idea to try a computer. It was! Binary thanks to you both.

Alicia Finkel
Spring 1996

Introduction

The stage is an optical point. Everything that exists in the world—
in history, in life, in man—should be and can be reflected therein,
but under the magic wand of art.
                    Victor Hugo, Preface to *Cromwell*

*I*N 1880 THOMAS HARDY NOTED IN HIS JOURNAL: "Romanticism will exist in human nature as long as human nature itself exists.
The point is ... to adopt that form of romanticism which is the mood of the
age."[1]

No better reflection of the Victorian romantic mood remains than the
scenery and costumes designed for some of the most notable productions
seen on the London stages in the second half of the nineteenth century. Well
beyond the 1830s, the conventionally accepted date for the demise of
Romanticism, the trends evident in theatrical design—pictorial techniques
on a massive scale, reliance on fantasy, history, and the ravaging forces of
nature as sources of inspiration—were all expression of the ideas found at the
core of the Romantic movement. The compulsion to escape into times and
places far removed from current reality; the deluges, tempests, and avalanches;
the historical reconstruction of dress and architecture; and the depiction of
exotic or mythical lands, seen both on stages and at art galleries—all are evidence that romantic subjects continued to find a sympathetic audience until,
and often beyond, the turn of the century.

Stage productions were dominated by visual elements that mirrored the
prevalent aesthetic concerns, and the emphasis placed on pictorial, evocative,
and spectacular settings revolutionized the significance that scenic artists had
in the context of dramatic presentation. Emerging from the obscurity that
had shrouded their profession during the Restoration and the Georgian
periods, designers evolved into highly praised artists whose contribution was
acknowledged by audiences and critics alike. Most of the scene painters at
work in the first half of the nineteenth century—David Cox, Clarkson
Stanfield, William Beverley, and the Grieves—were equally skilled as stage

1

designers and easel painters. By the late 1800s, artists who had acquired a reputation primarily as easel painters with the imprimatur of the Royal Academy—Lawrence Alma-Tadema, Ford Madox Brown, and Edward Burne-Jones—were engaged to display their talents as stage designers. Costume designers broke through the cloud of anonymity as well, to become active and recognized members of creative production teams.

From one generation to the next, from the late eighteenth century until the First World War, the uninterrupted allure of Romanticism is revealed by examining the creations of some of the most prominent actor-managers and the designers they employed.

Even though the scenery and costumes designed under the spell of the romantic potion were often derided for their extravagance, and were followed by a reaction against their excesses, these designs—like all other art styles in history—had to experience the process of birth, maturity, and eventual decadence before later generations, with the perspective that time provides, were ready to reassess their significance.

Chapter 1

The First Romantics

*C*LASSICAL AND ROMANTIC ELEMENTS have coexisted and overlapped throughout the history of art, but in the second half of the eighteenth century, the division between the two philosophies became deeper and more definite. The publication in 1756 of Edmund Burke's *Inquiry into the Origins of Our Ideas of the Sublime and Beautiful* gave expression to the ideas found at the core of the Romantic movement, ideas that subsequently manifested themselves in the visual and theatrical arts. The first Romantic generation, born in the midst of social and political unrest and thrust into a world of unfulfilled promises, rejected the no longer relevant classical models revered since the Renaissance. The past, the supernatural, the world of Celtic lore, remote and alien shores—all offered not only a refuge where contemporary reality could not intrude but also fresh sources of inspiration never before explored. In the theatre, the romantic compulsion to flee to spheres where dreams remained undisturbed resulted in the emphasis placed upon productions that evoked a world of myth, magic, and legend. The sensuous splendor of the Orient and the mysterious world of the Middle Ages became favorite destinations, as long as they were reproduced with as much historical accuracy as scholarship could provide.

The period from the late eighteenth to the late nineteenth centuries witnessed a revolution in set design spurred not only by the public's desire to find in the theatre more accurate depictions of bygone eras but also by a need to enjoy the beauty of exotic locations and spectacular fairylands. The scenery based on the system of generic wings, borders, and backdrops, which had been a convention in the English theatres since the Restoration, no longer satisfied the taste of playgoers influenced by romantic ideas.

Looking back with nostalgia, Godfrey Turner lamented in 1884: "I am aware that, a little before my time ... the scenic mounting of the drama was almost wholly confined to the painting of wings, flats and borders, the stage being meagerly furnished.... The only scenic backgrounds were flats, run on in pairs, and with greasy black finger-marks down the middle join, which divided, as often as not the trim perspective of a gravel-walk. Those dear, dingy old flats, only to be seen now-a-days at the merry matinees!"[1]

3

Early in the nineteenth century, outrage against those same conditions that provoked Turner's bout of nostalgia began to be heard. In reviews of productions, particularly for the provincial theatres, where mechanical systems were uncommon and scene shifts were achieved by manual labor, recurrent criticism referred to the dirty fingermarks made on the surface of the flats by the usually visible stagehands. Mishaps such as wings representing a palace being left on stage, by mistake, during a scene taking place in a forest or a hut were also frequently recorded. Moreover, the two sides of the back shutter did not always meet as planned, often leaving a vertical gap along the center of a landscape. At the sight of one such accident, a member of the audience loudly expressed his displeasure by screaming from his seat in the gallery: "We don't expect no grammar in here, but for God's sake join your flats!"[2]

The convention of achieving scene changes by the use of wings and shutters had been acceptable, and served well, during the seventeenth and eighteenth centuries, when dramatists and actors were the focus of the theatrical tradition and when the public did not demand elaborate visual effects to enjoy a performance. Restoration and Georgian scene painters were called on to provide a mere suggestion of locale, what Richard Southern called "good linings to the acting-box," within which the actors could perform unhindered by scenic effects.[3] The same stock scenery could be used interchangeably for Portia's house at Belmont, the audience hall of King John, or the Capulets' ballroom; equally, any flats showing battlements and a tower would do for *Hamlet* and *Othello*.

The lack of concern for the physical environment of the plays mirrored the lack of interest manifested by writers of those periods when describing the surroundings in which the action of their novels took place. This disregard for scenery, whether on stage or in fiction, was noticed by a late–Victorian journalist. In an article published in 1891, the author compared the scenery for one of Henry Irving's productions with that of earlier times: "The fact is that in the eighteenth century scenery in any true sense did not exist, not merely on stage, but in fiction, in poetry, in history. In Fielding's novels ... there are simply 'practical' gates, barns, and houses. ... In Scott on the other hand ... the scenery—the groups of people as well as the mere still life—is as important as the actors. This characteristic has found its way to the stage, where not only the chief actors but their environments, social and physical, are demanded.[4]

It is interesting to note that the name of Sir Walter Scott, the romantic novelist, was mentioned to define the contrast between the two periods, since it was the pervading influence of the Romantic movement that in no small measure precipitated the demise of traditional forms of set design. The demand for more specific indication of locale, historical accuracy, and spectacular, pictorial effects coincides with the early years of the Romantic movement and continued to increase unabated until the end of the nineteenth century.

The first glimpse at the changes that would eventually revolutionize the designing of scenery, and the position of the set designer, can be traced back to the collaboration between the actor-manager David Garrick and the artist Philippe-Jacques de Loutherbourgh. De Loutherbourgh was born in Strasbourg on October 31, 1740. He studied art in Paris under Carle Van Loo, and in a very short time his reputation was such that, in 1763, he was elected a member of the French Academy, in contravention of the rule against admitting anybody under the age of 30. While his fame increased as he exhibited land and seascapes produced during his extensive travels on the Continent, that experience also brought him in contact with the work of some prominent stage designers. In Italy, he saw the outcome of the Bibienas innovations, their use of scenery viewed from an angle instead of a central point; in Paris, where great attention was then given to the rules of scenic perspective, he became familiar with Giovanni Servandoni's sets for the Opera House. In his early years, De Loutherbourgh must have studied the work of his contemporaries, but his subsequent scenic creations for Drury Lane showed that he had broken free from the rigid rules of perspective as practiced on the Continent.

W. J. Lawrence affirmed, against the opinion of other historians, that Garrick, then manager of Drury Lane, secured De Loutherbourgh's services during a trip to Paris in 1765; his evidence in support of that date if based on the introduction of footlights at Drury Lane early in 1766, a change that "was made at the direct instigation and under the general superintendence of Loutherbourgh, whose knowledge of the possibilities of stage lighting was very complete."[5] The new footlights were widely spaced to aid in the even distribution of the still primitive candlelight. Previously, light came entirely from above, provided by four hoops with candles hung from the grid. Supplemental lamps and candles were brought in during the performance according to the requirements of the scene.

Whether the date was 1765 or 1771, as believed by some scholars, De Loutherbourgh accepted the position of exclusive scene designer for Drury Lane, with the stipulation that he would exercise absolute control over all visual aspects of the productions, including costumes and lights, thus embarking on the long struggle that designers after him would continue for a century: to achieve harmonious unity of the stage picture.[6]

De Loutherbourgh conceived his settings as gigantic paintings, breaking the rigidity of the wings with set pieces that could be placed at different angles and cut cloths that opened to reveal further views in the backdrop. His use of dramatic lighting effects to simulate moonlight, sunlight, and even volcanic eruptions reinforced the pictorial illusion of the scenery.

Lawrence attributes the sets for the Arcadian ballad-opera *Cymon*, in January 1767, to De Loutherbourgh, saying that it "proved a remarkable success, and so inaugurated a memorable series of spectacular *romances* [italics added] at Drury Lane."[7] From then on, hardly a season went by without the designer's innovations being noticed and praised by reviewers. For the 1773 Christmas pantomime *Pigmy Revels*, he painted extremely accurate views of some famous landmarks—St. Paul, Windsor Castle, Blackfriars Bridge—that were commended for their fidelity. In reference to *The Maid of Oaks*, a piece presented by Garrick in 1774, a critic wrote: "The landscapes of Claud are scarcely equal to some of the views exhibited; and if nothing beyond the bare merit of the paintings was held forth to attract the town, we should not be surprised at its bringing twenty crowded audiences."[8] The unreserved praise showered on the sets for *The Maid of Oaks*, with its celestial gardens, bathed in sunlight, leading to the Temple of Love, had very little precedent in the annals of dramatic criticism. De Loutherbourgh's work launched the trend toward recognition of the appeal that beautiful scenery exerted on the public, and for the next one hundred years, over and over again, some designers' creations were deemed to be the main attraction for attending a performance.

Whether for Christmas pantomimes or musical "romances" with Eastern overtones, such as *The Sultana* or *Selima and Azor* produced in 1775 and 1776, De Loutherbourgh's scenery illustrates the increased reliance on magnified pictorial techniques; his dramatic contrast of light and shadows echoed similar effects achieved in easel painting, to the point of blurring the boundaries between canvas and set design. His sets for *The Wonders of Derbyshire; or, Harlequin in the Peak*, the holiday pantomime for 1778, with mountains, gardens, and waterfalls seen under a variety of lighting changes, were based on views of that region he had made on the spot and were described as the most "romantic and picturesque paintings exhibited in that theatre."[9]

De Loutherbourgh remained at Drury Lane after Richard Sheridan took over the lease after Garrick's retirement, but in 1779 he grew dissatisfied with the financial arrangement and left to dedicate himself to the creation of the Eidophusikon, a theatrical exhibit from which players and playwrights were banished and in which the performances consisted of nothing but scenic effects. This extraordinary experiment was described in the *Whitehall Evening Post* of March 1, 1781:

> Mr. de Loutherbourgh's superior genius in the scenic line of his profession has led him to invent in the above Spectacle several of the most beautiful representations of nature that were ever effected by mechanism and painting.
>
> ...The first scene is *Greenwich Park* before dawn. It exhibits the college, the river, and a distant view of London at the dawn of day; and as the sun rises in the horizon, the sky and the whole landscape receive the various hues of light which, in a state of nature, that luminary casts upon the world. The tints of his sky are, in general, admirably managed; but nothing can exceed the amazing transition which the artist has contrived in changing the cool hue of verdure, which appears at dawn, to the refulgent warmth of the blushing morn. ... the *Moonlight* [seen after the progression from noon to sunset] is really beyond any idea that can be formed from description. ... The last

scene is a *Tempest*, which is progressively brought on by a variation of sky ... the wonderful sky ... the forked lighting pervading every part of it, together with the imitative peals of thunder, produces an effect that astonishes the imagination.[10]

To simulate clouds in movement, De Loutherbourgh stretched painted cloth on a frame 20 times larger than the stage and rolled it diagonally with the aid of cylinders; his wave machines, varnished to reflect light, turned on spindles and imitated the sound of water by the addition of a rolling octagonal box containing peas and pebbles. Hence, in an elegantly furnished room, on a stage only six feet wide and eight feet deep, unencumbered by the distraction that dramatic texts imposed, De Loutherbourgh produced a vision of beauty worthy of his reputation as a romantic set designer.

In 1782, in recognition of his talent as a landscape painter, De Loutherbourgh was granted membership in the Royal Academy. He lived until 1812, long enough to see other designers profit from his innovations and assert the preeminence of an English School of scenic artists. Some of his extant renderings and models may be seen in the collection of the Theatre Museum in London. His landscapes and battle scene are exhibited in the Tate Gallery and the National Maritime Museum, Greenwich.

Kenneth Clark diagnosed the taste for Gothic art as the clearest symptom of Romanticism and, with tongue in cheek, attributed the craze for the "picturesque" to picnickers who "following in the wake of some sentimental traveler, sought the shadow of a Gothic abbey; many who were young in the quarter of the eighteenth century must have associated these buildings with sweet and poignant moments, and through life Gothic must have kept for them some perfume of their poetic youth."[11] Nevertheless, anyone who has ever seen the Scottish mist set upon the ruins of an abbey church will grant that, even for a skeptical twentieth-century traveler, it is a sight to remember and cherish for a long time.

The fascination with the Middle Ages was, indeed, a symptom of Romantic fever; before the 1760s, eighteenth-century writers and scholars, convinced that no civilization worthy of their troubles had existed since Rome fell to the barbarians, had not been attracted to the uncouth Middle Ages. Although the Gothic revival initiated in the late 1700s was the most pervading, it was only the first manifestation of the romantic desire to explore the nonclassical past. The study of history, and the accurate historical reproduction of architecture and dress, would become overriding issues in the visual arts of the nineteenth century.

In its early stages, the interest in Gothic archaeology was confined to a group of amateur historians whose books were bought by subscription by a limited circle of aristocratic intellectuals. From 1780 onward, publications more easily accessible to the general public begin to show a greater number of illustrations depicting Gothic architecture. *The Gentleman's Magazine*, whose pages had been an encyclopedia of Greco-Roman art, included an article on the Gothic almost every month after 1783. By the last decade of the eighteenth century, the interest was widespread enough to justify the publication of Milner's *History of Winchester* (1798) and the *History of Gothic and Saxon Architecture in England* (1798) by Bentham and Willis.

Between 1791 and 1794, while the rage for the Gothic past expanded, the two Patent theatres, Drury Lane and Covent Garden, were rebuilt to accommodate larger audiences and larger scenery. The new Drury Lane, designed by Henry Holland, was the largest playhouse in Europe and could hold anywhere from 3,600 to 3,900 spectators; the opening of the stage was 43 feet wide by 38 feet high, with a backstage area of 83 feet by 92 feet and a height of 108 feet. It was the first building in London, other than a church, to rise above the skyline of domestic architecture. The advanced machinery installed both below and above the stage allowed the possibility of executing complicated scene changes without visible machinists.[12] That "vast wilderness," as the actress Sarah Siddons called it, required acres of scenery to fill the space, and the heirs to De Loutherbourgh were waiting in the wings to satisfy the ever-growing demand for their services.

Although dramatic literature was increasingly populated by medieval ghosts, and plays titled *The Castle Spectre*, by Matthew Gregory Lewis (1797), or *Feudal Times*, by George Colman the Younger (1799), were seen on stage, it was not until the actor-manager John Philip Kemble hired William Capon as his principal designer at the refurbished Drury Lane that the principles of strict historical research were applied to scenery. Capon had been a pupil and assistant to the architect Novosielski, with whom he worked on the decoration of the King's Theatre, the Royal Circus, and the Ranelagh Gardens between 1785 and 1789. As for his initiation into scene painting, Sybil Rosenfeld dates it to 1786, when he worked with Cornelius Dixon on sets for the new Royalty Theatre; he was also employed by Lord Aldborough to paint scenery and decorations in the private theatre in Aldborough House in the early 1790s.[13]

Kemble had already made some attempts to introduce accurate scenery in his production of *Henry VIII* at the old Drury Lane; by the time he chose William Capon as his chief scenic artist in 1794, both men shared a passion for the faithful re-creation of the Middle Ages. James Boaden, in his biography of Kemble, described Capon as "cast in the mould of antiquity"; Boaden went on to say that the artist's passion was Britain's ancient architecture, to which he dedicated himself "with all the zeal of an antiquarian ... as if he had been upon oath."[14] Capon was a meticulous researcher and draughtsman, recording in his sketchbooks not only architectural details but also the type of stone used and the effects of light in particular buildings.

The designer's initial contribution to historically correct scenery was a chapel with Gothic arches, for the oratorio that inaugurated the new Drury

Lane on March 12, 1794. Shortly thereafter, he collaborated with seven other scene painters in creating the scenery for *Macbeth* with authentic period details. Capon's crowning achievement that season was a set representing a fourteenth-century cathedral, with nave, choir, and side aisles, for Joanna Baillie's play *De Monfort*. The massive, superbly decorated interior, 56 feet wide, 52 feet deep, and 37 feet high, received universal acclaim. In 1798, Capon painted Milan Cathedral for the opening scene of James Boaden's *Aurelio and Miranda*, but in spite of the artistic value of his set, some claimed that "it was sacrilegious to represent a church upon the stage."[15] Nevertheless, this set, with slight alterations, was later used for other productions requiring medieval interiors.

In subsequent seasons Capon, in collaboration with other staff painters, provided scenery for *Richard III*, *Cymbeline*, and *The Winter's Tale*. All of his work was destroyed in the fire that consumed Drury Lane in 1809. When the playhouse reopened three years later with *Hamlet*, on October 10, he shared credit for the scenery with Greenwood, Marinari, and Dixon, among others. Sybil Rosenfeld believes that Capon painted the Anglo-Norman Hall for *Hamlet's* lobby from architectural fragments of the time of Edward the Confessor, William Ruffus, and Henry I.[16] Capon's work was not limited to the production of Shakespeare's plays; between 1809 and 1813 he contributed scenes for *All in the Wrong*, *Up All Night*, *The Wonder*, *Lionel and Clarissa*, and *She Wou'd and She Wou'd Not*.

Until the end of his career Capon remained faithful to his passion for historical accuracy, particularly the reproduction of medieval England. His last known work for the stage, *Woman's Will* for the English Opera in July 1820, showed a street with pointed arches inspired by Gothic remains.

Before the mid–twentieth century, only two of Capon's designs, preserved in the collection of the Shakespeare Memorial Museum at Stratford-upon-Avon, had been known to have survived. Rosenfeld's article "Scene Designs of William Capon," which has been quoted in several instances, is based on her study of a volume of Capon's finished drawings and rough sketches discovered and acquired by Francis Watson in 1956.

The vogue for scenery with panoramic views and romantic landscapes bathed by sun or moonlight, a trend initiated by De Loutherbourgh in the late 1700s, was sustained by other scenic artists well into the nineteenth century. Among the celebrated artists whose skills proved most influential in shaping the future of scene design, the name of Clarkson Stanfield may be placed at the top. That recognition was accorded to Stanfield in his own time; in playbills of the period his name was printed in larger type than that used for the names of the principal actors and much larger than the type used for the authors' names.

Stanfield, born in Sunderland in 1793, spent the early years of his life as a sailor, an experience that would later influence his painting of seascapes.

His stage career began in the minor theatres of London, among them the Old Royalty in Wellclose Square, a playhouse frequented by sailors; shortly after his initiation, he was engaged at Drury Lane, where his panoramas, used as background for his sets, became the center of attraction.

The panorama had been developed in 1787 by Robert Baker, an Edinburgh artist; in 1820 it made its appearance on the stage when it was seen in *Harlequin and Cinderella* at Covent Garden; subsequently, it became an integral part of the Christmas pantomime. The mechanism consisted of a large painted canvas rolled horizontally between two cylinders across the upstage area; a succession of landscapes could thus be shown, transporting the audience from one locale to another in the course of the performance. One of the panoramas painted by Stanfield in his early days at Drury Lane, for *Zoroaster*, was 482 feet long. The diorama, a similar but more elaborate device invented by Bontou and Daguerre, was first seen in London in 1823. Unlike the panorama, which was painted on a single layer of cloth, the diorama produced three-dimensional illusion by the use of two painted, transparent drops placed one behind the other.

Stanfield's panoramas and dioramas were one of the greatest inducements to attend a performance. He frequently made use of his talent as a seascape painter in the depiction of nautical subjects; his diorama for *The Queen Bee* in 1828 showed views of the Cowes regatta, the Portsmouth dockyard, a sunrise at Spithead, and Gibraltar.

A note in the program for William Macready's production of *Henry V* at Covent Garden in 1839 informed the audience, "The narrative and descriptive poetry spoken by the Chorus is accompanied with Pictorial Illustrations from the pencil of Mr. Stanfield."[17] The artist's panorama transported the viewers, as if aboard the ships of the English fleet, from "Southampton to Harfleur and from the camp at Agincourt back to London for the king's triumphal return. In another of Stanfield's designs for Macready, Handel's opera *Acis and Galatea*, the sea advanced toward the audience and broke in gentle waves of foam on the sand. This production was Stanfield's last work at Covent Garden; in spite of his success as a stage designer, he exchanged the paint frame for the easel and retired to devote himself to the painting of marine subjects. He abandoned his studio only once, sixteen years after *Acis and Galatea*, to paint an act drop for the Adelphi Theatre. That drop, conceived as an easel painting, was surrounded by a painted frame. It was said of Stanfield that "he taught the pit and the gallery to admire landscape and the boxes to become connoisseurs."[18] Without doubt, his influence was felt in the work of other designers and in the public's demand for ever more stunning scenery.

The history of the British theatre may one day become a case study for the importance of genetic inheritance in the choice of a career. The dynasties of actors and actresses are well known even in our time; likewise, scene design has also attracted successive generations of the same family, with the tradition handed from fathers to sons. Stanfield's father was a scene-painter, although his reputation was minimal compared with that of his son. Among other prominent families in the history of scene painting in the nineteenth century, the Fentons, the Gordons, the Telbins, and the Grieves are the most notable.

John Henderson Grieve, with his sons Thomas and William, reigned over the London Stage before and after Queen Victoria's accession to the throne. From John Henderson Grieve's first known production, *Richard III* at the Theatre Royal, Bath, in 1805, until 1879, when his son Thomas designed *Gulliver*, Thomas's last set at Covent Garden, this dynasty of scenic artists preserved the tradition of pictorial techniques on a grand scale. With only a brief interruption, between 1835 and 1839 when the scene painters worked at Drury Lane, most of the elder Grieve's scenery was produced for Covent Garden. Thomas, who had joined his father as an apprentice at the age of 18, painted scenery for Madame Vestris at Covent Garden and for her extravaganzas at the Lyceum; he later became one of the leading artists for Charles Kean's productions at the Princess's Theatre in the 1850s and continued to collaborate with the most notable actor-managers until the end of his career.

The Grieves carried the cut scenes, the transparencies, and the subtle effects of light introduced by De Loutherbourgh to new heights. Their panorama for *Harlequin and Cinderella* was the first seen in London, in 1820. In a later panorama they took the audience on a balloon excursion from London to Paris. Many of their innumerable designs were for opera and ballet, both fertile grounds for reproducing Gothic abbeys, oriental temples, and exquisite gardens, while the Christmas pantomime afforded opportunities for unrestricted fantasy. The list of their accomplishments in the art of scene design and painting is extensive; over 600 of their designs are in the collections of the University of London Library, and another 100 may be studied at the British Museum and in the Prints and Drawings Room at the Victoria and Albert Museum.

The description of just one of their productions, Milton's *Comus* for Mme. Vestris's company at Drury Lane in the early 1840s, seems to embody all the qualities of artistic imagination and craftsmanship for which they were so highly praised. George Vandenhoff, an actor in the company, sounds awestruck as he recounts this "most brilliant production of the season, presenting the most classical, and perfectly artistic *ensemble*, of all the spectacle-pieces brought out under the Vestris-Mathews management." Milton's masque was

> An honour to the theatre ... breathing the divine philosophy of virtue in tones of the highest poetry, with all the luxury of scenic display ... and all the aid that art could bring to delight the senses and to realize the great poet's picture. ... The groupings and the arrangements of the *tableaux* were admirable, and some of the mechanical effects were almost magical; especially

that exquisite scene in which Mme. Vestris as Sabrina appeared at the head of the waterfall, immersed in the cup of a lily up to the shoulders, and in this fairy skiff floated over the fall and descended to the stage!

There were forest scenes of the greatest pictorial beauty, equal in effect to the greatest efforts of Moreland or Gainsborough. ... This production ... was a thing to see, as a work of art, and to remember.[19]

The medley of wood nymphs, satyrs, grotesque monsters, and other fabulous beings who populated the set of *Comus*, according to Vandenhoff, was as much a reminder of the romantic attachment to the supernatural as it was a forecast of the fairy world that Mme. Vestris would bring to life in her productions of James Robinson Planché's extravaganzas at the Lyceum.

Chapter 2

Madame Vestris, James Robinson Planché, and William Beverley: Romanticism, Fantasy, and Spectacle

*R*OMANTIC FANTASY AND SPECTACLE flourished between 1847 and 1853 on the stage of the Lyceum. Long after the fairies had vanished from the boards of that playhouse off the Strand, the actor-manager Squire Bancroft wrote in his memoirs, referring to the Christmas piece of 1848: "I recall, but with a child's remembrance, being taken to see Mme. Vestris, and living in the fairyland of William Beverley's gorgeous scenery in Planché's extravaganza *The King of the Peacocks*."[1] Bancroft's cherished memories were quite possibly shared by a generation of London playgoers who had been entertained and delighted by the creative efforts of Lucia Elizabeth Vestris, James Robinson Planché, and William Beverley. The talents of manager, playwright, and set designer had converged and blended, in a unique moment of the mid–Victorian period, to create that world of unforgettable beauty fondly recalled by the actor.

The Lyceum, described at the time of Mme. Vestris's tenure as "the most elegant little theatrical temple in Europe," had a motley history dating back to the eighteenth century.[2] The foundation stone for the first building, designed for exhibitions of the Society of Artists of Great Britain, was laid in July 1771. Subsequently, through fires and rebuilding, Lyceum succeeded Lyceum on the same site, becoming, at one time or another, home to a bewildering assortment of activities ranging from puppet shows and a School of Eloquence to a Planetarium and the space to exhibit a 40-foot air balloon entirely overlaid with gold. Madame Tussaud transported, from across the Channel, her already famous waxworks to be shown there in 1802. In the early years of the nineteenth century the stage of the Lyceum saw burlettas, dramas, farces, and pantomimes interspersed with some attempts at producing English opera. One of Planché's earliest theatrical triumphs, *The Vampyre: or, The Bride of the Isles*, premiered at the Lyceum on August 9, 1820, to great critical acclaim. The decades of the 1830s and 1840s witnessed successive managers' fortunes fluctuate between brief spells of success and extended periods of failure. In October 1847, Mme. Vestris and her husband, Charles James Mathews, considered by some "the most alert and intelligent [managers] that ever conducted a London theatre," obtained the lease of the playhouse.[3]

One of the first women in management, Mme. Vestris had acquired her expertise during her former ventures at the Olympic, from 1830 to 1839, and Covent Garden, from 1839 to 1842. In both these settings—the little theatre in Wynch Street and the immense Patent house—she had established high standards for the presentation of her productions. The refined beauty and lavish splendor of her offerings had become as legendary as her talent as an actress and singer. A member of her company at Covent Garden described her as "the best *soubrette chantante* of her day; self-possession, archness, grace, *coquêtterie*, seemed natural to her; these, with her charming voice, excellent taste in music, fine eyes, and exquisite form, made her the most fascinating … actress of her day."[4] Besides her impeccable taste and bewitching charm, Vestris was endowed with perfectly turned legs and had made a career of playing parts "requiring a lady to invest herself in mannish integuments."[5] In the heyday of her beauty, her specialty had been to play "breeches" parts.

Mme. Vestris's partner in management was her second husband, Charles James Mathews, who had made his debut in her company at the Olympic, married her in 1838, and subsequently shared with her the triumphs, trials, and disappointments of theatrical ventures until her death in 1856.

When Mr. and Mrs. Mathews took over the lesseeship of the Lyceum, they invited their old friend James Robinson Planché to join them in the enterprise to fulfill responsibilities similar to the ones he had assumed earlier at the Olympic and Covent Garden. Due to his expertise in costume history—his *History of British Dress* had been published in 1834—as well as his growing reputation as a playwright, Planché was engaged to "superintend" the decorative departments, painting rooms, and wardrobe and to provide the managers with the Christmas and Easter plays. Madame's confidence in the talents Planché would contribute to the Lyceum was based on the long and happy history of their association; for over 15 years, since their first collaboration in *Olympic Revels; or, Prometheus and Pandora* in 1831, her presentation of one of the playwright's works had resulted in critical acclaim and increased audience attendance. By the 1840s Planché had acquired considerable fame not only as a pioneer of historical accuracy in stage costumes but also as the author of light comedies, vaudevilles, farces, and burlettas; above all, his name was associated with the success of his witty and elegant extravaganzas inspired by the fairy lore of France.

Although Planché's fame was based on his extravaganzas, he was not the originator of the genre; V. C. Clinton-Baddeley, in *The Burlesque Tradition in the English Theatre after 1660*, traces this form of entertainment to Charles Dibdin's *Poor Vulcan*, produced in 1778. In 1817, a decade before Planché's debut as a playwright, Thomas Dibdin's *Don Giovanni* had been billed as a "Comic, Heroic, Operatic, Tragic, Pantomimic Burletta—Spectacular Extravaganza." The characters and plots of the "burlettas-extravaganzas," well established on the stages of London before Planché began his career, were inspired by classical literature or mythological stories, but these gods and goddesses were inclined to use some of the traditional elements of the British burlesque—topical jokes, parodies and puns—more often than grandiloquent speech. Planché's early pieces, written in collaboration with Charles Dance for the Vestris' management at the Olympic, followed a similar pattern; although based on classical subjects, they were heavily influenced by the burlesque tradition. The mythological allegorical burletta—*Olympic Revels*, as well as his subsequent three plays for Mme. Vestris—*Olympic Devils; or, Orpheus and Eurydice* (1831), *The Paphian Bower; or, Venus and Adonis* (1832), and the "Burlesque Burletta" *The Deep, Deep Sea; or, Perseus and Andromeda* (1833)—were all examples of Planché's experimentation with the genre.

Planché's first attempt at adapting French fairy tales to create an extravanganza had been presented by Mme. Vestris at the Olympic Theatre on Boxing Night 1836. *Riquet with the Tuft*, as the London audience came to know the play, was based on the *féerie-folie Riquet à la Houppe*, which the playwright had seen produced in Paris in 1821. Of the next 21 "fairy" extravaganzas written by Planché after *Riquet with the Tuft*, 13 were adaptations from tales by the Countess D'Aulnoy. Charles Perrault's stories *Blue Beard* and *The Discreet Princess* were the sources for another two, Mme. de Beaumont furnished the plot for *Beauty and the Beast*, Mlle. de la Force for *Good Woman in the Wood*, and the Countess de Murat for *Young and Handsome*, the last of Planché's extravaganzas, which was presented at the Olympic exactly 20 years after *Riquet*, on December 26, 1856. Another three were based on popular, anonymous stories.

Planché's affinity with the French fairy tales induced a contemporary critic to conclude that the Countess D'Aulnoy's soul had taken refuge in Planché's body, suggesting metempsychosis, since the playwright had "that understanding of the structure and tone of her delicious fairytales, which, one would think can only be acquired by a second self." The unique personality of Mme. D'Aulnoy's characters, so well understood by Planché, was described by the same critic as belonging to "a totally distinct race from the shadowy beings of German tradition or the tiny midnight revelers who are called fairies in this island. They are thoroughly substantial courtly people, who, far from slipping into a house through a key-hole, a door-chink, or any other absurd aperture only make their appearance when they have been formally invited by the king of the country or some other grandee of the realm. ... The Countess

D'Anois [sic] 'fairies' are, in fact, actual ladies and gentlemen ... they eat, and they drink, and they marry mortals, without any evil consequences ... they dress themselves in the fashion of the time which, somehow or another, always happens to be about the period of Louis XIV."[6]

Planché enjoyed the company of this whimsical but extremely polite society whose penchant for sparkling wit and "delightful persiflage" he shared.[7] However, in his bringing of French fairies to the stage, the playwright also reflected the growing Victorian enthusiasm for folk tales, legends, and myths. The popularity of fairies as a subject matter in literature, painting, and the theatre increased progressively from the early decades of the nineteenth century to reach the proportions of a cult by 1900. The Grimm brothers' stories were first translated to English and published in the 1820s. Thomas Keightley's *Fairy Mythology* appeared in 1828, concurrently with T. Crofton Croker's *Fairy Legends and Traditions of the South of Ireland*. Some of the most gifted graphic artists of the period—George Cruikshank, Arthur Rackham, and Edmund Dulac—created the enchanting illustrations for those books and the myriad of others that continued to be published throughout the nineteenth century, providing readers with exquisite pictorial representations of the imaginary beings. The two great romantic fairy ballets, *La Sylphide* and *Giselle*, were first seen in London in 1832 and 1842 respectively, shortly after their original productions at L'Académie Royal de Musique in Paris, with two dancers, in the title roles, who epitomized the romantic ideal of the ethereal ballerina: Marie Taglioni and Carlotta Grisi.

Mme. Vestris was also well acquainted with the fairies; her production of *A Midsummer Night's Dream* at Covent Garden in 1840 had emphasized the fanciful, romantic elements in the play and may well be considered the harbinger of the subsequent spectacular revivals, from Kean's to Tree's, that gave concrete visual representation to fairyland and its inhabitants. The actress anticipated Charles Kean as well by setting the action of his play in ancient Athens.

The first of the fairy extravaganzas produced by the Vestris-Mathews management at the Lyceum opened for the Christmas holidays in 1847. *The Golden Branch* was an adaptation of the Countess D'Aulnoy's *Le Rameau D'Or*. It introduced to the London playgoers a new member of Madame's creative staff, William Beverley, destined to become one of the most distinguished set designers of the Victorian period.

William Roxby Beverley was born in a theatrical family: both his father and his grandfather, as well as his sister and two elder brothers, were actors. As a young boy, he kept company with some of the greatest luminaries of the English stage. Edmund Kean, with whom he stayed for nine months, was greatly attached to him, and Clarkson Stanfield, the famous set designer and landscape painter, took him on sketching trips. In 1831 Beverley appeared on stage, touring with his father's company, while at the same time he began developing his skills as a scenic artist. His first engagement as a scene painter, in London in 1839, was offered to him by his brother Harry, manager of the Old Coburg (later the Victoria Theatre). In 1842, at the age of 31, he was appointed principal scenic artist at the Theatre Royal in Manchester. Four years later he was back in London, where he worked at the Olympic and Princess's Theatres before being hired by Mme. Vestris in 1847.

The Golden Branch marked Planché's first collaboration with Beverley, and in the preface to the published edition of the play, he acknowledged Beverley's contribution to the production. The designer's admirable skills as a painter, in addition to his technical expertise, had made it possible to carry out effectively "the many complicated changes which were necessary for the comprehension of the rather intricate plot ... and which in less skillful hands might have endangered its success."[8] Planché's recognition of Beverley's abilities was echoed by the superlative tributes showered upon the designer in the press. The action of this extravaganza developed within a series of tableaux inspired by Antoine Watteau's bucolic paintings, giving Beverley full scope to display the lyric quality of his designs. Describing the second scene, the "Bowers of Arcadia," a critic declared it was "the most tasteful, fairylike composition ever seen on any stage." Carried away by all this beauty, he added: "It is impossible to describe in a few words the merits of many of these scenes. That which ends the first act is the most gorgeous exhibition imaginable, a very temple of flowers, designed, one would think, by an architectural Flora, and executed by magic hands, ... its brilliancy is like moon rays, and its tints ... those of the rainbow."[9]

Planché himself described the scenery as outstanding and so perfectly executed that, in spite of the fact that the last scene had never been rehearsed due to lack of time, the opening performance went on without a hitch. He also found the commendations from Edwin Landseer, one of Queen Victoria's favorite painters, extremely gratifying. He regretted only that the elaborate and costly mise-en-scène would discourage other managers from attempting future revivals of *The Golden Branch*.[10]

Seeking a subject for the Easter piece of 1848, Planché temporarily abandoned the French fairies, who did not seem to him appropriate company for the occasion, and returned to the classical world for inspiration. As he had done before, in *Olympic Revels* and *The Golden Fleece* among others, he concocted his new extravaganza from mythological Greek sources. *Theseus and Ariadne; or, The Marriage of Bacchus*, which premiered on April 24, was termed, in *The Era*, another "blaze of triumph" for the management. Beverley's scenery was considered extraordinarily beautiful, his best to date, and "quite equal to anything Stanfield ever produced upon the stage."[11] Evidently, Beverley had benefited from his youthful sketching trips with the unquestionable master of landscape painting.

Mme. Vestris played the role of Theseus, receiving once again the customary praises for the perfect symmetry of her legs, which "took the shine out of all other legs."[12] However, this was the last time Madame appeared in an Eastern piece; she continued to perform at all other times but could never be induced to take part in subsequent extravaganzas during the Easter season. Planché, who after his long association with Madame had given up any hope of understanding the reasons behind some of her decisions, was at a loss to explain the motives for her refusal to appear on stage at that particular time.[13]

La Princess Rosette, another fairy tale by the Countess D'Aulnoy, furnished the plot for The King of the Peacocks, the Christmas extravaganza of 1848. The scenery for this production gave Beverley a new opportunity to show his flair for spectacular effects, particularly in the last scene, which culminated with the display of an immense, brightly colored peacock-feather fan opening in view of the audience. Beverley's own recollection of this scene is a good example of the prominent position the set designer had acquired by the middle of the nineteenth century. In an interview given to the Times in 1885, he declared he had effected "the hit of the play by a pure piece of scenic art, without a soul on stage." He stated: "The house rose with enthusiasm at it. To end an act with merely a beautiful, fanciful scene, and no dramatis personae visible was daring. But those were the days when imagination in scenic art was valued."[14] From Philippe-Jacques de Loutherbourgh's Eidophusikon to Edward Gordon Craig's theatre without performers, the ambition to use the stage as a frame for displaying the designer's, rather than the actor's, art has haunted successive generations of scene designers.

On April 9, 1849, the Vestris-Mathews management presented yet another spectacular extravaganza that departed, however slightly, from the usual Easter fare. On this occasion, Planché forsook the French fairy tales as a source of inspiration and gratified his "own vaulting ambition by writing a drama with a loftier purpose in the hope of its being appreciated" by those who had "the best interest of the stage at heart."[15] The Seven Champions of Christendom, as this lofty drama was titled, was billed as a "comic fantastic spectacle," although Planché preferred the subtitle of "dramatic political allegory." The idea for this alleged comic fantasy was prompted by the generally atrocious state of affairs that Europe confronted in that fateful year of 1848: insurrection in Germany, revolution in France, famine in Ireland, and demonstrations in the streets of London. Planché believed it would have been in bad taste to allude to such calamities in a frivolous manner, although it would have been just as inappropriate to "comment upon them in a language more serious than the Easter Monday audience was accustomed."[16] His answer to this dilemma was to present the Seven Champions attacking and destroying the evil forces of tyranny, falsehood, ignorance, and superstition, which appeared on stage, presumably for the sake of spectacle and box-office revenue, in the guise of demons, dragons, ogres, and venomous vermin. Thus,

SCENE FROM "THE SEVEN CHAMPIONS OF CHRISTENDOM," AT THE LYCEUM THEATRE.

Scene from *The Seven Champions of Christendom* at the Lyceum. Engraving from the *Illustrated London News*. From the author's archives.

Saint Patrick of Ireland drove allegorical noxious reptiles out of the Emerald Isle and Saint Anthony of Italy destroyed a giant while Saint George of England was assigned the most thrilling adventure of them all: to kill the Dragon. This foul monster made his entrance—before being annihilated by Saint George, of course—merrily dancing a hornpipe and carrying his tail under his arm.

While the last scene in *The Seven Champions of Christendom* was being set up, Charles Mathews, in his closing address, prepared the audience for the visual marvels they were about to witness in the final "Tableau of Triumph":

> ...the spell is now broken,
> So to finish this rather long winded oration,
> I have only to request, as we really have done out best
> To add to your amusement and edification,

> That when, as I mean, I change to the last scene,
> Which, I think, you will own is a gorgeous decoration,
> You'll be kind enough to say, in your usual good natured way,
> That the scenery, by Mr. Beverley,
> Has been painted very cleverly.[17]

Neither critics nor audience needed Mathews's prompting to burst into an outpouring of praises for the scenery designed by Beverley. Words could not be found, according to *The Era*, to do justice to the beauty of the scenery, although the reviewer managed to find some to describe Beverley as "essentially a poet" whose creations were examples of extraordinary merit and the "highest art." The critic further declared that there was "more credit due to him [Beverley] than to half the dramatic authors of the day, and it would be but fair to remark that this extravaganza would be nothing without his aid. ... He produces half the effect and more than half the attraction." After a "half-hearted" attempt to recognize Planché's contribution to this production, the same critic continued by characterizing the final scene, the camp of the Seven Champions, as "the most delicately beautiful, spirited, and yet gorgeous tableau the eye ever rested upon."[18] The review in the *Illustrated London News* summarized the scenery as "transcendentally beautiful"; the critic reminded the public of the debt of gratitude they owed the management of the Lyceum for "improving the general taste, forcing other theatres, by comparisons generally made, to reform hitherto careless and ineffective methods of getting up spectacles."[19]

The hyperbolic commendations for Beverley's designs, and the conflict between the merits of the script and the visual elements of the extravaganzas, reached its climax with *The Island of Jewels*, the Christmas piece unveiled on December 26, 1849. The play was an adaptation of Mme. D'Aulnoy's *Serpentin Vert*; since no special tableau for the ending was suggested in the story, Planché, to his future regret, left it to Beverley's ingenuity to devise an appropriate final scene. The designer created a set for the splendid coronation of Queen Emerald and King Diamond; the leaves of an immense palm tree unfolded to reveal seven nymphs in shimmering dresses supporting a coronet of multicolored jewels while cupids flew about the air. This breathtaking scene, "worth paying to see were nothing else exhibited," initiated the tradition of the "transformation scene," which thereafter became a staple in the presentation of all Christmas pantomimes.[20] The sets were pronounced an unquestionable landmark in the art of scene design, and their dreamlike quality was seen as reminiscent of Turner's paintings. In short, the work was the most "complete picture of Paradise that [could] possibly be imagined."[21]

Planché was astonished at the effect the scenery had on the public; his reaction to the sweep of scenic brushes painting him off the stage was one of undisguised dismay. In the preface to *The Island of Jewels*, written 30 years later, in the collected volumes of the *Extravaganzas*, the playwright admitted that

Beverley's work had proved valuable to the management (the production had run for 135 performances) but added that it had also subsequently caused "serious injury to the Drama" by placing too much emphasis on spectacular effects. He concluded:

> Year after year Mr. Beverley's powers were taxed to out do his former out-doings. ... The epidemic spread in all directions. The *last* scene became the *first* in the estimation of the management of every theatre ... managers, blindly relying on these costly displays for the pecuniary success of their pieces are perfectly indifferent to the character of the dramas ... while, on the other hand, authors of well-deserved reputation, finding nothing is considered brilliant but the last scene, naturally become careless in the construction and dialogue of their pieces, and are unfortunately contented to profit by "unprecedented triumphs," as each production is invariably declared to be, obtained by no merit of their own beyond ... the suggestion of ... a title or subject affording opportunities to the scene painter.[22]

Planché looked back with nostalgia to his collaboration with the scenic artist Thomas Grieve, who, for Mme. Vestris's revival of *A Midsummer Night's Dream* at Covent Garden in 1840, had carried out "implicitly the directions of the author, and not sacrilegiously attempted to gild the refined gold."[23] Even though it would not be appropriate to suggest that Planché considered his own "gold" as refined as Shakespeare's, it seems evident from his comments that he felt deeply hurt by the ascendancy of visual effects at the expense of his own craft.

In spite of Planché's misgivings, year after year Beverley's imagination was called on to devise the dazzling spectacles in which the fame of the Lyceum rested. From a financial point of view, the lavish expenses thus incurred by the Vestris-Mathews management were perfectly justified. Whereas comedies and dramas seldom ran more than two weeks, the extravaganzas packed the house for months. *King Charming; or, The Blue Bird of Paradise*, the Christmas play offered in 1850, remained in the bill for 193 nights. The success of *King Charming*, an adaptation of Mme. D'Aulnoy's *L'Oiseau Bleu*, was due in part, no doubt, to Planché's script, said to be "crammed with puns like currants in a Christmas pudding."[24] However, Beverley's magnificent scenery was once again more extravagant than anything previously seen on the London stage; a bewildered critic described it as "grand, glorious, and splendid," painted by a master's hand. This review comes close to depleting the vocabulary of superlatives; after stating that all the beauty had to be seen to be believed, the author continued: "The pearls of Ormus are added to the rubies of Trebisond, and the emeralds of Viscapour glitter beside the diamonds of Golconda. ... Mahomet's paradise has been deprived of a score of Houries who sit in a semi-circle on thrones of beaten gold backed by fans of waving silver. ... Peru and California have yielded up their rubiest treasures to illustrate 'The Glorious Restoration of King Charming to the Throne of the Fan-Sea.'"[25]

Mme. Vestris as King Charming, with the chorus of ravishing beauties. "The King Charming's Quadrilles," lithograph for sheet music cover (Harvard Theatre Collection).

Mme. Vestris and her husband lavished as much care in the production of the Easter extravaganzas as they did during the Christmas holidays. In April 1851, two weeks before the opening of the International Exhibition at the Crystal Palace, they presented *The Queen of the Frogs*, Planché's adaptation of Mme. D'Aulnoy's *La Grenouille Bienfaisante*. The simple plot of this particular fairy tale required very little verbal explanation while it offered the opportunity for sumptuous scenery; this combination of elements made the extravaganza an ideal vehicle to attract the crowds of foreigners expected to overflow the city. The press commended Planché for his elegant taste and refined wit, but once again the star, "the pervading spirit of the scenery," was William Beverley. His sets for the Hall of Diana, the Quick-Silver Lake, the Garden of Prince Non-Pareil, and the Nuptial Bower of the Queen of the Frogs were "realised bits of romance," which "literally lap the spectator's mind in Elysium."[26] *The Era* synthesized in its review—quite possibly unintentionally—every romantic element evident in Beverley's scenery; the admiring critic considered the painting "so perfect" that the viewer would "regret its ephemeral character." The writer added, "It is full of poetry ... and realises all your notions of fairyland and of nature in its richest attire." The presence of some attractive ladies on stage was termed a dazzling sight that "blended with the limner's touches and the machinist's contrivances."[27] To the great disappointment of the Lyceum managers, attendance for this piece was low; in spite of their spectacular offering, sightseers seemed to have saved their energy and their farthings for the pavilions at Hyde Park.

During the next two years, three more of Planché's extravaganzas with scenery designed by Beverley were mounted at the Lyceum. *The Prince of Happy Land; or, The Fawn in the Forest*, adapted from the Countess D'Aulnoy's *La Biche au Bois*, opened on December 26, 1851. The following Christmas, Mlle. de la Force's *La Bonne Femme* inspired *The Good Woman in the Wood*, and on Boxing night 1853, *Once Upon a Time There Were Two Kings*, based on Mme. D'Aulnoy's *La Princesse Carpillion*, was presented.

Planché considered *The Prince of Happy Land* one of his most successful undertakings. He had seen a version of the original fairy tale that autumn in Paris and had been disgusted by the bawdy, tasteless manner in which the charming story had been presented. That experience made him wonder: "Is it too much to connect the low tone of taste and morals of a public that can patronise such frivolous and meretricious exhibitions with the decadence of national grandeur and the general disorganization of society."[28] Of course, no bad taste was ever displayed on the boards of the Lyceum under the Vestris management, and England's grandeur was intact and flourishing under the rule of Queen Victoria. The press agreed with Planché on the merits of his play; once more the latest extravaganza was considered "the best ever" and Beverley's sets were described as indescribable, as usual. The first scene took place in the chamber of a lady who had never seen the sun. Perhaps because candles were the only source of illumination for this poor soul, a gigantic candelabrum almost filled the upstage area of the room; the walls and backdrop were made of point lace. There was also a scene in a garden with golden palm leaves suspended from silver stems; the final tableau took place in the Golden Pinery, where different sections of a vast pine tree opened to reveal actresses attired in silver cloth and children surrounded by red and blue lights at the highest point of the tree. The golden pine suggested to one critic that California (this being gold rush times) had been "ransacked to produce this world of glittering wealth." The "blaze of splendour" of this closing scene produced

The Point-lace Chamber, from *The Prince of Happy Land* at the Lyceum. Engraving from the *Illustrated London News*. From the author's archives.

"unanimous astonishment and acclamation."[29] No less illustrious a critic than Queen Victoria, who devotedly patronized the Lyceum for the extravaganzas, was duly impressed with Beverley's glittering fairyland, although she found the production "too long, with much tiresome and bad singing."[30]

By 1852 time had begun to tell on Mme. Vestris, and neither fairy princesses nor young heroes in breeches were within her range any longer. She was performing less frequently, though she could still draw a crowd when her name was announced on a playbill, and during that cold winter of 1852 the Lyceum managers were in very great need of attracting an audience. Planché came to the rescue of his friend by creating, in the heroine of *The Good Woman in the Wood*, a character suitable for Madame's "appearance, style, and capacity."[31] The piece also gave Beverley another opportunity to create one of his magical "transformation scenes" that so fascinated the public. In the scene titled "Magnificent Testimonial," in which the entire array of fairies paid homage to the Good Woman, the audience saw "a large group of gems and flowers, the former all glistening in brilliant hues, the latter budding and afterwards blooming in various tints." *The Era* wrote: "These are borne by and garnished with living female figures, whose dark hair, and dainty limbs, and flashing eyes, add to the general effect. ... There is something supernatural in the fineness of everything, from the light dresses of the fairies to the leaves of the trees. Tulips open and expand in transparent colours; figures of reposing nymphs move without any perceptible effort, and the scene unfolds ... and grows before the eyes into something more and more wondrous, until a blaze of light is thrown upon the whole, and the curtain falls amid a burst of applause."[32] The spectators insisted on having Beverley receive the burst of applause in person, and the designer made his appearance on stage "in all the *deshabillé* peculiar to his craft."[33]

During the spring of 1853 Vestris and Mathews played to almost empty houses. Their financial troubles were compounded by the departures of Planché and Beverley. The playwright had left London to settle in the country at the home of his daughter, and the designer had found a more solvent management to pay his salary, which had been in arrears for some time. It was doubtful whether the Lyceum would reopen for another season with Madame at the helm, but Mathews, displaying great power of persuasion, convinced Planché and Beverley that they should all work together one more time. As a result, *Once Upon a Time There Were Two Kings* was unveiled on Boxing Night and became the last collaboration of the artists who, through their collective efforts, had transported the Victorian public to the romantic world of fairy tales.

In spite of their lack of funds, the managers did not hesitate to invest an enormous sum on this production in the hope that another grand spectacle would save them from bankruptcy. Beverley contributed his usual astonishing scenery, but his magic was to no avail: the hoped-for crowds did not materialize. After another season of agonizing failures, further aggravated by Madame's ill health, in March 1855 the last curtain fell on the Lyceum under the Vestris-Mathew lesseeship.

Mme. Vestris's care in the presentation of her productions had established a precedent that other managers could not easily ignore. As far back as 1842, her painstaking attention to detail, and her willingness to invest extraordinary sums to achieve visual perfection, had been commended for bringing a new dawn upon the drama, although, in the same article, other managers were warned not to fall for the temptation of considering scenery more a passion than a necessity.[34] Nevertheless, no warning could stop the tidal wave of elaborate romantic scenery that flooded the stages of the London theatres from mid-century onward, and William Beverley's talents continued to be in great demand for another 30 years.

While still on the staff of the Lyceum, Beverley had been appointed to succeed Thomas Grieve as scenic director of the Italian Opera at Covent Garden. In 1854 he began his association with Drury Lane, a relationship that would last until 1885. Season after season, Beverley's commissions alternated among operas, Christmas pantomimes, and Shakespearean revivals; he designed *King John, Macbeth,* and *Henry IV, Part I* at Drury Lane in 1855, as well as *Antony and Cleopatra* in 1873 and *Richard III* in 1876. His sets were also seen on the stages of the Adelphi, the Princess's, and Her Majesty's Theatres, as well as the Royal Theatre in Islington, among many others.

Beverley embarked on his career in an era when painted sets of great lyrical, romantic quality dominated unchallenged, and to the end of his professional life he continued to believe that only painting could convey the poetry of the drama. He dismissed with contempt, as "the reign of the pot and pan," the trend toward realistic scenery, a trend that had begun to appear at the time when his creations at the Lyceum brought him such universal acclaim. He continued to maintain, to the very end, his belief: "A well-painted scene ... stimulates the imagination."

> A "built-up" scene, full of elaborate realistic detail, distracts the attention of the spectator from the essentials of the drama. ... I condemn all this straining after realism because it serves no artistic purpose. The audience know that the scene is a sham, and no tricks of the carpenter, the "property" man, or the florist can convince them of its reality, though they may marvel at the ingenuity displayed. ... I do not approve of "building up" forest scenes. ... It is impossible to *make* a tree that will look like nature on the stage. A good painter, in painting trees, water, etc., endeavours to give them their natural atmosphere, and the light that would naturally be reflected upon them from the sky; but if you "built-up" a tree, and then turn the gaslight upon it, you cannot possibly give it the appearance of nature. ... Nowdays the carpenter and the property-man have as much to do with the mounting of a play as the scene-painter, and dramatic art must suffer as a consequence.[35]

Beverley believed himself to be, by the 1880s, the last of the dying breed that had included such great scenic artists as De Loutherbourgh, Stanfield, and Cox. He considered the painting room of the theatre the best training ground for aspiring young artists, and the fact that he had contributed watercolor renderings to the Royal Academy for 30 years was undeniable proof of his convictions.[36] Even in the most elaborate sets he ever designed, he insisted on conducting all the steps of scene painting himself; only the priming of the drops or flats was left to his assistants. The delicate atmospheric effects that had contributed so much to his fame were achieved through his mastery of watercolor technique; by painting on wet canvas as he would have painted on wet paper, he was able to duplicate the transparency of that medium on a massive scale.[37] The artistry of his drops earned him the title "the Watteau of scene painters," and the lyrical quality of his scenery led a critic to declare that Beverley must have dipped "his pencil in the rainbow itself," whereas other painters used "that compound which bears the vile name of "distemper.'"[38] Unfortunately, we have to re-create in our imagination, with the help of contemporary reviews and commentaries, the beauty of Beverley's scenery because, after a 50-year career, only two of his original designs have been preserved: a backcloth of Brussels for an unidentified play and a sketch for *Henry IV.*

The ephemeral fairyland created by William Beverley for Mme. Vestris's productions of J. R. Planché's extravaganzas vanished from the stage of the Lyceum to survive only in the memory of those who, like Squire Bancroft, were witnesses to that illustration of romantic fantasy in the history of nineteenth-century theatre.

The demise of the extravaganza was caused not only by the parting of the artists who had brought it to life but also by changes in the public's taste. By the late 1850s, Planché's elegant fairies were pushed off the stage by the coarser impersonations of the burlesque and pantomime, as well as by the realistic characters of the "cup-and-saucer" drama. Nevertheless, scenic illusion capable of transporting an audience to remote ages and exotic lands continued to be in demand for another 50 years.

Chapter 3

Charles Kean
and His Designers:
A Romance with History

*T*HE STUDY OF HISTORY AS A MEANS to understand the present began to be explored in the late eighteenth century and reached its summit in the nineteenth century. The romantic impulse to find in the past a refuge from contemporary reality, combined with the ever grow-ing desire to investigate the development of human activity, invaded every area of artistic endeavor. As Arnold Hauser states in his *Social History of Art*: "Without the historical consciousness of romanticism, without the constant questioning of the meaning of the present, by which the thinking of the romantics was dominated, the whole historicism of the nineteenth century and one of the deepest revolutions in the history of the human mind would have been inconceivable."[1]

In the theatre, historicism manifested itself in the proliferation of his-torically accurate scenery and costumes that first surfaced in the 1820s through the efforts of James Robinson Planché. Although John Philip Kemble had experimented with classic Roman costume earlier, it was Planché, in his capac-ity as designer for Charles Kemble's landmark production of *King John* at Covent Garden in 1823, who led the movement that would make historical research an indispensable ingredient in stage production. His work provided a turning point in the way plays were presented, making it impossible for most contemporary managers to ignore the demand for an "archaeologically cor-rect" reproduction of bygone eras. The reforms toward a faithful re-creation of the past initiated by Planché were adopted by Mme. Vestris when she pro-duced plays other than extravaganzas; her *Artaxerxes* at Covent Garden in 1839 had scenery and costumes inspired by Sir Robert Kerr's drawings of Persepolis. Historical accuracy became a feature of Macready's presentations in the 1830s and 1840s and was further carried on, with missionary zeal, by Charles Kean in the 1850s.

Kean understood, and shared with his audience, that extraordinary

Victorian thirst for education and information packaged in spectacular surroundings. The avowed purpose of Kean's endeavors was to entertain while educating by offering "dramatic representations conducive to the diffusion of knowledge."[2] In his preface to the acting edition of *Richard II*, Charles Kean declared: "Repeated success justifies the conviction that I am acting in accordance with the general feeling. When plays, which formerly commanded but occasional repetitions, are enabled ... to attract audiences for successive months, I cannot be wrong in presuming that the course I have adopted is supported by the irresistible force of public opinion, expressed in the suffrages of an overwhelming majority."[3]

The course that Kean had adopted, and that he felt compelled to defend time and time again, led him, during his tenure as manager of the Princess's Theatre, to attempt the most accurate re-creation of historical periods that current research would permit. He studded the leaflets attached to the playbills, and the editions of the plays printed to be sold to the public before the performances, with copious scholarly notes about the "authorities" he had consulted to ensure the utmost historical fidelity. In spite of some detractors, his efforts were rewarded by the public and lauded by the press; in 1855 a critic praised Kean: "[He has] not only essayed to dazzle the eyes of the spectators with a glittering show—though he does that most effectively—but he has sought to make his stage a vehicle for archaeological instruction, and thus keep pace with that tendency of the day to obtain the most information as to the life and habits of the past."[4]

Charles John Kean was the second son of the great, and notorious, Edmund Kean, an actor who had risen to success in the first decades of the nineteenth century performing some of the most demanding roles in the Shakespearean repertoire. Young Charles, after his academic education at Eton, made his stage debut at Covent Garden at the age of 16, on October 1, 1827, as Young Norval in John Home's *Douglas*. For the next 20 years his activities followed the pattern familiar to most actors of his time: provincial performances alternating with engagements in London, plus occasional tours to America. Kean's first trip to the United States took place in 1830; he returned in 1839 and 1845.

It was in New York, at the Park Theatre in January 1846, that Kean initially ventured to present one of Shakespeare's plays with all the accuracy and sense of spectacle that would become his trademark in the following decade. Never before had an American audience witnessed, at the monumental cost of $10,000, a production of *Richard III* in which such painstaking care had been lavished on the faithful reproduction of architecture and dress of the era of the hunchback king.[5] Kean's efforts were greeted with enthusiasm; *Richard III* played nightly to full houses for three weeks. However, when Kean offered an equally magnificent and accurate production of *King John* in November 1846, attendance was low. Whether because the novelty had waned or because the story of the landless king was not as appealing as that of the wicked Richard, the fickle New York playgoers—to Kean's great disappointment—remained indifferent to the six months of preparation and the $12,000 he had invested to educate them. Although this American tour had not been altogether unsuccessful from a financial point of view, the failure of *King John* discouraged Kean from attempting another revival in New York. He returned to London and joined Benjamin Webster's company at the Haymarket.

In the summer of 1848 Kean received instructions from Queen Victoria to devise a series of performances at Windsor Castle for the pleasure and edification of the royal family and their guests during the Christmas holiday. The presentation of *The Merchant of Venice* in the Rubens Room, on December 28, 1848, marked Kean's debut as director of the Windsor Theatricals; for the next nine years he would return every holiday season to entertain the queen and her court with productions of Shakespeare and other British playwrights.

In August 1850, Kean embarked on his career as actor-manager at the Princess's Theatre, a small but well-established playhouse in Oxford Street, where, until his retirement in 1859, he would dazzle the public with the historical accuracy of his Shakespearean revivals, produced on a spectacular scale never equaled on the English stage. Queen Victoria's patronage, combined with Kean's high standards of production, lent an aura of respectability to the actor's managerial endeavours, attracting the same upper- and middle-class audience that had remained, during the last decades, conspicuously absent from the playhouses that offered serious drama.

To carry out successfully his theories on the pedagogical value of massive historical reconstruction, Charles Kean solicited the assistance of scholars and antiquarians while at the same time he assembled a team of designers that included some of the most notable scenic artists of the period. William Telbin, Frederick Lloyds, William Gordon, Charles Fenton, Henry J. Cuthbert, and J. Dayes, all under the general supervision of Thomas Grieve, joined the enterprise. Following the practice of the time, designers worked in collaboration, with three, four, and sometimes five artists in the same production. Grieve, Gordon, and Telbin belonged to the bests tradition of the English landscape painting; all three had exhibited at the Royal Academy and were in charge of backdrops depicting romantic views of nature. Cuthbert and Lloyds specialized in historically correct architectural set pieces and properties.

A collection of over 200 watercolors, illustrating the scenery, properties, and in several instances the arrangement of crowds on stage for every scene of every one of Kean's productions at the Princess's, was rendered by Grieve and his colleagues and given to the actor-manager at his retirement. In 1900 this collection was presented to the Victoria and Albert Museum by Mrs. Paget, Mrs. Kean's niece, and was subsequently exhibited, for the first and only time, in 1902. These watercolors constitute the most comprehensive graphic evidence of settings created under the influence of the antiquarian-spectacular movement and are the only *complete* record of scenery designed for any management in the mid–nineteenth century. Moreover, when studied from a pictorial point of view, their careful composition and use of color schemes are also indicative of the interrelation between stage design and canvas painting.

Although Kean produced *Twelfth Night, The Merry Wives of Windsor,* and *Hamlet* in the first two years of his management, massive, historically accurate scenery does not seem to have been his priority at the time, perhaps due to budgetary considerations. However, in 1852 his devotion to archaeological reconstruction came into full bloom. *King John*, the same play that Kean had offered to the indifferent New Yorkers six years earlier, was presented, first to Queen Victoria at Windsor Castle on February 6 and three days later to the general public at the Princess's. John William Cole, Kean's friend and biographer, reported that *King John* was the manager's "first *great* attempt on the plan he ... carried out with such indomitable perseverance and triumphant success." According to Cole, Kean believed that "the time had at length arrived when a total personification of Shakespeare, with every accompaniment that refined knowledge, diligent research, and chronological accuracy could supply, was suited to the taste and temper of the age, which had become eminently pictorial, and unwilling any longer to believe themselves transported from Italy to Athens ... without the aid of scenic appliances."[6]

The scenery for *King John* had been inspired by thorough research of Norman ruins still in existence, remains of twelfth- and thirteenth-century architecture, and the Room of State in the first act had been copied from the Hall in Rochester Castle. There were fourteen different settings—six of them painted by Lloyds, five by Gordon, one each by Dayes and Cuthbert, and one done in collaboration by Lloyds and Gordon—all under the direction of Thomas Grieve. The interior locations were designed as box sets, with very elaborate ceilings achieved by a series of borders painted to match the architecture of the room. The exteriors were built on the principle of masking wings backed by drops depicting landscapes and skies.

The London press lauded the staging of *King John*, recognizing the attention to detail and historical accuracy that had been lavished on the piece. The *Times* called it "a medieval banquet on which no pains nor expenses [had] been spared."[7] George Henry Lewes, no great admirer of Kean's, reluctantly conceded that this "minutely antiquarian" spectacle was "truly pictorial and striking."[8] Nevertheless, this initial effort by Kean was to be eclipsed by his more magnificent subsequent productions; when the same *King John* was revived in 1858, the *Illustrated London News* considered it to be "one of the least elaborate" of the manager's presentations.[9]

To follow *King John*, Kean chose *Macbeth* as his next project. The play was performed before Queen Victoria at Windsor Castle on February 4, 1853, and ten days later it opened at the Princess's. On this occasion, Kean introduced the flyleaves in which he cited the authorities consulted to ensure accurate research and prepared the audience for the history lesson to follow. These leaflets, which became the preface to Kean's acting editions of the plays, were considered by J. W. Cole to serve as an introductory interpretation similar to "the Greek chorus elucidating the progress in the classical tragedy."[10] The flyleaf for *Macbeth* informed the public that due to the lack of extant remains from such remote times, the manager had gathered materials from Norway and Denmark in the eleventh century:

> In the four centuries and a half which intervened between the death of St. Columba [early seventh century] and the reign of Macbeth, it is reasonable to presume that considerable improvements took place among the Scotch, and that the fashion of their dress and buildings was borrowed from their more civilized neighbours. Under those considerations, the architecture, previous to the Norman Conquest, has been adopted throughout the play. During the five centuries that preceded the event, the Anglo-Saxons made great advances, and erected many castles and churches of considerable importance; they excelled in iron-work, and ornamented their buildings frequently with colour. On this subject I have availed myself of the valuable knowledge of George Godwin, Esq., F.R.S., of the Royal Institute of Architects, to whose suggestion I take this opportunity of acknowledging my obligation.[11]

Nineteen sets were designed for this production; Lloyds and Gordon painted five each, Dayes four, and Cuthbert two. Grieve was responsible for three settings, one of which, "View near the Castle of Dunsinane," act 5, scene 5, had no connection with the text but was probably used as a drop to cover the scene change that followed. There is no design in the Victoria and Albert Museum for the opening scene with the witches in the heath, but the reviews indicate that the scene was played behind semitransparent drops. The *Illustrated London News* remarked, "In treating the supernatural scenes, an abundant use has been made of gauze, so that the witches are continually presented enveloped in a thick mist ... and many of the scenes besides are so enveloped that the change from one to the other is managed almost with the effect of a dissolving view."[12] Another critic described the gaunt figures of the spectral creatures as standing "awfully against the morning sky" after the artificial fog dispersed. Their cave in act 4 was "no common cave, but the 'Pit of Acheron'—a hollow cone, lighted from the top, with a reddish lustre, in the midst of which they perform effective orgies."[13]

It is apparent that Kean had tried to emphasize the supernatural elements, so appealing to romantic sensibilities, with all the theatrical devices at his disposal. The banquet scene, painted by Dayes, was performed in a great hall with a sloping timber roof supported by round columns; an opening in the back wall showed a minstrel's gallery where seven old men in druidical costumes played their harps. Banquo made his appearance from a trap at the back of a table placed up center, his head backlighted by a pale blue light; as he turned around to pledge the guests, the inside of the column next to him became suddenly illuminated to show his menacing ghost within it while the lights were dimmed on the rest of the stage. This apparition of Banquo's ghost inside a pillar, which seems a considerable achievement given the limitations of lighting equipment at the time, was praised by the critics and taken as evidence of Kean's determination to present extraordinary visual displays. The *Times* remarked: "Whenever an opportunity is offered for a new striking treatment of the many strange subjects with which this wild and terrific tragedy abounds, it is sized on with avidity, and a remarkable picture is the result."[14]

When not using the scenery to accentuate the supernatural elements, Kean and his designers maintained visual unity throughout the play based on their studies of pre-Norman architecture. Some of the renderings at the Victoria and Albert Museum illustrate the massive but not opulent buildings appropriate to portray Anglo-Saxon times.

Macbeth played on alternate evenings, for a total run of 54 performances. Immediately following the end of this run, Charles Kean and his wife, the actress Ellen Tree, decided to exhume from oblivion Lord Byron's *Sardanapalus*. The Assyrian tyrant's violent death by fire had been a source of inspiration to the early romantic generation: Eugène Delacroix exhibited his painting *The Death of Sardanapalus* in Paris in 1829, and Byron's tragedy had been presented at Drury Lane in 1834. Although the original production of the romantic poet's play did not achieve great success, 20 years later it offered Kean an exceptional opportunity for performing antiquarian reconstruction in the service of the drama and for transporting his audience to the sensuous, exotic world of the ancient Middle East. The ruins of Nineveh had recently been discovered by the British archaeologist Austen Henry Layard and the French Paul-Émile Botta while excavating in Mesopotamia during the late 1840s and early 1850s. Therefore, Kean and his design team could base the scenery for *Sardanapalus* on unimpeachable, firsthand sources of information. The manager was hardly able to hide his excitement when he wrote in the flyleaf for the production: "To render visible to the eye, in connection with Lord Byron's drama, the costume, architecture, and domestic manners of the ancient Assyrian people, verified by the bas-reliefs, which, after having been buried for nearly 3,000 years, have in our own day been brought to life, was an object that might well inspire the enthusiasm of one who has learnt that scenic illustration, if it have the weight of authority, may adorn and add dignity to the noblest work of genius."[15]

The reconstruction of Nineveh was entrusted to Lloyds, Gordon, and Dayes; the five acts of the play were performed in three sets. In the first and second acts the scenery painted by Gordon showed a panoramic view of the city on the shores of the Tigris, with its tall, angular, highly ornate buildings

Frederick Lloyds's rendering for the Great Hall of Nimrod in *Sardanapalus*. Courtesy of the Board of Trustees of the Victoria and Albert Museum.

glowing under the rays of a rising sun. A grand procession of soldiers, priests, minstrels, and dancing girls in the first scene preceded Sardanapalus, who, dressed in scarlet and gold studded with jewels, made his entrance in a splendid chariot drawn by two horses. When the curtain rose for the third scene, the audience saw the Great Hall of Nimrod in the king's palace filled with the retinue of the Assyrian monarch "as if the sculptures in the British Museum had stepped on to the boards of the theatre by the power of a magician's talisman."[16] Frederick Lloyds's rendering for the Hall, where a great banquet and ballet took place, shows a massive diagonal wall, from downstage left almost disappearing out of view in perspective toward upstage right, made of five panels decorated with Assyrian figures and winged lions in shades of blue and gold. The first downstage panel backs a set of practical steps that lead to an entrance covered by a very elaborate tapestry of red and blue designs on gold background. The ceiling is indicated by tapestries that diminish in size as they recede, arranged horizontally across the stage above the flats. The exaggerated perspective of this design, emphasized further by a color scheme that turns cooler as the wall vanishes upstage, was a novel approach to the problem of creating the illusion of depth and received favorable comments from some critics. As spectacular as the early scenes were, Kean and his designers outdid themselves in the final act. The stage fire that consumed the palace chamber and the entire city in the "grand finale" was so realistically represented that a very alarmed insurance company sent some investigators to verify that the bursts of flames and blazing rafters falling from the roof were indeed harmless scenic effects presenting no danger to the structure of the Princess's Theatre. The watercolor in the Victoria and Albert Museum shows a very dramatic view of the scene, with bricks and stones flying from the sides toward the fires burning center-stage.

If Kean had any doubts about the validity of his theories on the didactic potential of his dramatic presentations, an article written by Douglas Jerrold, editor of *Lloyd's Weekly Newspaper*, must have been extremely reassuring. Jerrold expressed his approval: "Mr. Kean has been the noble teacher on this occasion, and he cannot be praised too highly for the generous spirit in which he has carried out and illustrated his pleasant teaching ... for many years to come, 'Sardanapalus' will be a beautiful picture to hang in the long, dreary hall of our dramatic recollections."[17] As Kean had intended, his productions were unquestionably becoming a living, pictorial lecture on the past. *Sardanapalus* had a run of 61 performances after its initial presentation and 32 additional evenings during the following fall season.

In the winter of 1854, on February 20, Kean offered another one of his Shakespearean revivals, *Richard III*. Although the manager was unequivocally dedicated to historical accuracy in scenery and costumes, his respect for Shakespeare's original texts was not equally intense. He opted for Colley Cibber's adaptation of *Richard III*, as his father and other great actors had done before him, and justified his choice by declaring: "There may be a question as to the propriety of tampering at all with the writings of our bard: but there can be none that as an *acting* play, Colley Cibber's version of 'King Richard the Third,' evinces great dramatic judgment, and a consummate acquaintance with scenic effect."[18]

Kean and his designers took the same pains to re-create the late fifteenth century as they had with other periods in previous productions. Most of the responsibility for creating the scenery was given to Lloyds, who designed 16 of the 19 scenes; two others were by Gordon and one by Cuthbert. Nevertheless, neither the spectacular sets nor the masses of supernumeraries, as many as 115 for the final grand tableau at Bosworth Fiend, were able to silence the critical objections to Kean's choice of Cibber's text. One reviewer wrote: "All that art and munificent expenditure can do for the illustration of the revived drama has been again accomplished on the boards of this theatre. We regret, however, that Cibber's 'Richard III' has been substituted for Shakespeare's 'Life and Death' of the same monarch. ... With all the store of scenery and costumes bestowed upon the present revival, more might yet have been done for the original tragedy restored in its ancient integrity."[19] The play had a very short and disappointing career, with only 19 performances.

Before his fourth season at the Princess's ended, Kean presented some other new pieces: *Faust and Marguerite*, a magical drama adapted from a French version of the well-known story; and a melodramatic tale of robbery and murder titled *The Courier of Lyons*. Between October 10, 1853, and August 9, 1854, Kean had mounted 18 different plays, in addition to eight shorter pieces and a pantomime.

In the spring of 1855, Kean undertook one of his most ambitious projects, one that proved to be his most successful Shakespearean revival. *Henry VIII*, presented on May 16, was performed on 100 consecutive evenings, an unprecedented record for one of the Bard's plays; it returned to the stage another 69 times in subsequent years and marked, in 1859, Kean's final appearance, in the role of Cardinal Wolsey, as manager of the Princess's. The sheer length of the play and the expense necessary to produce it had discouraged most managers in the past from attempting a revival. However, Kean saw in the required processions, banquet, masque, and trial scene abundant potential for didactic pageantry. To solve the problem of length, Kean omitted most of act 5, except for the christening of Princess Elizabeth at Grey Friars, and instead took advantage of the journey by the lord mayor and city council to the ceremony in Greenwich to end the play with a moving panoramic view of London as it had been in the sixteenth century. This panorama, painted by Thomas Grieve, was copied from Anthony Van Den Wynyerde's 1543 drawing, available in the Sutherland Collection of the Bodleian Library, Oxford.[20]

The playbill for *Henry VIII* credits seven artists for the scenery: Grieve, Gordon, Lloyds, Fenton, Seward, Jones, and Morgan, in addition to numerous assistants. Eight of the 13 scenes were played in box-set interiors, two were exteriors with three-dimensional units, two were conventional wing-and-drop arrangements, and the last was the grand panorama of the city. The antiquarian Francis Donce and the architect George Godwin served as historical advisers. The opening scene, the "Old Palace Yard at Westminster," was, as painted by Gordon, a copy of another one of Wynyerde's drawings in the Bodleian Library. Act 1, scene 2, "The Council Chamber," painted by Lloyds, was a restoration of the "Painted Chamber" at Westminster as portrayed in a drawing by the set designer William Capon in *Vetusta Monumenta*. The first act ended in "The Presence Chamber at York Palace," where a spectacular masque, involving 153 supernumeraries, took place. The illusion of extreme depth was achieved in this set, as it had been in *Sardanapalus*, by the diagonal treatment of a series of Gothic arches extending, almost to infinity, from down right to up left. Contemporary accounts referred to the quality and quantity of glittering ornament, real chandeliers among them, that graced this spectacular scene.

The scenery for acts 2 and 3 was massive and equally accurate; the locales were the King Stairs at Westminster, an antechamber in the palace, a hall at Blackfriars where Queen Katherine's trial took place, and the queen's apartment in the palace at Bridwell. In act 4, scene 2, Kean found yet another opportunity to display the artistry of his design team. "The Vision of Queen Katherine" in a room at Kimbolton Castle, painted by Lloyds, was described in the *Illustrated London News* as "perhaps the most beautiful effect ever introduced upon the stage—an effect so beautiful and dream-like, that it kept the audience entranced and hushed ... till the lovely group of floating figures had vanished from their eyes."[21] The effect that had so entranced the audience was the apparition of a number of angels gliding diagonally down toward the queen in a shaft of light coming from a window stage right. The system of rigging employed for flying the angels had been brought from Paris, where it was known as *les femmes volantes*, and had been improved upon by Kean's machinists. From the recollections of a contemporary writer it is possible to reconstruct the scene. Godfrey Turner said:

> The trooping angels in the slant of light which poured in at the Gothic window in Katherine's room ... were, one may reasonable guess, supported in iron frames or cradles, just as are the tinselled fairies in a transformation-scene; but ... we could then detect no trace of mechanism or even arrangement, all seeming so easy and yet so inexplicable. As a matter of fact, I knew, on the second occasion of seeing Charles Kean's *Henry VIII*, that the flood of light obliquely descending in Queen Katherine's chamber and peopled with white-winged angels, was not where it seemed to be—not in the room at all, but behind the transparency in the panelled wall at the back. Yet, for all my knowledge of the contrivance, the effect of prominence was the same as at first; the same as when I was ignorant of the means by which it was attained. This is the triumph of stage enchantment—to retain the admiration of those who are in the secret; to preserve the illusion for eyes enfranchised and on the watch for trick, blemish, or failure.[22]

This scene was followed by the moving panorama, suggesting the journey of the barges along the Thames, and the evening ended with Princess Elizabeth's baptism in the Church of Grey Friars, painted by Gordon from research on similar contemporary buildings, since no remains of Greenwich Palace existed. The crowd attending the christening of the future queen consisted of 149 supernumeraries.

Godfrey Turner, almost thirty years after the premiere of Kean's *Henry VIII*, called it "the most splendid revival, scenically and historically considered, ever placed before gods and groundlings."[23] Critics in 1855 had been equally enthusiastic, and for some, this production seemed to put to rest, once and for all, the ongoing controversy regarding the legitimacy of presenting

Opposite: Frederick Lloyds's rendering for the Masque, *Henry VIII*, act 1, scene 4. Courtesy of the Board of Trustees of the Victoria and Albert Museum.

Shakespeare in the midst of antiquarian realism and special effects. A reviewer maintained, "If the often-mooted question whether Shakespeare's plays should be subjected to all the means and appliances for their illustration that modern art can furnish has not hitherto been settled by that supreme and ultimate court of dramatic law, the playgoing public, we fancy the introduction of *Henry VIII* ... will put the question to rest forever." The writer believed Shakespeare himself might have used comparable scenic illustration if it had been available to him, "although the wildest dreams of the dramatist" could not have "anticipated the union of scene-painting, machinery, aerial suspension, and bude-light" found at the Princess's Theatre in the nineteenth century.[24]

The *Art Journal,* a publication dedicated to the visual arts, emphasized in its review the pictorial qualities of the production:

> The whole of the scenery is admirably painted by Mr. Grieve and his assistants, and as the views are taken from the best authorities who have left us records of ancient London, their fidelity cannot be questioned. But the great triumph in connection with the scenic display is in "Katherine's Dream," where the angels appear to her: this is a wonderful piece of stage illusion, and yet it can scarcely be called "illusion," for the beautiful spirits are real flesh and blood. The picture they present is one that Guido or Corregio might have painted, and yet Art could never reach the loveliness of this scene; we would heartily recommend every artist to go and study it—its groupings, attitude, and action, light and shade.[25]

With *Henry VIII,* Kean had firmly established Shakespeare on the boards of the Princess's Theatre and had raised much expectation among the public as to what he would do next to maintain his reputation. In the spring of 1856 the manager surprised most playgoers with the announcement of *The Winter's Tale* as his choice for the next revival. This play, full of anachronisms, without a defined time period or location, did not appear to be an appropriate vehicle for Kean's penchant for historical accuracy. Nevertheless, well aware of the difficulties involved and after much reflection, he decided to set *The Winter's Tale* at a time that, he noted, accorded "with the spirit of the play" but could "be considered the most interesting, as well as the most instructive."[26] Taking the pronouncement by the Oracle of Delphi as the cornerstone of the plot, Kean placed the action around 330 BC, the epoch when Syracuse rivaled Athens in magnificence and prosperity; consequently, he could reproduce the classical era and "place before the eyes of the spectator *tableaux vivants* of the private and public life of the ancient Greeks, at a time when the arts flourished to perfection."[27] The problem of "Bohemia," a country unknown to the Greeks and their neighbors, was solved by changing the

Opposite: Frederick Lloyds's rendering for "The Vision of Queen Katherine," *Henry VIII,* act 4, scene 2. Courtesy of the Board of Trustees of the Victoria and Albert Museum.

location to "Bithynia," as suggested by Sir Thomas Hamner in his edition of Shakespeare in 1744. This word in no way affected the incidents or meter of the play. George Sharf, author of the *Handbook to the Greek and Pompeian Courts at the Crystal Palace* and Fellow of the Society of Antiquarians, contributed his knowledge of ancient architecture in addition to his drawings of the vegetation peculiar to Bithynia. Under the direction of Grieve, the scenery was painted by Telbin, Gordon, Lloyds, Cuthbert, Dayes, and Morgan.

The *Winter's Tale* opened on April 28, 1856, with Queen Victoria present in the royal box. After the short introductory scene showing the Temple of Minerva at Syracuse, painted by Telbin, the action moved to Morgan and Cuthbert's rendition of "A Banqueting Room in the Palace." This room, of symmetrical design, was a massive box set, in an off-white color scheme, showing three enormous caryatids in each wall and matching painted figures in the backdrop. The first border was a painted red drapery, its rich hue repeated in the upholstery that covered the couches where the reclining guests were discovered at the beginning of the scene. As the action developed, 36 ravishing young women in full armor performed a Pyrrhic dance.[28] Act 2 opened in Hermione's chamber, a room designed by Cuthbert, who made use once more of diagonal composition to increase the illusion of depth. From slightly off-center, downstage, two rows of Doric columns vanished toward upstage right and left. The columns supported an elaborate ceiling formed by ornate square panels, each containing four additional panels painted blue. The scale of the set, according to the watercolor in the Victoria and Albert Museum, suggests a temple rather than the intimate environment of the *gynaeceum.* The following scene, another room in the palace, was performed in a box set of symmetrical design, with a back wall of columns spaced to reveal a distant view of hills, buildings, and palm trees painted by Lloyds. Act 3, Queen Hermione's trial, gave Thomas Grieve an opportunity to exhibit his exceptional skills as a scenic artist. Kean had selected the theatre at Syracuse as the locale for the trial because such buildings were frequently used for judicial proceedings in Greece but also because it afforded the possibility for dramatic scenic effect. Grieve's set suggested the colossal proportion of the amphitheatre with a backdrop representing a very steep section of the *koilon,* where the thousands of spectators on the benches were figures painted on the canvas. The two three-dimensional units downstage, a colonnade on the right, and a flat with a gate, which served as the facing for a staircase, on the left contributed to the illusion of distance. Leontes' throne was placed stage right, on a platform below the colonnade, facing the flesh-and-blood audience situated in the staircase downstage left.

Opposite: William Telbin's rendering for a view of Syracuse with the Temple of Minerva in the background. *The Winter's Tale,* act 1, scene 1. Courtesy of the Board of Trustees of the Victoria and Albert Museum.

Lightning and thunder raged as Antigonus deposited the infant Perdita on a wild and rocky spot on the coast of Bythinia, a set designed by Gordon. After the old shepherd discovered the baby, clouds descended to set the stage for an allegory representing the passage of time. Kean took full advantage of this scene for another one of his spectacular effects. As the clouds dispersed,

> *Selene*, or *Luna*, was discovered in her car accompanied by the *Stars* (personified by living figures), and gradually sunk into the ocean. *Time* then appeared, surmounting the globe, no longer represented by the traditionally bald-headed elder, with his scythe and hour-glass, but as a classical figure, more in accordance with the character of the play as now presented. He spoke the lines with which Shakespeare has connected the two separate epochs of this play. As *Time* descended, *Phoebus* rose with surpassing brilliance in the chariot of the Sun, encircled by a blaze of light which filled every portion of the theatre. The group appeared to be derived from that in the centre of Flaxman's Shield of Achilles. ... The statue-like grace and immobility of *Apollo*, as he stood in the car, reining in his impetuous steeds, impressed a universal conviction that this figure was also artificial; but the living reality was conveyed in the most startling manner, when, at the full height of his ascent, he suddenly raised his right arm to lash a restive courser. The effect baffles description. The entire allegory may be pronounced the greatest triumph of art ever exhibited on the stage.[29]

At the end of the allegory, after 16 years had elapsed, the audience was transported first to Polixenes' palace and then to a roadside landscape, rich in local and authentic vegetation, both sets designed by Cuthbert. The bucolic dance of the shepherds was followed by a festival in honor of Dionysus, frantically performed by a crowd of dancers in wild attires. The curtain went down on act 4 with the flight of Perdita and Florizel and rose again at the beginning of act 5 in the garden of Leontes in Sicily. Lloyds adapted the design for this set from a drawing found at Herculaneum, although the view in the backdrop is reminiscent of the Acropolis. The play ended in the peristyle of Paulina's mansion, painted by Dayes, where Hermione's statue was discovered within a round marble structure of classic Corinthian design.

The press greeted Kean's *The Winters Tale* with expressions of rapture. According to the *Illustrated London News*, Kean's interpretation was faithful to the intentions of the poet, since Shakespeare himself had devised the play for the introduction of pageantry.[30] *The Era*, after having reprinted Kean's flyleaf in its entirety for the benefit of its readers, declared—in upper-case letters to make sure the message was clear—that the production at the Princess's was "THE GREATEST TRIUMPH WHICH HAS EVER BEEN ACHIEVED UPON THE MODERN, AND, THEREFORE, UPON ANY STAGE."[31] The public agreed with the press and kept *The Winter's Tale* running for 102 consecutive evenings.

Opposite: Thomas Grieve's rendering for Hermione's trial, *The Winter's Tale*, act 3. Courtesy of the Board of Trustees of the Victoria and Albert Museum.

After a recess of only one week, Kean opened his seventh season at the Princess's on September 1, 1856, with a piece that John Kemble and his sister Sarah Siddons had made famous: Richard Sheridan's adaptation of August Friedrich Kotzebuë's *Pizarro*. That historical drama had not been seen in London for a long time; therefore, it presented Kean with the opportunity to depart from familiar territory and portray the Incas' recondite culture at the time of the Spanish conquest. As he explained in the flyleaf, *Pizarro* afforded a wide field "for the introduction of that historical detail which lends new interest to theatrical arts." He was convinced that the public preferred truth to inaccuracy, and he concluded, "When appropriate opportunity is embraced of blending instruction with amusement ... the drama is not likely to lose or be degraded by the attempted association."[32]

For the purpose of dramatic effect, Kean introduced dance, music, and song in the third act, during the festival of Raymi. Although the religious ceremonies were supposed to take place in the main square in Quito, Kean moved the action to Cuzco because more information on the ancient capital of the Incas was available for research. He filled the stage with a crowd of natives who, dressed in fantastic costumes, danced as the sun rose in the horizon, turning their jewelled garments into a blaze of light. Grieve and his associates were called on to illustrate the imposing mountainous landscape. For the exterior scenes Grieve, Lloyds, and Gordon painted masterpieces with rocks and torrents—the unleashed Nature dear to the Romantics—and for the gardens of the royal palace, Cuthbert created beds of golden plants shaded by golden trees. The great profusion of palm trees and giant ferns shown in the watercolors, however, is more reminiscent of the vegetation in a tropical forest than that of the snow-covered peaks of the Andes.

Just six weeks after the opening of *Pizarro*, on October 15, Kean presented another magnificent Shakespearean revival. Reluctantly conceding that no research, however arduous, could possibly reveal the exact time and location for *A Midsummer Night's Dream*, Kean decided to take the audience on an instructive tour of Athens in the fifth century BC and to show the city "as it would have appeared to one of its own inhabitants, at a time when it had attained its greatest splendour in literature and the arts."[33]

Grieve, Gordon, and Lloyds were the artists in charge of re-creating Athens, as well as the magical world of the fairies. The opening scene revealed a view of the Acropolis from Theseus's palace, with the Parthenon, the Erechtheum, Athena's statue, the theatre of Dionysus, and the temple of Zeus. The interior scenes in the palace were classically inspired, symmetrical box sets, not particularly imaginative. However, for the exteriors, the designers created whimsical landscapes in which legions of fairies, wearing romantic white tutus and with wings on their backs, performed their dances to Mendelssohn's incidental music. The diorama painted by Grieve and Gordon for act 2 allowed the scenery to glide from scene to scene through the

Frederick Lloyds's rendering for "Titania's Bower," *A Midsummer Night's Dream*, act 4, scene 1. Courtesy of the Board of Trustees of the Victoria and Albert Museum.

woods as if in a dream. The last view in the diorama, "A Wood near Athens by Moonlight," was painted by Grieve and was a copy of William Turner's "Golden Bough." "Titania's Bower" in act 4, designed by Lloyds, had a luxuriant tropical feeling, with gigantic ferns reaching to the sky.

It was irrelevant by then, both to the public and to the press, what approach Kean took to justify his choices; his hybrid version of *Midsummer* was hailed as an exquisite creation worthy of his lofty intellectual purposes. Moreover, he was praised as the savior of the British theatre, the individual primarily responsible for raising it to international acclaim. This exalted position was evidenced by "the expression of admiration uttered by foreign visitors, ever jealous of the dramatic excellence of their respective countries." The *Illustrated London News* continued: "Germany and France, especially the former, have borne ample testimony to the classical taste and information of Mr. Kean, and give vent to their opinions as if England had never until now possessed a theatre of the highest order. England at large is indebted to Mr. Kean for such an exercise of art, tending so powerfully to propagate a taste for all that unites instruction with refinement; and to redeem thousands from gross unintellectual recreations."[34]

Besides receiving such enthusiastic congratulations in print, Kean had been honored, on June 18 of that same year, with his election as Fellow of the Society of Antiquarians in recognition for his efforts to advance the cause of

historical research; from then on he was entitled, like J. R. Planché, who had been equally rewarded, to add the coveted letters "F.S.A." to his name.

With indefatigable energy, and what seems to have been unlimited funds, Kean revived another two works by Shakespeare in 1857: *Richard II* on March 12, and *The Tempest* on July 1. Kean searched far and wide for documents and illustrations dating back to the fourteenth century in order to depict the life and times of Richard II. Anthony Salvin, F.S.A., a scholar of medieval military architecture, advised Kean on the sets for the Welsh castles and the Tower of London; Henry Shaw, F.S.A., author of *A Series of Details of Gothic Architecture*, contributed his expertise for the Lists at Coventry and John of Gaunt's room at Ely House; in addition, George Godwin, F.S.A., lent his historical knowledge for the reconstruction of medieval London. Kean seized the opportunity offered by Bolingbroke's triumphal entrance to the city with the defeated king to interpolate a historical scene of massive proportions. In the original text the description of Richard being led back to the city by his cousin is related by the Duke of York to his wife in a moving but very short speech in act 5, scene 2. Kean anticipated that description by visually re-creating the actual episode between the third and fourth acts. The set for that scene represented a street corner with four-story houses; the houses in the center and at stage left were evidently flats backed by platforms, built to accommodate the crowds of curious onlookers peering through every window and balcony; the illusion of depth was achieved by a painted view of other buildings vanishing diagonally from the house in the center toward upstage right and left. There is no attribution in the rendering as to which artist painted that scene; it may have been Morris, since his name appears in the program but is not mentioned as having designed any other set.

Multitudes stood in the street and on the rooftops in expectation of the arrival of Bolingbroke, who made his entrance mounted on a white charger and followed by Richard on his humble little dark horse, utterly subdued by the insults of the crowd. J. W. Cole estimated the number of people participating in that scene to have been between 500 and 600, but it seems unlikely that the stage at the Princess's, for which no extant dimensions exist, could have accommodated such a large crowd.[35] Nevertheless, even with half that number, the effect must have been magnificent, judging from the space devoted to its description and the comments it elicited in contemporary periodicals. The *Art Journal* summed up the general opinion in its review: "Never before ... was archaeology so elaborated for dramatic purpose as in the Princess's version of 'King Richard,' and never before out of elaboration came such actual graphic and emphatic life. If archaeology be, as has been said, the dry bones of history, in Mr. Kean's hands 'these dry bones' do verily and

Opposite: **Historical episode from *Richard II*. Courtesy of the Board of Trustees of the Victoria and Albert Museum.**

undeniably *live*—live their own glowing, peculiar and many-coloured life. ...
The dust was shaken from the dry facts of antiquity and these were arranged
into pictures."[36]

Although the "historical episode" was the crowning glory of this production, all the other scenes, 15 different settings in all, had been given the
same lavish attention. The locales alternated between extremely elaborate box
sets for the interiors and wing-and-drop arrangements representing the outdoors. Act 3, scene 3, the exterior of Flint Castle as painted by Cuthbert, was
a combination of backdrop with sky and a three-dimensional fortress, surrounded by a moat, with a practical drawbridge. Cuthbert had painted six of
the scenes, Dayes four, and Lloyds two; Gordon, Telbin, and Grieve were
responsible for one each.

Two months to the day following the opening of *Richard II*, on May 13,
a fire broke out on stage just before the beginning of act 5. The velvet curtains, being used instead of the usual act drop, caught fire from the gaslights
on the side; the flames spread to the borders, and in seconds the proscenium
was ablaze. Mrs. Kean, about to make her entrance in the role of the queen,
approached the footlights and, with great self-possession, entreated the
alarmed audience to remain in their seats. This extraordinary gesture elimi-
nated the potentially tragic consequences of a sudden rush to the doors. At
great risk to their lives, some carpenters took down the borders while others
used all the water available to extinguish the fire, though not fast enough to
avoid the destruction of the scenery. Kean appeared in the midst of the debris
to announce the inevitable cancellation of the last act. A few days after the accident, the manger rewarded the bravery of his stage crew with a bonus, and the
staff presented Mrs. Kean with a framed testimonial for her heroic conduct.

For the second revival of the 1857 season Kean had chosen *The Tempest*,
another Shakespeare play that was not easy to fit within the boundaries of
any historical period but that afforded opportunities for dashing visual effects.
There was almost a tone of apology in Kean's declaration in the flyleaf: "A
purely imaginative drama does not admit of those historical details which have
been so accurately observed in earlier revivals." In any case, he had endeav-
oured "to impact a generally new character" to that lofty play.[37] The manager,
incapable of missing a chance to reproduce some remote era, found some
moments when it was possible to derive inspiration from ancient art and
mythology, if not for the scenery at least for the costumes. The "strange
shapes" that were to bring the banquet at the end of act 3 were transformed
into dancing naiads, dryads, fauns, and satyrs; the demons that were to tor-
ture Caliban, Trinculo, and Stephano were copied from furies depicted on
Etruscan pottery. The betrothal masque in act 4, when the Greek goddesses
Juno, Iris, and Ceres fly in to celebrate "the contract of true love" between
Miranda and Ferdinand, offered a ready-made opportunity for mythological
extravagance.

Thomas Grieve's rendering for the sinking ship in *The Tempest*, act 1, scene 1. Courtesy of the Board of Trustees of the Victoria and Albert Museum.

While visiting with Charles Dickens in London, Hans Christian Andersen attended the opening night of *The Tempest* and reported his impressions in the Danish daily *Berlingske Tidende*. The great storyteller's description of the staging provides valuable information on the astonishing effects devised by scenic artists and machinists:

> During the overture, which expressed the tempest and during which thunder rumbled, shouts and cries were heard from behind the scenes.
>
> The entire opening scene was shouted out in this way while the act curtain was still down, and when it rose, great, heavy waves rushed forward towards the footlights. The entire theatre was a raging sea, a large vessel tossed forth and back, filling nearly the whole stage. ... The masts fell, and soon the vessel itself disappeared beneath the heavy seas; this was managed, as Dickens told me, by means of a complete ship of air-tight canvas which had been pumped up, and from which they suddenly released the air. The great body collapsed like a rag and was hidden by the waves, which towered to half the height of the stage....
>
> Ariel's first appearance was highly poetic and lovely. As Prospero called him forth, a shooting star fell from heaven and touched the turf; it shone in blue and green flame, in which one suddenly saw Ariel's beautiful, angelic form. All in white he stood, with wings from his shoulders to the ground. ... Each revelation of Ariel was different and beautiful. At one point he suddenly appeared hanging by his hand from festoons of vine leaves; at another he floated across the stage in a mechanism which was hardly possible to discern, no rope no metal bar in sight, and yet there was such as apparatus that held him from below in a flying position.[38]

Besides descending in a ball of fire, Ariel made some other spectacular appearances: rising gently from a tuft of flowers, sailing on the back of a dolphin, gliding over sand as a water nymph, and riding on a bat.

Andersen's account of the production continued with the transformation scene in the third act: "We saw deserted, wintery surroundings which, as rays of sunshine grew stronger and stronger, were transformed to the most luxuriant scenery. Trees became green, blossomed, and brought forth fruit. Streams flowed quicker and fuller, and down a mighty waterfall river nymphs now danced as lightly as swan's down on the water."[39]

The mythological masque with the Greek goddesses was played in front of a moving panorama in which landscape followed landscape in a fantastic kaleidoscope as the lovers sailed in a gliding boat. But Kean saved the most brilliant effect for the closing scene. As Andersen described it:

> The entire stage represented the open sea, ruffled by the wind. Prospero, leaving his island, stood in the bow of the ship, which moved from the background to the footlights. The sails swelled and after the farewell epilogue was spoken, the ship glided quietly into the side wings. Then Ariel appeared, hovering over the surface of the water and waving goodbye. The full lighting fell upon him, with the result that he seemed ... to be something which, like a meteor, gave the entire stage its brilliance. A lovely rainbow shone out from him over the mirror-like water. The moon which was visible became merely a full circle of fire in the sunlight and the rainbow splendor which Ariel emanated at the moment of parting.[40]

The scenery for all these extraordinarily elaborate effects had been conceived by Grieve and Telbin, assisted by Gordon, Lloyds, Cuthbert, Dayes, and Morris. Even with a crew of 140 stagehands, the scene changes caused the performance to run from seven o'clock in the evening to after midnight. This fact did not deter the audience from giving Kean a lengthy standing ovation when the curtain fell in the final tableau.

Between April 1858 and March 1859, Kean produced another four plays from the Shakespearean repertoire: *King Lear, The Merchant of Venice, Much Ado About Nothing,* and *Henry V.* Kean selected the Anglo-Saxon eight century as a background for the tragic events in the life of the old King Lear and his three daughters. As Kean explained in the preface to the play, the incidents were "presumed to occur when the land was peopled by rude Heathens and the minds and hearts of men, as yet unreclaimed by the softening influences of Christianity, were barbarous and cruel."[41] Perhaps these "barbarous and cruel" men, in addition to the painful nature of the tragedy itself, were too disturbing and unpleasant for Victorian sensibility. After only 32 performances *King Lear,* which had opened on April 17, was removed from the repertory due to lack of audience interest. Not even the 13 historically accurate sets created by Grieve and his colleagues were attractive enough to entice the public.

William Telbin's rendering for the exterior of Shylock's house, *The Merchant of Venice,* **act 2. Courtesy of the Board of Trustees of the Victoria and Albert Museum.**

On June 12, two days after the final curtain ended this run of *King Lear,* *The Merchant of Venice* was unveiled at the Princess's Theatre. Once again the scenic artists were called on to create beautiful, historical illustrations as a background for the play. The first scene opened in the heart of Venice, the Piazza San Marco, and showed the buildings that surrounded the square. To set the mood, throngs of supernumeraries, all most accurately costumed in sixteenth-century fashions, gradually filled the stage to witness a ceremonial procession of the doge and his attendants, a set copied from a Josse Amman print in the British Museum. Portia's room at Belmont in the second scene was a box set of relative simplicity, particularly compared with the other interior of her mansion presented in act 3, scene 1. That set, all red and gold painted by Dayes, showed two diagonal walls, with two arches each, converging up center. One of the arches upstage framed a staircase of Versaillesque proportions; the other opened into a gallery overlooking a canal. Three massive chandeliers hung from the ceiling.

Act 2, designed by Telbin, was played entirely in front of Shylock's house at the edge of a canal. A large bridge, with an arch wide enough to allow a gondola to glide underneath, ran parallel to the facade, slightly slanted from downstage right to up center, and seemed to touch land at the other side of the waterway, in front of a four-story building. A painted drop, with a view

William Telbin's rendering for the avenue to Portia's mansion in Belmont, *The Merchant of Venice*, act 5. Courtesy of the Board of Trustees of the Victoria and Albert Museum.

of more buildings in perspective and another bridge, backed the practical flats and platforms placed downstage. All the characters involved in the scene arrived and departed by means of gondolas, a much more "Venetian" effect than the customary exit toward the wings. Kean took the mention of a masque as a cue to stage a spectacular carnival in this set. Immediately following Jessica's elopement with Lorenzo, groups of masquers rushed over the bridge, singing parties entered in gondolas, and neighbors appeared in the lit windows of the practical buildings. That ending to the act was rewarded with a burst of rapturous applause from the audience and was compared to the historical episode in *Richard II* by some critics.

The settings for the other scenes were painted with their customary artistry by Grieve, Telbin, and their colleagues. A particularly beautiful one was created by Telbin for act 5, in what seems like a perfect poetic illustration of the lines:

> The moon shines bright. In such a night as this,
> When the sweet wind did gently kiss the trees,
> And they did make no noise...

The watercolor in the Victoria and Albert Museum shows a terrace by moonlight, with a staircase leading up to an avenue of trees at stage right and two smaller ones descending toward a canal on the left. Portia's house at Belmont is seen at some distance, painted in a backdrop. The moon shines bright in the evening sky.

The only surprise in *Much Ado About Nothing*, presented on November 19, 1858, was perhaps the fact that Kean had chosen to produce it at all. After so many seasons of devoting his resources to antiquarian spectacle and lofty roles, the audience had almost forgotten that he could play light comedy.

Not much scenery was required for this play, although Cole described the opening view, the city and harbor of Messina, as "quite a pictorial gem." He also remarked, "The gradual illumination of the lighthouse and various mansions, in almost every window, the moon rising and throwing her silver light upon the deep blue waters of the Mediterranean, were managed with imposing reality."[42] On this occasion, Mr. and Mrs. Kean, acting as Benedick and Beatrice, received much more attention from the press than did the visual elements of the production.

Kean chose *Henry V*, presented on March 28, 1859, for his last Shakespearean revival as manager of the Princess's. Not only was the play the story of England's favorite monarch, but this "song of triumph" also enabled him to attempt antiquarian spectacle on an even larger scale than that used in his previous productions. Kean had thrilled his audience with processions, masques, mythological ballets, supernatural apparitions, and sinking vessels. However, *Henry V* offered incidents never before encountered: battle scenes, a siege, and the storming of Harfleur. He declared in the preface to the play that accuracy, not show, had been his intent, although in this case one was inseparable from the other. His authority for historical reconstruction was an obscure Latin manuscript; accidentally discovered in the British Museum, it had been written by a priest who had accompanied the English army throughout the campaign and who had witnessed the battle of Agincourt. The return of the victorious monarch to London, related in Shakespeare's text by the Chorus, became an opportunity to interpolate another historical episode to rival the one in *Richard II*.

The scenery, described in the *Illustrated London News* as "superb," was designed by Grieve, Telbin, Gordon, Lloyds, and Dayes, and a score of anonymous helpers.[43] Lloyds painted three of the most spectacular scenes: the storming of the breach; the background for the king's address to the army in act 4, scene 3; and a view of the old London Bridge, from the Surrey side of the river, for Henry's triumphal return to his capital. Grieve rendered, among others, a haunting night scene for the English camp before Agincourt. All props, banners, pieces of furniture, horse blankets, and the most minute accessories were specially designed and built for the production.

The members of the press, who after nine years of spectacular revivals

had grown accustomed to Kean's lavish display, were nevertheless at a loss for words to describe the magnificence of this production. The *Times* warned its readers not to expect a run-of-the-mill siege, with a small group of soldiers playing against "a very red background," as had been done in other theatres. In *this* storming of the fortress, a crowd filled the stage, pushing and shouting in the midst of the smoke produced by the cannons. So realistic was the action that the reviewer stated, "Mr. Kean has got up a faction among his supernumeraries, that they may pommel each other in good earnest."[44] The king's speech before the battle was addressed to a large mass of soldiers, each of them directed to express his emotions in a different and moving manner.

Kean had yet another surprise to end the play and crown his achievements as manager. Arrayed in full suit of armor and riding a real charger, he made his triumphal entrance as King Henry returning to London while the sound of church bells resounded in the theatre. The entire reconstruction of the historical episode was based on the account of the priest who had been an eyewitness to the event. The crowd of citizens gathered to welcome their beloved ruler exceeded, in number and animation, any previous crowd onstage. Besides common people and high dignitaries, there were venerable prophets, twelve kings of England with golden scepters and crowns, children dressed as angels, and a chorus of beautiful young girls who were attired in white to symbolize their chastity and who showered silver leaves on the king. Thus, with that paradigm of the stage as a medium for educational entertainment, Kean's term as a manager drew to a close.

The superlative tributes paid to Kean by the press were innumerable; the *Theatrical Journal* concluded a two-page account of his accomplishments by saying, "His great and good deeds have shone out with a lustre that will not dim as long as the British drama and Shakespearean memories exist or hold a place in the British Empire."[45] More than a century later that prediction may sound bombastic, particularly in view of the fact that in the early twentieth century, Kean's extreme attachment to archaeology was derided and finally rejected in favor of making accuracy subservient to aesthetic concepts.

Even in his own time, Kean was not without detractors; more than once he was accused of smoothing the poetry and sacrificing the text for the sake of accuracy and scenic effect. Hans Christian Andersen, an enthusiastic but perceptive observer, could not hide his misgivings at the sheer scope of the spectacle involved in *The Tempest*. He confessed that after all that wealth of pictorial illustration, "one felt overwhelmed, tired, and empty. Shakespeare was lost in visual pleasure; the exciting poetry was petrified by illustrations; the living word had evaporated. No one tasted the spiritual banquet—it was forgotten for the golden platter on which it was served."[46]

Opposite: **Frederick Lloyds's rendering of "The Storming of the Breach,"** *Henry V,* **act 3, scene 1. Courtesy of the Board of Trustees of the Victoria and Albert Museum.**

Regardless of how our own time may judge Kean's adherence to the extremes of historical reproduction, it is impossible to deny that he was very much in tune with the Victorian public's proclivity for the painless acquisition of knowledge presented as entertainment. Before his revivals, Shakespeare's plays had not enjoyed extended runs on the stages of London; the artistic excellence of Kean's antiquarian presentations made them successful by attracting that segment of the public interested in "culture" while the spectacular elements appealed to those in search of entertainment.

Kean's vision was by no means original; Charles Kemble, William Macready, and other managers had attempted to satisfy the public's clamor for accurate representation of the past; however, before Kean, no other manager had manifested such unshakable belief in the intellectual benefits derived from watching the plays performed in appropriate settings, with appropriate properties and costumes. It might be possible to blame him for superficiality, for trusting the picture more than the word, but it would be difficult to deny his influence on the subsequent development of theatrical practice. The antiquarian movement, of which Kean was the strongest proponent, not only created demand for historical accuracy in classical drama but also, by its very presence, prepared the way for the trends in later decades, when attention to detail was equally lavished on settings required for modern plays.

Kean's determination to blend all aspects of production—scenery, lighting, costumes, music, and choreography—in the service of the text went a long way to advance the concept of visual unity, sorely lacking in Victorian mise-en-scène. Both the watercolors preserved in the Victoria and Albert Museum and the contemporary reviews suggest that the settings became in some instances protagonists of the plays at the same time that the performers were integrated into the scenery to produce carefully planned pictorial compositions. Although Kean's manipulation of stage crowds was masterful, and preceded the Duke of Saxe-Meiningen's practice by two decades, he has received little credit for his endeavors in this area.[47]

Due in part to the fact that so many talented artists collaborated in all the productions, no single artist was individually accorded the accolades that were bestowed on William Beverley; they performed as ensemble players for a manager who firmly believed in ensemble playing. Most of them enjoyed long and successful careers after Kean's retirement. Thomas Grieve continued the tradition begun by his father, John Henderson Grieve, and trained his own son in the techniques of scene painting; they worked together until Thomas Sr.'s death in 1882. Frederick Lloyds wrote a treatise on the art of scene painting, published in 1875, and practiced his craft until the 1890s. William Telbin also founded a scenic dynasty; his youngest son, William Lewis, designed scenery well into the twentieth century.

Shortly after Kean's retirement, the *Saturday Review* expressed dismay at having been left "without any actor or manager" who could "do for Shakespeare what was done by Mr. Kean in Oxford-street." The paper added, "There is no one to follow in his steps, even at a long interval."[48] The long interval would end almost a quarter of a century later, with Wilson Barrett's productions at that very same Princess's Theatre, Henry Irving's at the Lyceum, and Herbert Beebohm Tree's at her Majesty's Theatre.

Chapter 4

Wilson Barrett and Edward William Godwin: Another Romantic View of History

*I*N THE YEARS BETWEEN Charles Kean's retirement from management and the mid–1870s, the romantic drive toward historical re-creation seems to have lost focus, temporarily, as an important issue in the presentation of stage plays. It was instead the tendency toward contemporary realistic interiors, as practiced by the Bancrofts at the Prince of Wales Theatre, that defined the style of scenery prevalent at the time. In their joint memoirs, Squire and Marie Bancroft congratulated themselves for the "elaborate and careful *dressing*" they had used for the first time in Tom Robertson's comedy *Society*, which they had premiered on November 11, 1865.[1] They mentioned as well that slovenliness was rampant in other playhouses and that consequently their own commitment to realistic sets astonished theatregoers and was a revelation to the critics. However, their claim at being "first reformers" disregards the reforms instituted by Mme. Vestris when she presented *The Conquering Game* at the Olympic in 1832 and *London Assurance* at Covent Garden in 1841. Thirty years before the Bancrofts applauded themselves for their success, Mme. Vestris had introduced real furniture, as opposed to properties painted on the scenery, and had dressed the stage with carefully chosen carpets, draperies, and decorations. Whenever Madame was not producing light musical pieces or spectacular extravaganzas, her attention to realistic detail in interior settings was evident and much praised by reviewers.

The scenic artist Charles Stanfield James was responsible for the scenery of *Society*, as well as for the realistic interiors of another two plays written by Tom Robertson and offered by the Bancrofts: *Ours* in 1866 and *Caste* in 1867. In the third act of *Ours*, a winter scene in Crimea, snow blew inside the hut each time the door was opened—to the great surprise of the audience. In 1868 Hawes Craven, later to become Henry Irving's principal scenic artist, joined the staff of the Prince of Wales to provide designs for *Play*, another one of Robertson's comedies.

During the next five years the Bancrofts continued to acquire a reputation as scrupulous managers who lavished a great deal of attention on the visual aspects of their productions. By 1873 they believed their recent successes in contemporary pieces had given them a good background to attempt the production of a classic play, and they decided to revive Richard Sheridan's masterpiece *The School for Scandal* "as an exact picture of its period."[2] George Gordon, a member of the Royal Institute of Architects who had been consulted on pre-Norman architecture for Charles Kean's production of *Macbeth*, was commissioned to design the scenery. The faithful reproduction of eighteenth-century interiors was accomplished by careful study of prints from the period and by a pilgrimage to Knole, the great country house in Kent built by Thomas Bourchier, archbishop of Canterbury, in 1456 and later greatly extended by the Sackville family, to whom it was granted by Queen Elizabeth I. The admiration of the critics for the Bancroft's accurate portrayal of high life in the eighteenth century suggests that attempts of this nature were indeed rare at the time, outside of the Prince of Wales Theatre.

Encouraged by the warm reception *The School for Scandal* had received, the Bancrofts embarked on an even more ambitious enterprise. On April 7, 1875, they opened *The Merchant of Venice*. In the long months of preparation for that production, the managers were assisted by Edward William Godwin, as historical adviser, while George Gordon and William Harford were engaged as scenic artists.

Between October 1874 and June 1875, E. W. Godwin's insight and erudition regarding Shakespeare's work were being displayed in a series of 30 articles he contributed to the *Architect*. "The Architecture and Costumes of Shakespeare's Plays" was the outcome of his exhaustive research not only on the architecture and costumes but also on the furniture, customs, and manners most appropriate for the presentation of the dramatist's plays. Both the artist and the scholar are evident in those articles; the thorough study of original sources is applied to the interpretation of the text, while at the same time all participants in a production, from actor to property master, could find some sound and sensible advice.

Edward Craig, Godwin's grandson, declared in a speech given to the Society for Theatre Research on December 15, 1976, that his grandfather "loved the theatre because he was at heart a romantic." Craig added: "In the theatre he could see the past recreated, and that fascinated him. He, like so many of his generation, had acquired a taste for the Gothic, which Sir Kenneth Clark tells us 'is an essential expression of Romanticism.'"[3] As is evident in Godwin's many articles on a variety of subjects, he loved history because he saw it as the unbroken chain that binds together all times and human experiences.

Godwin's passionate interest in the theatre in general, and Shakespeare in particular, began in Bristol, where he was born in 1833. He trained as an architect and had his first major national success in that field when he won, in 1861, the competition to design the Northampton town hall in the Gothic Revival style. However, his busy career was no impediment to his frequent visits to the theatre. In 1862 Godwin persuaded the editor of the *Bristol Western Daily Press* to publish his comments on the performances at the Theatre Royal; his "Theatrical Jottings," as his reviews were entitled, first appeared in the newspaper on October 16 of that year and continued intermittently until October 11, 1864. As he would do later on, throughout his prolific activities as a writer, he turned his "Jottings" into a pulpit to chastise theatrical managers for allowing a lack of accuracy and inconsistencies in scenery, properties, and costumes to debase their productions. Godwin's denunciations, usually expressed in very strong terms, irritated some readers and brought about the charge of "unpardonable egotism and vanity" against him, forecasting the pattern of controversy that would follow him for the rest of his life.[4]

Godwin's attacks on managers who neglected the visual elements in their presentations turned into bitter condemnation when the disrespectfully treated plays belonged to his revered Shakespeare. In the autumn of 1864 James Henry Chute, lessee of the Theatre Royal, offered a production of *Romeo and Juliet* that unleashed one of Godwin's most vitriolic diatribes. After denouncing scenery, costumes, and properties as utterly inadequate, Godwin aimed his rage at the main culprit:

> Surely, if *Romeo and Juliet* is worth acting at all, it is worth *some* expenditure on the part of the manager. A sensation piece or a pantomime would soon set painters, costumers, and property men to work, and the manager would be active in superintendence—but Shakspere! [sic] who is he that we should care for him? What has he done for us, the stage or the drama that we should spend a shilling to render his work attractive to, or popular with the common people? But we should humbly submit to Mr. Chute and his craft that to Master William Shakspere they are indebted for whatsoever respect or interest their art may still inspire. On him the miserableness of ignorance and the intolerance of bigotry furiously rage in vain, for the fact remains that the greatest genius produced in any age was a player and a dramatist. I simply ask you, both manager and actor, as well as playgoer, to approach him at least with reverence.[5]

These comments, which generated a storm of rebuttals and requests for retractions, illustrate Godwin's proclivity for so inspiring animosity that the real issue—the validity of his views—was often diffused and lost in a barrage of recriminations and countercharges. However, when Godwin was able to state his theories outside of the context of a review, without attacking anybody, the quest for consistency and visual unity outweighed historical accuracy in his own scale of values. Referring to paintings shown at the Royal Academy in 1865, Godwin remarked, "Accessories of costume, etc., in pictures, whether on canvas or on the stage, should be either altogether wrong or wholly right."[6]

This statement indicated that he did not reject the possibility of an inaccurate or imaginative approach to design, whether in sets or costumes, as long as it was thoroughly consistent throughout. Godwin's biting criticism of contemporary practice was directed mainly toward those productions that pretended to be historically correct but that in reality suffered from the introduction of anachronistic elements, resulting in a pastiche of periods and styles that jeopardized the visual unity of the presentation, for it was visual unity that would become Godwin's lifelong quest. In spite of his reputation for uncompromising devotion to historical research, Godwin was willing to subordinate faithful historical reproduction in design to achieve visual unity and considered the requirements of the stage to be "superior to *strict* archaeological accuracy."[7] His purpose was to persuade theatre practitioners to use historical research in the service of dramatic presentations, as a means to interpret the periods to be portrayed, and not to become mere slaves of accuracy.

In 1865, after the death of his first wife, Godwin moved to London, where he established his architectural practice and renewed his friendship with Ellen Terry, whom he had known as a young girl in Bristol. Three years later the actress and the architect settled together in the country, first in Wheathampstead and later in a house designed by Godwin in Harpenden. In 1873 Ellen Terry was persuaded by Charles Reade to return to the stage with a role in his new play *The Wandering Heir*, and the couple moved back to London with their two children, Edith and Edward (Gordon Craig). When the Bancrofts cast Ellen as Portia in *The Merchant of Venice*, Godwin was engaged as "archaeologist" for the production.

In his articles on *The Merchant of Venice* (March 27 and April 3, 1875), Godwin had dealt at great length with the staging of the play. He had determined the year 1590 to be best suited for the action. He had also reduced the number of required sets to no more than five: a street or public place; the street before Shylock's house; a court of justice for the scenes in Venice; a grand hall; and a garden in Belmont. As for the architecture, the three styles prevalent in the late sixteenth century—Byzantine, Gothic, and Renaissance—were to be used throughout. His preference for the treatment of the scenery was to make it three-dimensional to avoid the conflict usually generated by the combination of painted false perspective and structural units, a conflict offensive to "artistic minds." Godwin considered the court of justice to be "one of the most difficult problems among the scenic questions of Shakespeare's play," due to the great number of people involved. He proposed for that locale a diagonal set with raised platforms, reminiscent of the *Sala dello Scrutinio*, with architectural elements inspired by Venetian interiors of similar character and covered with gilded, carved wood panels.[8]

It is difficult to determine Godwin's specific influence on the scenery of *The Merchant of Venice*, since his position was simply that of adviser. The actual sets were designed by Gordon and Harford, who had traveled to Venice for firsthand research. But it might be appropriate to assume that Godwin's sense of visual unity and historical consistency had a beneficial artistic effect. Most critics praised his contribution to the production; the *Building News* declared that the interior of Portia's house in Belmont surpassed "everything yet produced upon the English stage; not for gorgeousness, nor size, nor any sensational belongings, but because if [was] a true picture of a stately hall, likely to have been erected by Portia's kinsfolk, two, or perhaps three, generations before her time."[9] Herbert Beerbohm Tree, in an address to the Oxford Union Debating Society in 1900, called that presentation of *The Merchant of Venice* "the first production in which the modern spirit of stage management asserted itself, transporting us, as it did, into the atmosphere of Venice, into the rarefied realms of Shakespearean comedy." He added, "Since then, no doubt millions have flocked to this class of production."[10]

The millions who may have flocked to see that kind of production in later years were conspicuously absent in 1875. The play ran only three weeks, the failure due mainly to Charles Coghlan's performance as Shylock. As Ellen Terry pointed out in her memoirs, Coghlan "spoke as though he had a sponge in his mouth, and moved as if paralysed."[11] Godwin also had opinions about the acting; in his copy of the opening night program he scribbled some notes grading the cast on a scale of 0 to 100. Mr. Bancroft as the Prince of Morocco rated 5; Mr. Lyn Ryne as Gratiano received a 0, with an emphatic "vile" written next to the number; Miss Terry was granted a 60.[12]

In his next theatrical experience, John Coleman's revival of *Henry V* at the Queen's Theatre in September 1876, Godwin encountered mainly frustration. His scholarship and his desire for harmonious unity were affronted by the inconsistencies and inaccuracies that permeated the production in spite of his efforts to advise the manger, who had engaged him as "archaeologist" for sets and costumes. Although the scenic artist George Gordon had used Godwin's sketches with "tolerable fidelity" to render some of the sets, others, like the palace of Charles VI, totally disregarded historical research and even common sense. Godwin described the exterior of the palace: "[It was] one of those architectural surprises we used to be familiar with, but of which I had hoped we had seen the last. Perhaps the particular artist that assisted Mr. Gordon on this scene may remember, if told in print, that when a building is of various dates, it is not usual to find the *whole* of the *sub*structure later than the rest by about three centuries."[13]

The designer's attempts at preserving the integrity of the visual elements in *Henry V* had been completely ignored by John Coleman. In a letter addressed to the manager before opening night, Godwin had tried, in an unusually diplomatic manner, to point out some errors observed during rehearsals. Wanting to avoid even the slightest suspicion of interference, Godwin stated his misgivings as "queries." Some of those "queries" indicate that

Godwin's well-justified concerns went beyond the accuracy of sets and costumes. One of them reads: "Is it wise to use dummy horses in prominent positions, (I hear you are going to be seated on one of them) when they are so abominable modelled as those I see in the theatre? However short a time a tableau may be on view somebody will be sure to spot them and must laugh per force."[14]

Godwin's desire to control every detail of the stage picture, rather than merely to provide the manager with "archaeological" advice, was a radical idea in the mid–1870s, and even a decade later the controversy created by his dispute with Coleman as a result of *Henry V* continued to be aired in the press. When, in 1885, Godwin contributed a series of articles on "Archaeology on the Stage" to the *Dramatic Review*, he referred once more to Coleman's refusal to accept suggestions that would have improved the unity of the stage picture.[15] In the same publication, Coleman replied that Godwin had at the time been engaged "not as an artist, but as an archaeologist," not as a creator but as a copier.[16] Coleman had previously stated, in terms that left no room for doubt, the prevalent view about the ultimate authority of "a competent manager." It was the responsibility of the manager "to point out to the archaeologist the particular archaeological 'cram' required; to the costumier the shape, material and colour of the costumes; to the property man the make, size, dimensions and date of the furniture and properties."[17]

The position of copier was not one that could be willingly accepted by Godwin. He stated, "The archaeologist ... must be *an artist*, endowed with a sense of form and colour, ... and in sympathy with the dramatic purpose."[18] Though his desire to create new standards for harmonious visual unity was far too advanced to be understood by his contemporaries, the opportunity to put his theories into practice increased slightly when he was entrusted by the actor-manager Wilson Barrett to furnish set and costume design for several productions.

Wilson Barrett, born near Chelmsford, Essex, in 1846, spent a childhood of Dickensian squalor working as a laborer in a corn exchange in London, where his family had settled in 1857. One evening, while still a young boy, he was offered a ticket to the Queen's Theatre, and his immediate reaction to that newly discovered, fascinating world was the determination to become an actor.[19] His ambition increased further when he attended a performance of Charles Kean's *Henry V* at the Princess's Theatre and was so entranced by the spectacular production that he decided on the spot to make a name for himself "as the chief actor-manager of that very Princess's Theatre."[20]

Before Barrett could fulfill that wish, he served the usual apprenticeship with small parts in provincial companies. Between 1864 and 1878 Barrett acquired experience as an actor and a manager performing in towns, large and small, in England and Ireland. By 1878 he had become successful enough to attempt a London season with his own company; at the Princess's, under

Walter Gooch's management, he presented Charles Reade's *It's Never Too Late to Mend* and William Gorman Wills's *Jane Shore*, as well as *Uncle Tom's Cabin* and several comedies.

The following year Barrett acquired a lease for the Royal Court, a small theatre in Sloane Square with a seating capacity for 728 patrons, and set out to win audience and critical approval with both classic and contemporary plays. In 1881, Barrett engaged Godwin for the first time to create sets and costumes for William Gorman Wills's gloomy new tragedy, *Juana*. The heroine of the title, played by the Polish actress Helena Modjeska, was a young Spanish princess rescued from dishonor by a heroic friar who had once been her admirer. Barrett's commitment to excellence in the presentation of the play is evident from the cast of luminaries he hired to paint the scenery: William Beverley for act 2, a wood near Juana's castle; Stafford Hall for acts 1 and 3, the loggia in the castle; and Walter Hann for act 4, the crypt in the convent.

The program for the play, which opened May 7, included a note from Godwin explaining the sources of his research: "In preparing the drawings for the scenery, costumes, etc., of MR. WILLS' Play, I thought it more logical to gather, whenever possible, the designs from one contemporary Artist, rather than from various sources, as being more likely to conduce to the preservation of unity of time and place. I have selected as my authority a very fine illuminated work made for Isabella of Castile, after the union. In the architecture, I have referred to existing buildings, and to mark the age, I have introduced a Loggia, the then new style of the Renaissance."[21]

Godwin's own copy of the play, dedicated to him by Wills as a tribute for the manner in which he had conveyed the "semblance of past times," is covered with notes and pencil sketches concerning his research.[22] Although Godwin eventually decided to use one single source, he had consulted a number of manuscripts and books of hours produced in Spain in the late fifteenth century, as well as the work of the Italian artists Pinturicchio, Crivelli, and Pollaiuolo. Among the sketches are a map of Toledo, ground plans for acts 1 and 2, and numerous studies for ecclesiastical vestments and properties. The volume also contains the color scheme for the costumes.

The painstaking research conducted by Godwin did not save *Juana* from failure. The play closed in four weeks, but the association with Barrett, who had been supportive of the designer's efforts, opened the doors for future collaborations.

The Princess's Theatre had become available for leasing in the spring of 1881, giving Barrett the opportunity to move out of the Royal Court and finally settle in the playhouse of his childhood dreams. To carry on Kean's tradition of spectacular mise-en-scène, Barrett mounted, between 1881 and 1883, three extremely elaborate melodramas by English authors: George Sims's *Lights o' London* and *The Romany Rye*; and *The Silver King* by Henry

Arthur Jones and Henry Herman. The formula—good acting surrounded by spectacular scenery—had proven immensely successful for the manager. His next enterprise, *Claudian* by W. G. Wills and Henry Herman, would capitalize on that success, with the added attraction of presenting a "classical revival" melodrama in which elements in the plot of *The Last Days of Pompeii* were combined with the legend of the wandering Jew. To secure an accurate reproduction of Byzantium in the fourth century, Barrett commissioned Godwin to design the sets and costumes.

Since the story of *Claudian*, a Roman aristocrat cursed to be young forever and live in despair as punishment for murdering an old man, evolves through 100 years, Godwin consulted sources covering the period from AD 360 to 460, "when classical art was *in-extremis* and Byzantine art had scarcely come to birth."[23] He studied paintings of the Catacombs, consular ivory diptychs, mosaics, coins, and sculptures. He also obtained, from the Museo Nazionale in Naples, a series of large photographs showing the only known example of a Roman litter chair, which would be faithfully reproduced to carry Barrett on stage.[24]

Claudian opened December 6, 1883, to mostly rave notices. The *Times* praised it as a play that did honor "to the authors who wrote it and the manager who produced it" and that shed "lustre upon the theatre" where it had "seen the light."[25] The reviews suggest that Godwin not only had been consulted in matters of scenery and dress but also had influenced the arrangement of the stage picture. After remarking that no detail, however insignificant, had escaped attention, the *British Architect* described in glowing terms the opening scene:

> The foreground is like a bit of Constantine's forum, to the left, solidly built, and of true dimensions, is the end of a doric portico, to the right of a portion of a circular ionic portico; a low wall bounds the plateau, and over this we see the tops of dark cypresses ... and, on a rising hill beyond, stately, many pillared structures, while in the far distance, the blue waters of the Bosphorus and the hilly shore beyond complete the picture [painted by Walter Hann]. In the walls beneath the porticos we recognize the *opus sectile*, or large mosaics, of which Mr. Godwin speaks in his pamphlet. The capitals and friezes reveal the coarse carving of time, and the marble and gilding exhibit something of the costly splendour. Under one portico is a marble statue of Venus with gilded drapery, and in the center of the stage there is another similarly treated. At the foot of this ... statue is a group of slaves. ... In another group there are boys wrestling, and gladiators waiting for the hour of the games, or for a chance engagement; in another we have the townsfolk discussing the news of the day, or idling the golden hours away in dreamy indifference ... forming altogether a scene of vivid reality never surpassed.[26]

That cosmopolitan crowd, dressed to indicate the many nationalities and social ranks in the population, was "brought into play with so skillful an eye to composition that not a mere picture, but rather a succession of pictures melting into each other in imperceptible gradations, [were] presented to the eye."[27] Godwin may have contributed his aesthetic sense to the arrangement of the crowd into a carefully planned pictorial composition. When, in 1881, he had reviewed the Meiningen Company performances for the *British Architect*, he admired the precision of their blocking, which resulted "emphatically in pictures, as if painted by one master hand," and he may have been able to influence Barrett's direction.[28] In a follow-up review, the drama critic of the *Times* indicated that *Claudian* typified "the close connection now established between art and the stage."[29]

As impressive as the opening of the production was, it paled by comparison with the scenic triumph of the evening, the last scene in act 3, when Claudian's palace was destroyed by an earthquake. When the moment arrived for the massive structure to collapse, "with a might upheaval of the walls, pillars and arches shook, then split up and fell with a crash; and in a quarter of a minute, the magnificent palace was reduced to fearful desolation, amid which Claudian stood pale, dignified and unharmed."[30] London audiences had never seen a better or more realistic earthquake than the one on the stage of the Princess's.

Although Barrett had refused to wear some of the costumes designed by Godwin for Claudian—as strongly as he had rejected the idea of being carried in the very accurate littler chair—he was one of the very few managers in London willing to grant Godwin a measure of freedom and the funds necessary to explore ideas concerning the relationship between historical accuracy and the unity of the stage picture. When Barrett decided to revive *Hamlet*, he engaged Godwin once again as "archaeologist" for scenery and costumes.

Faced with the prospect of designing *Hamlet*, Godwin realized that he had several options regarding the time period. He could place the action of the play at the time when it was written, the late sixteenth century, or he could dress the cast in contemporary fashion (Gertrude in a bustle), as Garrick and others had done previously. The third choice, and the one he had favored ever since he had published his 1874 article on *Hamlet* in "The Architecture and Costumes of Shakespeare's Plays," was to re-create the look of the early eleventh century, "just before the reign of Cnut."[31] Godwin was well aware of the difficulties that setting the play in the Dark Ages would entail, but he considered this approach to be no more riddled with dangers of inconsistencies and anachronisms than the other two.

In an interview granted to *Life*, Godwin related in detail the method he had followed for his research. He had traveled to Denmark, where he had visited museums and done full-size drawings of weapons and ornaments so that they could be reproduced. He had systematically looked at objects, buildings, and landscapes before consulting literary sources; in his estimation, the reverse process would have meant "putting the cart before the horse" and "tending to create a prejudged opinion."[32] Armed with all his notes and drawings,

Godwin had returned to London determined to create "an image in all its bearings, and a picture of the people as they lived, with their leather-banded legs, their huge personal adornments," and "bold embroideries."[33]

Barrett unveiled his unconventional production on October 16, 1884. The actor-manager introduced new dimensions to the interpretation of the role by playing the prince as much younger and more energetic than portrayals of the prince by previous actors. By restoring to the text lines that had traditionally been cut and by carefully stressing all the references to Hamlet's youth, Barrett found the means to justify his novel approach. Hamlet's younger age made it possible, as well, for Claudius and Gertrude to be at what was considered by the Victorians to be the prime of life, adding an unexpected erotic suggestion. A reviewer remarked: "The amorous toying of their Majesties in public—hardly possible on the assumption that the Queen is 50— adds gall to Hamlet's bitterness, and the text of the Ghost's exhortations as now given leads him furthermore to believe that the guilty *liaison* dates even from his father the late king's lifetime."[34]

The innovations introduced in the production were not limited to the interpretation of Hamlet's character. The scenery also departed from well-established traditions, most notably in the play scene, act 3, scene 2, which was placed outdoors in a courtyard of Elsinore Castle. Godwin's rationale for the choice of that unusual location was the potential it offered for dramatic lighting effects. He explained that Denmark is as warm as England and that "since the play is taken to extend between Spring and Autumn," it presented "the possibility of Summer moonlight."[35] The scene was divided into two parts: the first was played in front of a drop, painted by William Beverley, depicting a view near the castle, which served as a background for a procession of torch-carrying attendants and courtiers on their way to the performance; the second, by Walter Hann, revealed the full stage courtyard behind the drop. A small stage was placed in the courtyard, hidden at first by a curtain hung between two fir trees; in this setting, lit to create the illusion of the summer moon, the king and queen sat to watch the players, sitting not on a throne but on a rustic bench placed at an angle stage right. Hamlet and Ophelia were on another bench upstage center between the king and the stage.

The change of locale was deemed to be "a vast improvement" on what had "always been a somewhat absurd scene when presented indoors, from the necessity of ranging the King and Queen and the courtiers diagonally across the stage, so as to leave the view of the audience uninterrupted." The *Times* wrote, "Now the whole depth of the scene can be utilized."[36] Another reviewer called the scenery, painted by William Beverley, William Telbin, Stafford Hall, and Walter Hann, "exquisitely beautiful" but added: "The scenic artists, under the direction of Mr. Godwin, have taken some liberties with the natural features of Elsinore. It so happens that Elsinore itself is flat, while the neighboring coast is rocky and precipitous. Mr. Godwin, therefore, to do a

From neck cut the
length of coat—is
3′–2½″ to allow
for sticking up
thro' belt.

Hamlet

E. W. Godwin's pencil sketch for Hamlet's costume. Courtesy of the Theatre Museum.

great right, did a little wrong, and enabled us to enjoy the highly picturesque view presented at the Princess's by sacrificing geographical accuracy to the demands of scenic effect."[37] It seems apparent that Godwin, if he was indeed responsible for the landscape, was willing to subordinate not only strict historical accuracy but geography as well for the benefit of dramatic values.

Another scene that provoked favorable comments was the ghost's

Wilson Barrett as Hamlet. From the author's archives.

Hamlet. .... *Nymph in thy orizons*
Be all my sins remembered " *Act II. sc. 2*

HAMLET AND OPHELIA AT THE PRINCESS'S THEATRE.

Bernard Partridge's engraving of a scene from *Hamlet*, with Barrett as the prince and Mary Eastlake as Ophelia. Courtesy of the Theatre Museum.

entrance. The dead king appeared "draped in a mysterious filmy grey, without the classical armour," and seemed to be "a shade emerging through the stones of the castle battlements before Horatio and Bernardo."[38]

As in most other instances of Godwin's participation in a production, it is difficult to assess the exact extent of his influence on the visual aspects of *Hamlet*. The program credited him for "the archaeology of the costumes, properties and furniture," although some reviews praised also his innovations regarding the scenery. Obviously, he did not have the final design authority that is associated with the creative work of a modern set designer. When he provided ideas and sketches, it was still the prerogative of the scenic artists, in this case four of the most notable Victorian painters, to follow or disregard his wishes. From the notes that Godwin scribbled in his opening-night program, it would seem that his ideas were more often rejected than followed; only some of the sets met with his approval, and he deemed the final act unsatisfactory, although there is no explanation attached to the criticism.[39]

Godwin's ambition to exercise control and unify all elements of the stage picture was apparent in his planned color scheme. The costume sketches extant in the Theatre Museum show the characters dressed in intense colors, with a predominance of reds and blues, presumably to separate and give relief to the actors against the muted browns and grays of the scenery. The only exception to that palette was Hamlet's costume, generally all black except for a touch of red in his cloak for the graveyard scene. Godwin's pencil sketch shows the Prince of Denmark as he would have looked in the tenth century, with long hair and mustache, heavily embroidered tunic, and leg wrappings. However, Barrett was no more submissive to Godwin's ideas on historical accuracy than the scenic artists had been. The photographs of the actor in costume for the role show him in a very different garb; all traces of the "barbarian" look Godwin had envisioned had vanished, leaving an idealized romantic figure in a low-cut doublet over an open neck Byronic shirt. One reporter's sensibilities were affronted by Barrett's exposed neck, which he considered "wholly unsuited to artistic effect as well as to the Northern latitudes," though he admitted at the same time that Godwin had, "with no violation to historical accuracy, produced some fine effects of colour."[40]

Barrett's rebellion must have been rather discouraging for Godwin, whose compulsive drive to influence every detail of the production was not limited to sets and costumes. An envelope covered with notes penciled by Godwin during the course of a dress rehearsal quite strongly indicate that he longed to take on the responsibilities associated with the work of a modern stage director and thus to achieve complete artistic control of all aspects of the production. Besides comments on costumes and properties, his notes refer to gestures, groupings, and even sound: "speech to kneeling King too passionate and too jerky"; "Ghost/swear deeper tone"; "bell too harsh." He remarked as well that the crowd attending Ophelia's funeral "should show amazement at Hamlet's behaviour."[41]

Hamlet played at the Princess's until February 21, 1885, for a total of 110 performances, and was followed by Lord Bulwer-Lytton's *Junius; or, The Household Gods* on February 26. Despite their occasional disagreements in matters of costumes and historical accuracy, Barrett and Godwin seemed to have overcome their differences and continued their collaboration in this new attempt at classic-revival melodrama. Once more, Godwin contributed his vast knowledge of the classical world, and his efforts were considered so successful that a newspaper article advised everyone eager "to form a clear idea of how the Romans looked and lived to pay a visit to the Princess's Theatre."[42]

Percy Fitzgerald wrote in his review of the production: "In this labour of love nothing has been spared either in the training of the crowds ... or in the truly sumptuous character of the scenery ... nothing more stately, imposing, or in the Antique Roman spirit, inspiring with a sense of dread and awe has yet been attempted. The Princess's has now taken first rank in these daring efforts, which are directed by the profound archaeological gifts of Mr. Godwin."[43]

Although some members of the press stressed the educational significance of the sets and costumes—reminiscent of the comments that had greeted Kean's productions—most neglected to elaborate on the dramatic values of the play itself. Perhaps because there was too much "dread and awe" in this play to attract an audience, *Junius* was a dismal failure and was taken off the boards after only five weeks.

In May 1886 an article printed in *The Stage* remarked: "In fashionable and artistic circles there is a sudden mania for Greek plays. Plays from the Greeks, and imitated from the old Athenian plan, theatres exactly copied from classical models, occupy alike the labour and love of University professors and eminent archaeologists. Young ladies 'divinely tall and mostly divinely fair' are sought far and wide to impersonate Helen or Minerva. Noble-featured maidens are implored to put on clinging robes and appear as the vengeful Clytemnestra or the fateful Cassandra. Youths with shapely limbs are carefully scrutinized with a view to selection for Apollo or Orestes."[44] Leaving aside the fact that the author could not differentiate between the names of the Greek and Roman gods and goddesses, this comment had its origin in the wave of Greek or Greek-inspired plays about to flood the London stages in just one week. Professor G. C. Warr's metrical version of *The Oresteia* was offered at the Prince's Hall, followed shortly by Dr. John Toadhunter's *Helena in Troas* at the Hengler's Circus and soon thereafter by Wilson Barrett and Sidney Grundy's *Clito* at the Princess's.

The production of Greek plays in London was nothing new. As early as 1845, Sophocles' *Antigone* had been presented at Covent Garden, and some efforts had been made to approximate the original stage arrangements and

achieve a satisfactory effect.[45] However, the fascination that Greek plays held for managers and audiences in the mid–1880s seems to have been stronger than ever before. Both Godwin and Barrett were swept into that Aegean wave, the former as producer, director, and designer of *Helena in Troas* and the latter as coauthor and star of *Clito*, for which he engaged Godwin once more as historical adviser.

Barrett opened *Clito*, a tragedy in five acts set in Athens in 404 BC, on May 15, 1886. The play was as handsomely mounted as all his previous offerings, but the concern displayed in the visual elements does not seem to have been extended to the text itself. Barrett and Grundy, in their capacity as playwrights, had difficulty divorcing themselves from their Christian background and introduced ideas alien to the Greek frame of mind. There were reported mentions of angels, devils, heaven, and hell, and charity was hailed as the queen of virtues, a concept as un-Greek as the Vestal Virgins who appear in one scene. *Clito* was as much a failure as *Junius*. Barrett's serious financial troubles made it impossible for him to carry on another season. On July 23, 1886, he officially ended his tenure as manager of the Princess's with a farewell benefit, and two months later he departed for a tour of the United States. Even though his six years at the helm of the Princess's concluded on a sad note, Barrett had received recognition for achieving, with Godwin's assistance, high standards of theatrical production, and for as long as it lasted, he had fulfilled his childhood dream of becoming the heir to Charles Kean.

Godwin had only a few months to live after his last collaboration with Barrett; he died on October 6, 1886. But in that short time before his death he came as close as it was possible, in the late 1800s, to exerting complete control over all aspects of a stage production. By creating for himself duties and titles unknown in the Victorian theatre—art director and producer—he provided himself with the opportunity to apply his theories in a manner thus far unattainable in his previous enterprises.

Two days after *Clito* premiered at the Princess's, Godwin opened a production for which he not only had assumed the duties of producer, director, and designer of sets and costumes but also had drawn on his expertise as an architect to remodel the space. The Hengler's Circus was the location chosen to present *Helena in Troas*, in an environment Godwin transformed to approximate the plan and dimensions of the Theatre of Dyonisus in the Acropolis. Toadhunter's play was a poetic re-creation of the Trojan War, though Oscar Wilde attributed the fact that it was in blank verse "more to the courtesy of the printer than the genius of the poet."[46]

Godwin redesigned the interior of the Circus following the standard arrangements of a Greek theatre, with *skene*, semicircular orchestra, and central

Opposite: A scene from *Helena in Troas*, with sets and costumes designed by E. W. Godwin. Courtesy of the Board of Trustees of the Victoria and Albert Museum.

altar. On the raised platform, he placed the entrance to Priam's palace, con-
cealed by a dark-red curtain and flanked by pillars and ramparts. Stage right
and left, behind that gate, a drop showed a landscape of distant hills. The
facing of the platform, painted to imitate marble, included panels with figures
in relief; a six-step unit gave access from the *skene* to the orchestra, where the
floor was painted in geometric patterns on a reddish, marbleized background.
The introduction of a crimson, plush front curtain, which was raised from a
trough on the stage floor at the end of each act, was a departure from archaeological accuracy, as was the absence of cothurni and masks in the designing
of the costumes. An even more intriguing lapse in historical reproduction was
the design for the royal door, which exhibited the motif of lions and leop-
ards—symbols more closely identified with the Royal Arms of England than
with the Royal House of Troy. These deviations from historical truth may be
an example of Godwin's willingness to subordinate *strict* accuracy to dramatic
effect; they were certainly not due to his ignorance of Greek art and architecture, since he had read and written extensively on the subject. Another
justification may be found in a remark by Oscar Wilde: "The performance was
not intended to be an absolute reproduction of the Greek theatre in the fifth
century before Christ: it was simply the presentation in Greek form of a poem
conceived in the Greek spirit; and the secret of its beauty was the perfect cor-
respondence of form and matter, the delicate equilibrium of spirit and sense."[47]

As a fellow aesthete, Wilde understood that Godwin's aspirations went
beyond subservient compliance with the conventions of historical accuracy
and that *Helena of Troas* demonstrated the validity of Godwin's theories. The
playwright wrote in his review of the production: "Mr. Godwin is something
more than an antiquarian. He takes the facts of archaeology but converts
them into artistic and dramatic effects, and the historical accuracy, that under-
lies the visible shapes of beauty that he presents to us, is not by any means
the distinguishing quality of the complete work of art. This quality is the
absolute unity and harmony of the entire presentation, the presence of one
mind controlling the most minute details, and revealing itself only in that
true perfection that hides personality."[48]

That "presence of one mind controlling the most minute details," not a
radical concept by any means in the late twentieth century, was Godwin's
lifelong ambition in a period when, if there was one mind in control, it
belonged to the actor-manager and not to a designer. Even the position of
"designer," as we understand it today, was ambiguous, when not nonexistent.
It is not surprising, then, that Godwin's desire to assume the positions of
both designer and director—positions that would have given him the means
to influence all aspects of a production—was met with resistance by most of
his contemporaries. In spite of the generally favorable reviews that greeted his
efforts, a segment of the press insisted on deriding his "archaeological tyranny."[49]
In some instances the criticism was aimed at the elitist connotations of his work.

The *Illustrated London News* remarked that *Helena in Troas* had been produced "for the sake of airing Mr. Godwin's experiment, and for pleasing the aesthetic and literary crowd."[50]

Jacques Barzun, in his study of classic, romantic, and modern art, argued that the "exploration of reality was the fundamental intention of romantic art" and that "against the assumption that no civilization had existed since the fall of Rome, [the Romantics] rediscovered the Middle Ages and the sixteenth century and made history their dominant avocation."[51] If that postulation is compared with Godwin's statement that the purpose of the archaeologist is "to make history a reality,"[52] it becomes apparent that Godwin indeed belonged to the romantic tradition that continued to influence stage design in England until the last decades of the nineteenth century. Planché, Kean, and others before him had followed the path of historical research, but it was Godwin who expressed most strongly the need to understand the past to better serve the intentions of the dramatists. He wrote, "If the science of archaeology supplies us with the materials of a bygone time that seem in harmony with the plot of the drama or the intention of the poet, the artist cannot do better than accept them as the foundation of his work."[53] The application of those tenets would result in "the great principle which must underlie all good art—*Unity of Design*."[54]

In 1910, Edward Gordon Craig wrote about the pioneering ideas of his father: "His work was the natural realistic link between the unimaginative and the imaginative. In the immediate tomorrow comes the next link in which the accessories shall be not only correct in date but correct in spirit; when we shall not realise but suggest. The day after that we shall move still forward, from suggestion to symbolism, until in time, by taking step after step, we restore to the Art of the Theatre its liberty and royalty. On that day there is no doubt we shall remember the debt we owe to E. W. Godwin."[55]

Godwin's theories created controversies more often than praise because they were so far ahead of his time. Few could foresee that in the future his methods of research would be applied routinely, by directors and designers, to the interpretation of plays and that unity of the stage picture would become the natural result of collaboration among theatre artists. It is regrettable that Godwin's efforts did not make an impression commensurate with their importance. Considering the knowledge he devoted and the talents he contributed to the theatre, in addition to his pioneering theories on unity of the stage picture, it would not be excessive to state that he was one of the most influential figures in stage design in the late Victorian period.

Chapter 5

Henry Irving:
A Romantic Actor
and His Set Designers

*T*HE TREND FOR SPECTACULAR SCENERY based on accurate historical research and pictorial techniques favored by Charles Kean in the 1850s, persisted well into the last decade of the nineteenth century. Henry Irving, as manager of the Lyceum Theatre in the 1880s and 1890s, preserved the tradition of giving scenery a voice to state romantic aesthetic principles when he not only engaged for his productions some of the same scenic artists that had collaborated with Kean but also commissioned set designs from painters whose reputation rested on the creation of the sweeping romantic canvases habitually exhibited at the Royal Academy.

Laurence Irving remarked in his grandfather's biography, *Henry Irving: The Actor and His World*:

> Henry Irving took his place in the front rank of English actors when Ruskin was the arbiter of artistic taste, when Tennyson was the Poet Laureate, and when the replicas of Roman and Italian palaces which Leighton and his fellow academicians were building in Fulham and St. John Wood, bore solid testimony of the esteem in which their peculiar art was held by the intelligentsia and the public.
>
> The English drama had lagged behind in the romantic revival which, in the sister arts of painting and poetry, was now in full swing. Every year visitors to the Royal Academy were stirred by vast canvases whose literary message and architectural accuracy suggested the final tableaux of well produced plays.
>
> ...with no other choice of entertainment than the all too robust melodramas and the everyday realism of the Bancroft school, the public, who sighed over the Pre-Raphaelites and whose dreams were realized by Burne-Jones, found little to satisfy them in the theatre. Suddenly there appeared at the Lyceum a man who embodied the very spirit of romance, who brought to life the engraved pictures which hung upon their walls and in whose every word and gesture they found their ideal of the long-awaited romantic actor.[1]

The late Victorian audience found in Irving not only the "long-awaited romantic actor" but also a manager who envisioned the playing space as a vast canvas on which actors, sets, costumes, and light performed a function in terms of pictorial composition. He asserted his conception of the stage as a painting when he declared in an interview with the *Pall Mall Gazette* in 1886: "Each scene is like his picture to a painter. You have to combine colours, group figures, and arrange the mountings."[2]

Like most actors of his generation, Irving spent the early years of his professional life in provincial theatres, among them the Theatre Royal Stock Company in Manchester, where he remained from 1860 to 1865. After leaving Lancashire for London, he continued to develop his skills in a variety of roles under several managements. In 1871 he was hired by Colonel H. L. Bateman as a permanent member of the Lyceum, to perform on the very same stage that had seen the triumph, and later the demise, of Mme. Vestris and J. R. Planché's extravaganzas.[3] His interpretation of the sinister, middle-aged innkeeper Mathias in Leopold Lewis's *The Bells*, on November 25, 1871, mesmerized the audience, secured his reputation as a notable actor, and set him on the course that would eventually lead to international fame and the first knighthood ever bestowed on a member of his profession.

When Bateman's widow retired from management in 1878, Irving acquired the lease of the Lyceum and chose *Hamlet* as the first production in the playhouse for which he would be the sole master for the next 24 years. The opening night of *Hamlet*, December 30, 1878, with Ellen Terry as Ophelia, inaugurated the actor-manager's tenure and the beginning of one of the most successful acting partnerships in the history of the theatre. The Irving-Terry reign at the Lyceum was, as well, another link in the chain of the romantic trends that influenced stage production until the early years of the twentieth century. A survey of Irving's productions from that time forward indicates that he chose to ignore the latest Continental developments toward naturalism, favoring instead Shakespearean revivals and costume melodramas and selecting for his repertoire those pieces that allowed him to display the fascinating romantic aura that held his audience spellbound. The actor-manager's choices were founded in his deep belief that the ultimate aim of art is to create beauty. "Truth itself is only an element of beauty, and to merely reproduce things vile and squalid and mean is a debasement of Art."[4]

George Rowell, in his study *Theatre in the Age of Irving*, asserts that the actor "established and sustained in England a Romantic drama comparable to that of Goethe and Schiller in Germany and Hugo and Dumas in France half a century earlier" and that, paradoxically, he achieved this romantic renaissance without the physical characteristics of the romantic actor and without romantic dramatists.[5] Furthermore, it was not only his hypnotic power as a performer, or his selection of plays, that contributed to Irving's reputation as a romantic; the designers who created the backgrounds for the actor's art brought with them the romantic mood that had remained a driving force in the visual arts since the early nineteenth century. From the very beginning of his management, his associates belonged to, or were heirs to, the romantic tradition in set design. Hawes Craven, who designed that first *Hamlet*, had worked with William Beverley at Drury Lane and was an established painter of river and coastal scenes; his watercolors were exhibited at the Royal Society of British Artists. Craven remained at the Lyceum with Irving until 1902, both as designer and as scene painter for productions designed by other artists.

In 1881, the talents of several romantic artists converged on the stage of the Lyceum for Irving's production of *The Cup*. The playwright was the poet laureate Lord Tennyson, and Edward William Godwin was one of the historical advisers whose research on ancient Greek art was applied to create the sets painted by Hawes Craven and the costumes worn by Ellen Terry. William Lewis Telbin, the son of one of Charles Kean's principal scenic artists, and Henry Cuthbert, a former member of Kean's design team, also collaborated with Craven. Some critics compared the scenery to Sir Lawrence Alma-Tadema's accurate pictures of the classical world; the painter himself, a member of the opening-night audience and a future collaborator with Irving, exclaimed at the sight of such beauty: "Ah! how poor my art is after this."[6]

Between 1881 and 1884 Irving produced four Shakespearean revivals, which established him as the indisputable heir to Charles Kean. He presented *Othello* in May 1881, *Romeo and Juliet* in March and *Much Ado About Nothing* in October 1882, and *Twelfth Night* in July 1884. On the subject of *Romeo and Juliet*, a critic wrote: "Playgoers with retentive memories will be able no longer to point to the Shakespearean revivals of Charles Kean at the Princess's Theatre as priceless and unexampled in picturesque design and archaeological accuracy. *The Winter's Tale* and *Richard the Second* pale before the beauty of the new *Romeo and Juliet*, which is probably the grandest production of a play by Shakespeare that the stage has ever seen."[7] However, like E. W. Godwin, Irving was willing to subordinate archaeological accuracy to the needs of a dramatic presentation, particularly when the choice was between accuracy and beauty. As he stated, "The first duty of anyone who mounts a piece is to produce a beautiful and pleasing effect."[8]

More than most managers of his time, Irving understood the dramatic potential of footlights, battens, and vertical standards fed by gas, instruments that in other playhouses had no more purpose than to crudely illuminate the stage. His masterful use of the limited lighting equipment available to him further emphasized the pictorial beauty of the scenery by applying the media of "coloured lights as a painter uses his palette."[9]

The play selected by Irving as the big "draw" of the 1885 winter season, *Faust*, had all the romantic elements certain to attract him and the public: set in Gothic Nuremberg, it offered infinite possibilities for a wide range of supernatural stage effects plus the opportunity to create spectacular scenery based on accurate historical research. When the previous season ended in July, and before departing for Germany on a working holiday in search of locations to reproduce, Irving embarked on an ambitious renovation of the Lyceum, reconstructing the stage and completely redecorating the auditorium.

The width of the proscenium arch—33 feet, 5 inches—and the depth of the stage—40 feet raked ½ inch to the foot—remained unchanged, but to fly the scenery planned for *Faust* without having to roll the drops, Irving raised the roof of the theatre from 48 feet to 60 feet.[10] Another addition to the playhouse was a full-sized organ, deemed necessary to provide background music for the scenes outside Nuremberg Cathedral and to accompany the heavenly choirs.[11]

Irving was joined by Ellen Terry and her children, Edith and Edward Gordon Craig, for his visit to Germany. The travelers settled in Nuremberg, but it was mainly in Rothenberg, another well-preserved medieval town, that Irving found the inspiration he was seeking for the decor of *Faust*. Hawes Craven, his set designer, was summoned from London, and together, scenic artist and manager explored and recorded the architectural gems they observed in the winding, narrow streets. A buying spree through antique dealers' shops resulted in the acquisition of authentic furniture and bric-a-brac destined to serve as stage properties in the forthcoming production.

The lengthy preparations and careful research culminated with the opening of *Faust* on December 19, 1885, in William Gorman Wills's free adaptation, with prologue and five acts, of Goethe's dramatic poem. Irving, like a master puppeteer, or a "ruthless autocrat" as his grandson Laurence dubbed him, had orchestrated the work of his creative staff to achieve "the angelic visions, the heavenwards ascents, the descents into sulphurous infernos, the magical appearances and the trap-door vanishings, the lycopodic brimstone, the gauzy treacle, [and] the calcium arcs," without "drowning the words of the poet or overwhelming the actors."[12]

The curtain rose to reveal a despondent Faust, sitting in his study full of strange beasts, birds, and skeletons and pondering the meaning of life and the futility of all human effort. His only living companion was a dog he had rescued from the streets, but as the audience was soon to discover, this was no ordinary mongrel. In a burst of flames the dog vanished, and out of the sulfurous smoke appeared Irving as Mephistopheles, first in the guise of a traveling scholar and immediately after in a bright-red costume with a long cock's feather in his hat. After signing the pact on a book that glowed with a mysterious light, Faust and the devil were borne away through the air to Saint Lorenz Platz in Nuremberg; this scene, in front of a church square, was in the grand tradition of Charles Kean and was reminiscent of the prologue in Wilson Barrett's *Claudian*. Against the background of medieval architecture, constructed with both modeled and painted set pieces, bright with light and full of life, Irving choreographed the crowds of wealthy ladies in brocaded gowns with their trains carried by pages, soldiers off to war having the last rivets fixed in their armor, and beggars, burgomasters, and Franciscan friars in travel-stained robes, all slowly making their way to the church for the prayers announced by deep-toned bells.

The following scenes moved between Margaret's moonlit bedchamber and garden, Martha's cottage, Nuremberg's city walls, and a street in the city in front of the cathedral, where a well was the gathering spot for a group of young women to draw water and exchange gossip. In that street, Irving staged the spectacular duel between Faust and Valentine, introducing—with the assistance of Colonel Gouraud, Thomas Edison's partner—the use of electricity to produce sparks every time the swords clashed. The two actors playing Faust and Valentine each wore, in one of their boots, a metal sole electrically connected to their swords by means of insulated wire. When each actor placed his foot on a plate set on stage, they generated a 90-volt intermittent current that produced sparks as they crossed their weapons.[13]

However, not even sparkling swords had prepared the audience for what was to come in act 4, on the summit of the Brocken where the witches gathered to seek the Evil One. Amid thunder, hail, and rain, with flashes of lightning that brought into relief giant rocks with menacing crags, the witches, flying on broomsticks, appeared and disappeared in an instant at Methistopheles' command while emitting moans, shrieks, and hellish laughter. The tree trunks groaned, the branches crashed, the wind howled, the clouds swept by, and once more, the critics avowed their inadequacy to find appropriate words to describe the wizardry of these stage effects.[14] One reviewer, after stating that no exhibition of the supernatural "as weird, fantastic, and thrilling" had ever been seen before, declared that the scene was so short that the audience had no time for speculations. "When it has ended amidst a shower of gold, and the rocks pierced through and through with the brilliance of forked lighting, the audience is left breathless with astonishment ... this act alone would be enough to secure the success of the production had it no other merits than this marvelous display."[15]

The final scene took place in a dungeon where Margaret (Ellen Terry), in chains, fell dead at the foot of a cross while a heavenly group of winged angels appeared against a star-studded, dark-blue backdrop to carry her soul to the realm of eternal bliss. At the end of the performance, in response to the persistent applause, Irving addressed the audience, thanking them for the warm reception and noting that the production had lasted longer than the three hours it was meant to run. But he added, "As the Prince of Darkness, I am glad to be able to tell you that it is not yet twelve o'clock." He ended his speech with an astonishing declaration: "Perhaps after this work has run for four or five or six hundred nights, I may introduce some new scenes, such as Auerbach's Cellar or the Witch's Kitchen. But this is an affair of the future."[16]

The future came sooner than he had promised: for the 244th performance on November 15, 1886, the witch's kitchen was added to the show between the prologue and the Saint Lorenz Platz scene. The set was a dark, smoky cavern with a great cauldron downstage right. five hissing monkeys frolicked about the dimly lit cave, and the grotesque broom-flying witch made her entrance cursing and howling, before being ordered by Methistopheles to concoct the magic potion intended to restore Faust's youth. The incantation was performed within a circle ringed by candles, with the aid of dead snakes, lizards, and other paraphernalia associated with evil deeds.

Faust was an artistic and commercial success. It was performed 577 times in London, 128 in provincial tours, and 87 times in the United States, with a total box office revenue of over a quarter of a million pounds. The largest audiences in the 1888 American tour congregated in Boston, New York and Philadelphia. But in Chicago, a city that "neither fears the devil nor troubles its head about him or all his works," as Bram Stoker explained, "the receipts were not much more than half the other places."[17]

Besides Hawes Craven, credit for the scenery was due to Cuthbert and Telbin, who had previously worked for Kean, plus Stafford Hall and Thomas Ballard. The sets were burned in 1898 in a warehouse fire that destroyed all of the company's stock, but they were reproduced for another run in 1902.

One of the most successful productions in Irving's repertoire, *Faust* ran almost continuously for the next two seasons, until December 29, 1888, when *Macbeth* opened. Irving, always eager to collaborate with artists who could contribute fresh ideas to his productions and who shared his aesthetic sensibilities, commissioned Keeley Halsewelle, A.R.S.A. (Associate of the Royal Scottish Academy), to design the scenery for *Macbeth*. Halsewelle, a landscape painter and illustrator of romantic books, was well versed in historical accuracy. His preliminary sketches and models met with the approval of Irving, who consented to the artist's expressed desire to do the actual scene painting himself. However, Halsewelle had absolutely no experience in the field or any notion of the difficulties inherent in painting on a massive scale. After the flats and drops had been built, primed, and delivered to the paint room at Coven Garden, Halsewelle apparently panicked at the sight of acres of white canvas and resigned his commission without leaving behind him as much as a brush stroke on the pristine surfaces. Hawes Craven, assisted by T. W. Hall, Walter Hann, and Joseph Harker, the last a newcomer who would eventually work for all the leading managers of the time, completed the task.

The first scene in *Macbeth* showed a dark, desolate heath backed by blood-red clouds, intermittently lit by flashes of lightning that revealed the witches. As the weird sisters concluded the scene with their line "Hover

Opposite: Hawes Craven's sketch for the banquet hall in *Macbeth*. Courtesy of the Board of Trustees of the Victoria and Albert Museum.

through the fog and filthy air," they were flown out of sight, as they had been in Kean's production. Except for the "Hall in the Palace" where Macbeth held audience with Banquo's murderers, a scene painted by Hall, and the banquet scene, painted by Hann, credit for most of the sets went to Craven, sometimes in collaboration with Harker. Craven designed a solid masonry interior for Macbeth's castle, where Lady Macbeth was seen in her first appearance, reading the letter from her husband by the light of an open fireplace, and an eerie cavern for the witches in act 4, scene 1, where Hecate entered with an electric star on her forehead.

Irving made imaginative use of the supernatural effects the tragedy required, particularly in the second scene of act 4, when hundreds of gray-draped supernumeraries wandered about with lifted arms against an awesome sky-drop, so wild in appearance that, once again, reviewers were left speechless.[18]

Although Irving's interpretation of Macbeth as a character, as well as of Ellen Terry as his murderous wife, stimulated controversy, there were no dissenters regarding the magnificence of the production. The heir to the tradition of romanticized, spectacular Shakespeare had surpassed his predecessors. As was stated in *Truth*, "Mr. Irving has proved that he is the first of living stage-managers, a man with a mind to conceive and a head to direct, for all the boasted Shakespearean revivals of Macready, Phelps, and Charles Kean pale before the new Lyceum splendour."[19]

At a luncheon given in his honor in Birmingham, Irving defined for his audience his ideas about scenery:

> The value of the aids and adjuncts of scenery and costume have ceased to be a matter of opinion; these have become necessary. They are dictated by the public taste, and not by the desire for mere scenic display. Mere pageant, apart from the story, has no place in any play although there may be a succession of harmonious pictures which shall neither hamper the natural action nor distract the judgment from the actor's art.
>
> Scenery there must be, and if you are able to offer the truth, why be content to submit the false ... the truth is the best, and better than anything we can invent.[20]

Truth, and the beauty derived from truth, were undoubtedly in Irving's mind when he commissioned Sir Lawrence Alma-Tadema to design another of his Shakespearean revivals, *Henry VIII*. Alma-Tadema's work was a panorama of romantic painting in which the themes of Victorian domestic life were often superimposed on images inspired by the splendors of Imperial Rome. His devotion to historical accuracy in architecture and dress was unquestionable, as was his skill in rendering highly reflective surfaces—luminous marbles, metals, and silks. Though the Tudor architecture for *Henry VIII* did not belong to the period Alma-Tadema was most closely identified with, his archaeological expertise ensured that the decor for that production would meet Irving's expectations for absolute truth. Moreover, by engaging Alma-Tadema, Irving was closing the circle that had begun in the early nineteenth century, when scenic artists, even though they might also have been accomplished easel painters, became famous mainly for their theatrical achievements. Alma-Tadema was already a respected painter, a member of the Royal Academy, who would contribute his talent and the prestige of his name to the stage.

Henry VIII opened on January 5, 1892. Just as Charles Kean had done in his revival, Irving played Cardinal Wolsey, dressed in costumes designed by John Seymour Lucas, another painter belonging to the Royal Academy. Lucas was famous for his accurate portrayal of British life in the seventeenth and eighteenth centuries. The *Daily Telegraph* summarized the production, stating:

> It would tax the imagination to believe what can be done on the modern stage until this splendid revival has been witnessed. There are fourteen complete scenes, elaborately set, and they change almost without descent of the curtain as if by magic. The lights are turned down; there is a momentary darkness, and a gorgeously equipped scene, complete with furniture, is changed to another equally rich, literally in the twinkling of an eye. What would our ancestors not have given for these marvelous mechanical appliances which … have enabled a capable manager to add beauty to beauty, and to bring the theatre as near to nature as it is conceivably possible to do.[21]

The technical support required to change scenery "in the twinkling of any eye" was extraordinary. Backstage crews, often over 100 strong depending on the production, had to be drilled with military discipline to coordinate the timing of the innumerable tasks assigned to each individual.

Henry VIII played to full houses until the end of July. In the fall of 1892, his 15th season at the Lyceum, Irving felt ready to present his own interpretation of another Shakespearean character, the tragic King Lear. The new production opened on November 10.

Ford Madox Brown, 70 years old at the time, had been engaged by Irving as designer and historical adviser. Brown had impeccable credentials as a painter of romantic subjects; in the early years of his career, Byron's poetry had inspired his *Manfred on the Jungfrau* and *Manfred on the Chamois-hunter's Hut*, both painted in the 1840s. Although never a member of the Pre-Raphaelite Brotherhood, his friendship with Dante Gabriel Rossetti exercised a deep influence in the artistic movement that flourished in the 1850s and continued to cast its spell on the public's imagination for another two decades. Opulent beauty, fantasy, and the romance of the unspoiled past were subjects dear to the Pre-Raphaelite brothers William Holman Hunt, John Everett Millais, Rossetti, and later Edward Burne Jones, who would also design scenery for one of Irving's productions. Thus the uninterrupted chain of Romanticism continued to link the generations until the end of the century.

At the suggestion of Ford Madox Brown, who designed three scenes in the first and second acts of *King Lear*, Irving chose the period between the departure of the Romans and the coming of Arthur. His Lear was "long-locked and grey as the lichen on an apple-tree." There could be no doubt about who he was, "this weird and gaunt old man"; he was "a priest-king, a Druid grown ancient in mystery, the monarch from whom Merlin obtained his crabbed text. He has pored over mystic lore until the wall which divides ghosts from shadow-casting men has grown as glass."[22]

Brown was responsible for the scenery of Lear's palace and Gloster's and Albany's castles. The king's lodgings were of rugged red stone, with Romanesque arches borne on pillars, arms trophies on the walls, and hangings simulating early attempts at tapestry. Since, apart from some thunder and lightning, the play did not require any of the spectacular effects the Lyceum was famous for, or perhaps because Irving's performance, in spite of his looks, was disappointing, the critics did not spend much ink praising the scenery. At best, they found Brown's contribution as good as could be expected from an artist of his reputation.

Lear, which had a run of only two months and was never revived, was followed in February 1893 by Lord Tennyson's *Becket*, another romantic escape into the Middle Ages. The always reliable Hawes Craven, with William Telbin and Joseph Harker, was in charge of the scenery.

London journalists were becoming aware of the highly specialized skills required to create those sets that they habitually admired so fervently, and they were also becoming intrigued by the secluded—and often subterranean—world of scene painting. One of them paid a visit to the Lyceum with the purpose of revealing to his readers the mysteries of the paint shop:

> There is one gentleman who plays a very important part in the proceedings, yet never appears in public, and that is *Mr. Hawes Craven*, the scenic artist. ... Down many steps beneath the stage is a winding passage ... a little beyond is a narrow flight of stone steps leading to Mr. Craven's painting room, which is about fifty feet long and about thirty feet wide. It is lit by a skylight extending the full width of the roof. On each side of it there are stretched huge canvasses, eighteen feet high and forty-seven feet long. These canvasses are extended on frames, which can be raised or lowered by means of a winch to suit Mr. Craven's convenience. ... It takes Mr. Craven four hours to "prime" one cloth ready for painting. [It is doubtful that the head scenic artist primed the flats himself.]
>
> In times of emergency he often works fourteen hours at a stretch. The floor of the room is bespattered thickly with paint; Mr. Craven's clothes are all the hues of the rainbow; so are those of his assistants, one of them unconsciously having decorated himself with a blue nose. The centre of the room is occupied by huge tables, on which stand earthen pots containing paint by the half gallon, and brushes of all shapes and sizes. Indeed, some of the brushes will

Illustration after a drawing by Bernard Partridge of Henry Irving as King Lear. Courtesy of the Board of Trustees of the Victoria and Albert Museum.

hold two pounds weight of paint at a single dip, and Mr. Craven's implement for sketching in outlines is a thick stick of charcoal fastened to a long pole. The artists's method of painting is to walk to the center tables, take a huge dip of paint, and speed back again to his canvas, which represents a huge ash tree. Mr. Craven, besides sporting as much woad on his person as an ancient Briton, wears a white handkerchief round his brows. When he is very much pressed for time, he exchanges this handkerchief for a red one, and the joke goes around that this means blood.

Mr. Craven, in addition to his artistic knowledge, is a perfect ambulatory enciclopaedia, his work requiring an intimate acquaintance with architecture, botany, history. He is, above all things, an artist, with an intimate knowledge of the shapes, the hues, the seasons of flowers, the colours and the habits of birds, their varied forms, and another thousand and one things which he is called upon to depict at a moment's notice.[23]

Not much has changed since that description was published over 100 years ago; any late-twentieth-century set designer or scenic artist would have felt very much at home in Craven's paint room and might even today adopt his red handkerchief as a warning to the crew.

Irving had intended to produce *Becket* for a long time. After years of delays, revisions, and consultations with Lord Tennyson, the play was finally ready for public view on February 6, 1893. The scenery required even less spectacular effects than *Lear*. It called instead for the artistic touches that Craven and his colleagues were so adept at providing: accurate architecture, sweeping views of woods and plains, and Rosamund's bower in the second act, "a lovely picture by Hawes Craven, with shady trees, and winding paths and mossy banks, and flowers in wide profusion."[24]

Becket was a great personal triumph for Irving as an actor; it played to enthusiastic, full houses 388 times—in London, the provinces, and America. On March 18, 1893, Irving gave a command performance for Queen Victoria and her guests at the Waterloo Chamber at Windsor Castle, the same venue where Charles Kean had presented many of his productions for the queen in the 1850s.

The Lyceum company spent the autumn in Canada and the United States; during the tour, Irving made plans for *King Arthur*, a forthcoming excursion into the realms of magic and fantasy. This romantic medieval story, which had also been in Irving's mind for some time, was finally presented in a blank-verse version by Joseph Comyns Carr. Laurence Irving, commenting on his grandfather's production of *King Arthur*, stated, "Under Irving's hand the arts and sentiments, which distinguished mid–Victorian England, reached their apotheosis in the theatre, springing together into glorious life at the very moment when new artistic ideas and intellectual forces were getting ready to sweep them impatiently into the dustbin of discarded aesthetic principles."[25]

Totally oblivious to the new aesthetic trends, Henry Irving engaged Sir Edward Burne-Jones, a painter who epitomized the unmitigated hold of

Romanticism on the visual arts, to design sets and costumes for *King Arthur*. Mundane reality never intruded into Burne-Jones's canvases; his subjects were drawn from the regions of romance and legend, with titles that left no room for doubt: *Le chant D'Amour, Love among the Ruins, The Beguiling of Merlin, Cupid and Psyche*, and *The Mirror of Venus*.

The usually impressive first-night audiences at the Lyceum, with royalty and literary luminaries in attendance, witnessed an addition to the galaxy for the first night of *King Arthur*, on January 12, 1895: The painters assembled to congratulate Burne-Jones on his stride from the studio to the stage, a sure sign that the theatre had become a legitimate environment for a member of the Royal Academy to explore.

Burne-Jones had furnished sketches for the play's prologue and four acts; Hawes Craven and Joseph Harker had done the actual painting of the scenery. Harker, reminiscing in later years about his relationships with some of the famous painters with whom he had worked, Burne-Jones among them, remembered them as "genuinely anxious to create designs worthy" of the scene painter's art. "What impressed me still more was that none of these great artists desired to teach me my job."[26] This collaboration between artists who respected one another's skills and talents resulted in scenery of unparalleled beauty for *King Arthur*.

From the opening in the Magic Mare, a remote lake populated by water nymphs and where Merlin leads Arthur in search of Excalibur, through the garden of Queen Guinevere, a mass of spring blooms in a forest of old trees, to the king's final apotheosis in the barge that will take him to Avalon, the isle of sleep, every scene transported the audience to a universe of enchantment, as if the paintings by Burne-Jones had come alive and the characters had stepped out of the frames.

The reception and praise accorded to *King Arthur* demonstrated that Irving, without ever wavering from his firm belief in the meaning of beauty and truth and with the most absolute disregard for the "new wave" of dramatic trends, fulfilled the public's desire for romantic antidotes to the drudgery of their daily lives. Between the closing of *King Arthur* and the opening of *Coriolanus*, his first production in the twentieth century, Irving presented a series of plays that reaffirmed his—as well as his audience's—preference for romantic historical dramas with very large casts: *Don Quixote* and *A Story of Waterloo* in 1895, *Cymbeline* and *Richard III* the following year, and *Madame Sans-Gêne, Peter the Great*, and *Robespierre* in the next three seasons.

For *Cymbeline*, which opened on September 22, 1896, Irving commissioned Alma-Tadema once again to advise on the details of sets and costumes. The 18 scenes designed by the artist, and interpreted for the stage by Craven and Harker, were evidence of a careful search of "archaeological scripture," and the stage picture "was a lesson in Celtic construction and ornament, which must have sent many of the curious to their books for explanation of its odd decorations and mysterious monolith."[27] The pictorial quality of the set received as much praise as the historical reconstruction; *The Stage* described the act drops as "admirable exercises in artistic composition" on which "as much care and skill" had been expended "as if they were to remain on view for a long time."[28] *Cymbeline* was not one of Shakespeare's most popular plays. In spite of its educational potential and the beauty of the scenery, after 72 performances it had failed to recover the production expenses; although it was intermittently revived during the season, the temporary absences of Irving and of Ellen Terry from the cast, due to illnesses, compelled the manager to withdraw it from the repertoire.

The scenery for the Lyceum productions under Irving's management was stored, at great expense, in a warehouse in Southwark, beneath the railway tracks of the Chatham and Dover line. On the early morning of February 18, 1898, the contents of the warehouse—the sets for 44 plays—were completely destroyed by fire. The £6,000 insurance policy, which had recently been reduced from the previous £10,000 because the building was considered absolutely safe, could not even begin to pay for the material loss. Tragically, furthermore, the flames consumed not only Irving's assets but also the irreplaceable creations of some of the most notable designers and scenic artists of the late Victorian period.

Irving's financial situation in the last year of the nineteenth century bordered on desperate. He was 61, and his health was undermined by illness, the burdens of management, and the stress of provincial tours. Aware of the actor's situation, Joseph Comys Carr offered to relieve him of financial responsibilities by establishing a syndicate that would take over the management of the Lyceum for the remaining eight years of the lease in exchange for Irving's services. In return for £26,000 in cash and £12,500 in shares of the company, Irving was to appear in at least 100 performances at the Lyceum and tour for no less than four months every year, in addition to bearing 60 percent of the cost of new productions and paying all stage expenses. For the actor, who had been forced to sell his collection of theatrical memorabilia in order to pay off his most pressing debts, the offer was tempting; against the advice of his closest collaborators, his stage-manager Loveday and Bram Stoker, Irving accepted the proposal.[29]

At the close of his second season at the Lyceum in 1879, 20 years before, Irving had announced his intention to stage *Coriolanus* and had made up his mind at the time to invite Alma-Tadema to design the production. The long hiatus between his original plans and the actual presentation of Shakespeare's play did not alter Irving's desire to benefit from the painter's expertise in Roman archaeology. Under the banner of the new management, the Lyceum Ltd., *Coriolanus* opened on April 15, 1901, with sets and costumes by Alma-Tadema.[30]

In an interview published by the *Daily News* the day after the premiere, Alma-Tadema elaborated on his designs:

Coriolanus presented difficulties far beyond the other plays for which I have designed the background. In the first place our accurate knowledge of such a distant past is necessarily very limited. In the second place, what we do know places serious obstacles in the way of presenting that dramatic contrast which is so essential in the theatre. For the information which the discovery of the monument beneath the Lapis Nigra afforded proves almost conclusively, what indeed was known before, that the early roman civilization was mainly Etruscan. ... But it was necessary in this play to mark a contrast between the inhabitants and the buildings of Rome and Corioli, and to make the Rome of Marcus more distinctively Roman, and I was obliged to avail myself of a little artistic or poetic license. In the Volscian scenes I have made some attempt—necessarily founded mainly in conjecture—to reconstruct the known characteristics of the Etruscan architecture. In the Roman scenes, while partly reserving the same character, I have allowed myself a little latitude in bringing the date of the play a little nearer to the period which can be recognized as definitely Roman, while I have sometimes assumed that the earliest forms in furniture and other accessories were not so far different in earliest Rome than in earliest Greece.[31]

From these comments it is evident that Alma-Tadema had no difficulty thinking in theatrical terms and was willing to subordinate accuracy to the requirements of the play. Another excerpt from the same interview demonstrates that his concerns extended beyond the historical period to include the need for appropriate lighting. He ended his comments: "I have often noticed that the points on the stage from which light is supposed to come, a lamp, a window, never appear to be giving any light at all. They are in fact flooded by other light coming from elsewhere. I have tried to assist in the correct effect by illusion more than once in this play, but particularly in this scene [the hall of Aufidius's house, decorated with painted Etruscan figures and lit by four lamps standing against the walls]. I have painted on the wall something of the effect of light that these feeble lamps give in the darkened chamber."[32]

Sybil Rosenfeld, in her article "Alma-Tadema's Designs for Henry Irving's *Coriolanus*," indicates that Alma-Tadema's method of work was to make a model of the Lyceum—two feet wide by one foot, ten inches high—in which he set his scenic elements designed to scale, with watercolor sketches representing backcloths and wings. The backcloths were cut out in silhouettes of distant buildings against sky-drops, which could be painted to represent different times of day.[33] Although most theatres were already showing "built up," heavily three-dimensional scenery, Alma-Tadema's sets for the Lyceum, sets painted by Craven, Harker, and Walter Hann, conveyed a remarkable illusion of solid reality due, no doubt, to the skills of the scenic artists as well as to Alma-Tadema's painstakingly accurate use of perspective.

Even though the audience knew that the scenery for *Coriolanus* had been designed by the famous painter, *The Stage* conceded that "few were prepared for the pictorial treat" that followed the raising of the curtain. The reviewer proclaimed: "It was like studying Alma-Tadema's work through a magnifying glass; it was as if the celebrated artist in miniature (so to speak) had suddenly become scene painter. Admirable and enjoyable alike were the street views and the 'interiors,' all obviously based upon an exhaustive archaeological knowledge, but all thoroughly interesting and singularly real in the effect produced. The Rome of that time was brought before us as if by magic. Nor did it look coldly sculptural, with an ancient, far-off air. It was a habitable and inhabited Rome, with plenty of colour and brightness, and with all kinds of humanizing accessories."[34]

Irving had made some drastic cuts to the text, reducing the action from 27 to 17 scenes; nevertheless, the cost of producing and running *Coriolanus* was overwhelming. Moreover, the audience did not find the conflicts of the Tribune very appealing, and the play was withdrawn after 33 performances. This was to be Irving's last production at the Lyceum. The London County Council had embarked on a program to ensure strict compliance with safety regulations against fire hazards; the alterations required to meet the new standards would have involved an expenditure of £20,000, which neither Irving nor his nearly bankrupt associates could afford. At the end of the 1902 season, on July 19, Irving played his last role at the Lyceum as Shylock in a matinee of *The Merchant of Venice*. After his departure the contents of the theatre were auctioned off, and the house was refurbished as a music hall.

The loss of the playhouse he had transformed into a national monument did not deter Irving from attempting yet another spectacular production, this time at Drury Lane. The play he chose was *Dante*, an adaptation of the *Divine Comedy* by the French playwright Victorien Sardou. The scenery, which included a moving panorama designed to give the illusion of Dante's and Virgil's travels as it rolled behind them, was build and painted in Paris. When it was set up on the stage, Irving, unhappy with its garishness, discarded most of it.

Irving spend the last two years of his life in farewell tours of America and the provinces. On Friday, October 13, 1905, after a performance of *Becket* at the Theatre Royal in Bradford, he died in a hotel room. A week later his coffin was laid at the feet of Shakespeare's monument in Westminster Abbey.

The period between 1878, when Irving took over the management of the Lyceum, and 1902, when his tenure expired, marks the acceptance of set design as a legitimate art. E. W. Godwin's efforts to assert the importance of adequate scenery—accurate as well as dramatic—opened the doors for a new understanding of the contribution that visual arts could make to play production, and Irving's influence was vital in promoting this development. As far back as 1879, when he first thought of inviting Alma-Tadema to design sets for *Coriolanus*, he realized that the participation of an accomplished artist would provide not only historical accuracy but also unity of purpose and, above all, his longed-for beauty based on truth. The critic William Archer recognized Irving's talent for creating beautiful visual images, even in the early stages of his management. Archer wrote: "As one thinks of the past five years at the Lyceum there rises to the mind's eye a whole gallery of scenic pictures, each worthy of minute study as any canvas of the most learned archaeological painter. ... He works over every inch of his canvas, leaves no corner without its little illustrative or merely decorative touch."[35]

By the end of the nineteenth century, no manager would have attempted to offer a play with the slovenly decors that had been seen at some London theatres 50 years earlier. Whether designed by a Royal Academician or a scenic artist, scenery had come of age, nurtured by the care that Irving lavished on his productions.

It is true that Irving, as much as Mme. Vestris, Charles Kean, and Wilson Barrett, was sometimes taken to task for his reliance on "paint and upholstery." But it is also evident, considering the scope of some of their successes, that all of them had a better understanding of their contemporaries' need for romantic, spectacular entertainment than did the critics who derided their endeavors.

Chapter 6

Romantic Swan Song

*I*N SPITE OF THE RECURRENT CRITICISM often heard in the 1800s regarding scenic excesses, the romantic fascination with spectacular staging survived well into the twentieth century. As late as 1916, the most popular, record-breaking show in London was *Chu-Chin-Chow*, a musical tale of the East described as "an excursion into the regions of the fantastic, polyphonic, polychromatic Orientalism … a kaleidoscopic series of scenes, now romantic, now futuristic … but always beautiful."[1]

Chu-Chin-Chow, seen by over three million people during its 2,238 performances, was presented at His Majesty's Theatre, the same playhouse that, under Herbert Beerbohm Tree's management, had become the heir to Irving's Lyceum. Even though this musical extravaganza had been produced by Oscar Asche and not by Tree, the actor-manager's tenure from 1897 to 1915 may be regarded as the last stage in the development of spectacular scenery with strong romantic overtones.

As a young actor, Herbert Beerbohm Tree performed only once in Irving's Lyceum, in Lord Byron's *Werner* on June 1, 1887, at a matinee benefit for the playwright Westland Marston. Although the production was meant to be seen only once, and by a rather small afternoon audience, Irving spared no expense in the presentation: new sets and elaborate costumes executed by the finest armorers and dressmakers in Paris were prepared. Whether or not this brief and unique experience planted the seeds for Tree's determination to outshine Irving as an actor-manager, as Laurence Irving believes, is a matter of conjecture.[2] On the other hand, it is clear that Tree, born in 1852, had come of age at a time when, regardless of the controversies, spectacular scenery still dominated the Victorian stages. Besides, Tree had been a friend and admirer of E. W. Godwin, with whom he shared a belief in the dramatic importance of historical accuracy.

Tree spent his first ten years as an actor-manager, from 1887 to 1897, at the Haymarket Theatre, where he presented, among a great variety of contemporary plays that included works by Wilde and Ibsen, three by Shakespeare: *The Merry Wives of Windsor* (1889), *Hamlet* (1892), and *Henry IV, Part I* (1896). Later on, during his management at Her Majesty's (His Majesty's after 1901) Theatre, he demonstrated his commitment to the Bard by producing another 13 of Shakespeare's plays. In addition, from 1905 to 1913, he organized the annual Shakespeare Festival, where visiting companies, as well as his own, offered 60 productions over a period of eight years.

Ever since Charles Kean's spectacular revivals at the Princess's Theatre, managers who followed in his steps had been accused of burying Shakespeare beneath acres of scenery and gallons of paint. However, the audience, the only important critic for a manager dependent on box-office revenue, had consistently bestowed its approval on those productions. Tree, the victim of similar criticism, felt compelled to defend his ideas as well as the taste of the audience. In an address to the Oxford Union Debating Society on May 28, 1900, he declared: "We have, in fact, two contending forces of opinion: on the one side we have that of the literary experts, as revealed in print; on the other we have that of the public opinion, as revealed by the coin of the realm. ... The few experts who arrogate to themselves the right to dictate what the public taste should be are exactly those who ignore what it really is. Now, there is only one way of arriving at an estimate of the public taste in 'things theatric,' and that is through the practical experience of those whose business it is to cater to the public."[3]

As unquestionable proof of the public appeal of his elaborate productions, he cited the success of his Shakespeare revivals in his first three seasons at Her Majesty's Theatre: 242,000 people had attended *Julius Caesar*, over 170,000 bought tickets for *King John*, and nearly 220,000 saw *A Midsummer Night's Dream*, for a grand total of 632,000 tickets sold. Tree refused the notion, voiced by some detractors, that the great majority of playgoers were ignorant fools because they had demonstrated such decided preference for productions presented with all the embellishments that art and current technology could provide.

An added attraction for the loyal public attendance was certainly the playhouse itself. Her Majesty's was the most beautiful theatre in London: a building of Portland stone and red granite, with interior decoration inspired by French styles of the seventeenth century. The patrons were welcomed like guests by ushers in blue livery, red breeches, and white hose. There was no charge for either programs or cloakrooms. The acting area, 50 by 70 feet, had a proscenium opening of 29 feet, six inches, by 35 feet. The distance above the flat, trapped floor to the grid was 60 feet and below to the cellar was 23 feet. The electric system of footlights, instruments in battens and vertical stands, all controlled from a single dimmer board, was one of the most sophisticated in Europe.

As an heir to the tradition of pictorial scenery faithfully inspired by archaeological research, Tree engaged some of the same designers who had collaborated with Irving at the Lyceum. Alma-Tadema was responsible for his production of G. Stuart Ogilvie's *Hypatia* at the Haymarket in 1893 and rendered his services once again for *Julius Caesar* at Her Majesty's in 1898. G. B. Shaw, whose sharp pen could be counted on to find fault in most of Tree's productions, called Alma-Tadema "the real hero" of *Julius Caesar*.[4] Another critic mentioned, "It was less a drama than an immortal page from world's history ... unrolled in a series of gorgeous Tadema pictures."[5]

Among all of Shakespeare's plays, *A Midsummer Night's Dream* was quite possibly the most attractive to managers and designers wanting to embark on a voyage to fairyland. In the mid–nineteenth century, Mme. Vestris and Charles Kean had offered their vision of Titania and Oberon's world; Tree unveiled his own on the first days of the twentieth century, on January 10, 1900. The set designers—Hawes Craven, Joseph Harker, and Walter Hann, who had also traveled extensively in enchanted landscapes—were well qualified to create an atmosphere resembling those "elegant pieces of arabesque where little genii with butterfly wings rise ... out of flower-cups" and assist nature in "embroidering her carpet with green leaves, flowers, and glittering insects."[6] All the scenes in this production were praised for their poetical and exquisitely pictorial qualities. The woods near Athens were populated by real rabbits, in addition to fairies who had electric lights in their wings and who flew over and around the trees. A sudden, magic transformation took place in the last scene: after the pomp and pageantry at Theseus's court faded into darkness, Titania and Oberon entered with their fairy attendants as the columns and steps of the palace became aglow with supernatural light emanating from inside. Gradually, their songs and dance ended, the elves dispersed, the lights dimmed down, and the final curtain descended on an empty stage.

Following the triumphal run of *A Midsummer Night's Dream*, on October 31, 1900, Tree exchanged the sixteenth-century costume of Bottom for that of a biblical character in Stephen Phillips's *Herod*. Tree would eventually produce three more plays by the same author, who showed a marked tendency toward the mythical, historical, and supernatural: *Ulysses* in 1902, *Nero* in 1906, and *Faust* in 1908.

The actor-manager had considered engaging James McNeill Whistler to design the scenery for *Herod*, but a meeting with the artist dissuaded him from the idea on the grounds that the setting would probably become merely an exhibition of Whistler's paintings. Once again Craven was called to provide the design, consisting of a single scene of the palace atrium with an imposing staircase leading to the royal chambers. Tree's production of *Ulysses* on February 1, 1902, was credited with rehabilitating the Greek gods, who had been out of favor with the audience for some time. As was expected, the scenery for this presentation was based on the most painstaking research of Mycenaean architecture, interpreted for the stage by Craven, Harker, and William Telbin. Telbin painted wide stretches of misty mountains for the opening scene at Mount Olympus; Harker provided views of the seacoast near Ithaca and the banquet hall in Ulysses's palace; Craven was responsible for Calypso's sun-baked island and the gloomy depths of Hades. This last scene, like so many others influenced by the romantic attachment to the supernatural, was yet one more example of an actor-manager's applying all the means at his disposal to bring the audience to the brink of terror. *The Stage* described how Ulysses, groping his way down a flight of broken steps, descended to the world of disembodied spirits, a world lit only by a dim ray of light that barely allowed him to see Charon's barge in the Stygian stream below. In the chilling silence, broken only by the wails of phantoms shrouded in gauzy tunics, he encountered the ghosts of men and women who had acquired fame on earth—Agamemnon among them—and who, with muffled sobs, vainly implored him to take them back to earth.[7]

Tree's reputation for sumptuous staging increased with each production. Whether in the guise of a biblical character, a Greek hero, or the comical Malvolio, the actor-manager continued to offer the kind of spectacle his audience had come to expect. For his *Twelfth Night* in February 1901, Hawes Craven and Joseph Harker designed the romantic, dreamy scenery with their customary skill. Craven painted Olivia's house for the first act with views of the sea in the background as well as her magnificent garden for act 2, scene 2, showing several levels of grass-covered terraces, red flowering shrubs, and an avenue of trees.

Almost half a century after Kean's production of *Richard II* at the Princess's, the superb revival of the same play by Tree at His Majesty's in 1903 demonstrated he could match and surpass his predecessor in matters of historical re-creation. For scholarly advice on heraldry and ceremony, he engaged G. Ambrose Lee of the Herald's College; to depict the fourteenth-century architecture, Craven, Harker, Hann, and W. T. Hemsley lent their expertise. Critics had difficulty choosing which one of the 13 sets was the most spectacular; *The Era* mentioned in particular Harker's "picturesque" landscape of the coast of Wales and the architectural beauty of Westminster Hall and Westminster Cathedral, while Hann's Langley Garden, with its lovely bowers and flowers, was also a favorite.[8] As Kean had done before him, Tree turned the Lists at Coventry—with real horses included—and Bollingbroke's London entrance into rich, animated tableaux of city life in the late Middle Ages.

Storms at sea and shipwrecks, especially when in conjunction with spirits and magical forces, retained the same fascination for the early-twentieth-century public that they had in earlier days, and the luxuriant imagery of *The Tempest* continued to provide opportunities for a manager like Tree to display ever more elaborate scenic effects. His production of that play opened to rave reviews on September 14, 1904; as was customary, it was said that nothing as fine as this triumph of modern stagecraft had ever been seen before. The opening scene showed a vessel as large as the stage itself, a ship similar to those that had carried sixteenth-century explorers in their voyages of discovery. The ship rocked as the waves splashed on the deck and the wind tore its sails; the timber seemed to creak and the main mast snapped like a feeble match.

The idyllic masque was just as appealing to Tree and his audience as the storm; the manager reported at great length in his program notes—another vestige of Kean's tradition—about the ballet he had devised to illustrate this scene, described by Shakespeare only as the entrance of "certain reapers, properly habited—[who] join with the Nymphs in a graceful dance."

> The Naiads of the winding brooks are discovered disporting themselves in the water among the rushes and the water-lilies. Iris calls on them to leave their crisp channels to dance on the green turf. Nothing loth, the Naiads leave their native element and dance as mortals dance. The sudden appearance of the boy Cupid interrupts their revels—the Naiads modestly immerse themselves in the water. Cupid, ever the matchmaker, brings in his train the sunburnt sicklemen who, leaving their long furrow, are enjoined by Iris to make holiday with the nymphs "in country footing," Taking advantage of the chaste amiability of the nymphs, the reapers endeavor to embrace them, but their advances are indignantly repulsed, the maidens very rightly pointing to their ringless wedding-fingers, it being illegal (in fairyland) to exchange kisses without a marriage certificate.[9]

Of course, since everybody does live happily ever after in fairyland, Cupid intervened to solve the moral problem: the reapers gave wedding rings to the nymphs, the maidens donned their wedding veils, and they all cheerfully took part in the ceremony celebrating the betrothal of Miranda and Ferdinand.

William Telbin, son of the scenic artist who had painted some of the scenes for Kean's *Tempest*, was responsible for the shipwreck; other painters credited with several sets were Richard Douglas and W. T. Hemsley.

In following seasons Tree presented a series of Shakespearean revivals: *Much Ado About Nothing* (1905), *The Winter's Tale* (1906), and *Antony and Cleopatra* (1906), all with the same attention to historical accuracy and, when appropriate, the customary pageantry. The return of Antony to Alexandria, in *Antony and Cleopatra*, was an occasion for a superb display of "total theatre," with music, dance, colorful crowds, and spectacular scenery.

Henry VIII, in 1910, marked Tree's pinnacle as a producer and heir to the romantic tradition, initiated by Kean and followed by Irving, of historicism wrapped in spectacle. Shortly before the play opened on September 1, Tree made press statements affirming that to accomplish an absolutely realistic representation of the Tudor period, he had consulted every available source in order to obtain the best possible exactitude, a declaration that echoes similar ones made by Charles Kean in the 1850s. To achieve that exactitude, Tree secured the services of Percy Macquoid, a scholar on English costume, furniture, and applied arts, who designed the scenery for Wolsey's banquet hall

Above and opposite: Two views of the trial scene in *Henry VIII* at His Majesty's Theatre. Courtesy of the Board of Trustees of the Victoria and Albert Museum.

in act 1 and counseled Joseph Harker on architectural details for the other scenes. The banquet and masque in act 1, scene 3, was one of the most elaborate scenes Tree ever presented in his 20 years of dedication to spectacular theatre. The procession of guests entered a set with a vaulted ceiling and stone walls hung with velvet tapestries; musicians and singers, placed in two upstage galleries, waited to entertain them. The tables, dressed in gleaming goldplate, offered an abundance of dishes copied from original sources in museums and galleries. Over 200 items of furniture and properties were used in this one scene. The trial scene at Blackfriars was played in a great hall with a beamed ceiling and a large stained-glass window; seats for the large cast of lords, ladies, monks, and prelates were arranged in three tiers below the window. Three consecutive processions of principals and their attendants slowly made their entrance to the hall: Wolsey, led by four halberdiers, walked under a canopy held by four boys; the king, resplendent in jewels and gold embroidery, was preceded by courtiers carrying his crown, orb, and scepter; and Queen Katherine entered accompanied by five ladies-in-waiting. The chamber in Kimbolton where the rejected queen had her vision—the angelic *femmes-volantes* in Kean's production—was a paneled room simply furnished. The transparent back wall, when lit from behind, revealed a constellation of stars made of shimmering sequins attached to a dark drop. The production ended with yet another spectacular procession for the king's coronation in the nave of Westminster Abbey.

To his detractors who maintained that Shakespeare had once again been

buried under an excess of scenery and pageantry, Tree had already responded some years before. In 1900, he had advised them to carefully read the stage directions for *The Tempest* and *Henry VIII* and ask themselves "why, if Shakespeare contemplated nothing in the way of what we term a production, he gave such minute directions for effects which, even in our own time of artistic and scientific mounting, are difficult of realisation. Surely no one reading the vision of Katherine of Aragon can come to any other conclusion than that Shakespeare intended to leave as little to the imagination as possible, and to put upon the stage as gorgeous and as complete a picture as the resources of the theatre could supply.[10]

It was not the first time that an actor-manager attributed to Shakespeare a desire for spectacle and pageantry similar to his own. Whether or not Shakespeare himself felt limited, at least in practical terms if not in imagination, by the resources at his disposal, it was clear that dazzling displays were still very much in favor in Edwardian London. *Henry VIII* had a run of 254 performances, all to near capacity in a playhouse with seats for 1,720 spectators. Although the expenditure involved was exorbitant, it was Tree's most successful play from a financial point of view.

Tree presented only one more of Shakespeare's plays before his retirement: *Macbeth* on September 5, 1911, with sets by Craven, Harker, and McCleary. Although on that occasion he had tried to concentrate on creating "that awe-inspiring atmosphere suggested by the poet," without stressing the historical aspects of the period or insisting "upon archaeological detail of scenery and costumes," the production was nevertheless described as "elaborately spectacular."[11]

In the early years of World War I, Tree traveled to the United States to raise funds and promote American support for the war efforts. During his absence from London, his playhouse was booked by other producers who continued to present plays; in some instances these were light but spectacular entertainment like *Chu-Chin-Chow*, intended to give the public a chance to escape, even if for only a few hours, from the anxiety of the conflict on the Continent.

The romantically inspired emphasis on fantasy, spectacle, and historical accuracy was rejected after World War I, to be replaced by the exploration of abstraction, symbolism, selective realism, minimalism, and other "isms" deemed more appropriate for the twentieth century. The process of collaboration between directors and designers, a collaboration that started in the 1800s, had more lasting consequences. Its positive influence may be recognized in the work of modern director-designer teams, whose particular styles have defined the visual aspects of the theatre in the last decades.

Chapter 7

Romantic Fairies
and Medieval Knights

*T*HE SAME AESTHETIC CONCERNS that influenced the styles of scenery in the nineteenth century contributed to the development of costume design. The desire to create appropriate backgrounds for the action of the plays, whether historically accurate or purely imaginative, ran parallel to the will to dress the actors in harmony with their surroundings. Moreover, just as set designers acquired a prominent position in the context of the productions, costume designers also became indispensable members of creative teams, although the process took longer to evolve. Whereas set designers had been anonymous partners to theatrical managers until the late eighteenth century, the position of costume designer did not even exist until the late 1800s.

Before the romantic period, the lack of interest in specific and descriptive detail extended from the scenery to the actors' wardrobe. The tradition of performing in contemporary dress, regardless of the time frame of the play, was no more objectionable to the audience than the "one-style-fits-all" stock scenery seen on the English stages from the Restoration to the end of the eighteenth century. The public did not mind seeing Othello and Macbeth make their entrance, periwigs on their heads and gold lace stockings around their necks, wearing the red, full uniform of an English regiment, any more than they minded the generic sets.

For aesthetic as much as practical reasons, contemporary dress was accepted and even encouraged, since many clothes seen on stage were the discarded fineries of wealthy patrons, clothes sometimes loaned or donated directly to the actors and sometimes given to a servant who subsequently sold them to an actor. Performers were expected to wear the garments received as a gift whenever the donor was present in the playhouse, and not even the most vain thespian would have refused to don Charles II's coronation robes, loaned by the king to Thomas Betterton for a production of *Henry V*. Similar generosity was displayed by Mary of Modena, James II's second wife, who presented her wedding and coronation dresses to Elizabeth Barry. Actors who lacked aristocratic patrons were reduced to buying or renting at secondhand clothing stores or, even worse, to wearing the shabby, moth-eaten stock stored in some theatre wardrobes. In the very rare instances of new costumes being provided for a production, they were under the supervision of either the playwright or the manager. The tradition of cast-off theatrical costumes survived well into the mid–eighteenth century; George Anne Bellamy, an actress who had joined Covent Garden in 1749, wrote in her memoirs: "The dresses of the theatrical ladies were at this period very indifferent. The Empresses and Queens were confined to black velvet except on extraordinary occasions, when they put on an embroidered petticoat. ... The young ladies generally appeared in a *cast* gown of some person of quality."[1]

David Garrick made some advances toward appropriate costume; he played both Richard III in the 1740s and King Lear in the 1770s, in fairly accurate versions of historical dress. And as the romantic influence increased, so did the desire to investigate the history of dress. As with the history of architecture and applied arts, the first signs of interest in fashion history began to appear in print; one of the earliest was Thomas Jeffery's *A Collection of the Dressed of Different Nations, Ancient and Modern*, published in 1757. In the late 1700s, three volumes by Joseph Strutt appeared: *Regal and Ecclesiastical Antiquities of England* in 1773; *A Compleat View of the Manners, Customs, Habits, etc., of the Inhabitants of England* in 1776; and *A Compleat View of the Dress and Habits of the People of England* in 1796–99. C. A. Stothard's *Monumental Effigies of Great Britain* and Sir Samuel Meyrick's *A Critical Inquiry into Ancient Arms and Armour* were published early in the next decade, followed by Frederick William Fairholt's *Costume in England* in 1834 and Henry Shaw's *Dresses and Decorations of the Middle Ages* in 1836.

The evolution from contemporary dress to accurate and appropriate stage costume, a process generated by the romantic desire to reconstruct the past, may be followed through the work of the same actor-managers who were instrumental in reforming set design. Indeed, John Philip Kemble did not limit his interest in historical accuracy to the presentation of Gothic sets designed by William Capon; in the 1790s he appeared in Roman toga, "then for the first time exhibited on the English stage," to play *Coriolanus* and *Julius Caesar*.[2] Following in his steps, nineteenth-century managers increasingly used costume design to express their own aesthetic values.

Theatre and archaeology found two enthusiastic devotees in James Robinson Planché and Charles Kemble. Heir to his brother's reforms while manager of Covent Garden, Kemble produced *King John* in November 1823, traditionally considered to be the turning point in the way theatre practitioners viewed the designing of stage costume. For the first time an entire cast, not just the leads, appeared in medieval costume, designed specifically for that production and based on the most painstaking research of historical sources. This approach to presenting a production was revolutionary enough to warrant an unprecedented advertising campaign; Londoners saw their city papered with playbills announcing:

The Publick is respectfully informed that

Shakespeare's Tragedy of King John

is in a forward state of revival at this Theatre, and will shortly be produced with an attention to Costume which has never been equalled on the English Stage. Every Character will appear in the precise habit of the Period—the whole of the Dresses and Decorations being executed from copies of indisputable authorities, such as, Monuments, Sels, illuminated Manuscripts, painted Glass, etc.

The Proprietors request permission likewise to state, that should their exertions in this instance obtain the patronage of the Publick, it is their intention to produce, in succession the rest of Shakespeare's Plays in the same splendid, novel, and interesting style.[3]

The person in charge of supervising the authenticity of this "splendid, novel, and interesting" production was J. R. Planché. Although by then he had established his reputation as a playwright, it had been a subject of regret to him that despite some halfhearted attempts at accuracy, his contemporaries had not paid much attention to appropriate dress for Shakespeare's plays. In a letter to the editor of *The Album*, shortly before *King John* opened, he denounced this fact: "The acting plays of Shakspeare [sic] are incorrectly dressed at both the patent theatres, and ... more care is taken in the production of a pantomime for Christmas ... more expense lavished to render nonsense palatable ... than would worthily decorate the immortal monuments of the genius of our first poet."[4] In addition, he advanced the theory that every drama, whether ancient or modern, should be presented with the same attention to historical accuracy. He acknowledged one argument occasionally heard against strict adherence to accuracy, the argument that some periods were odd enough to risk turning actors into objects of ridicule, but he was convinced that "a little ingenuity and taste" could avoid the caricature just as easily as a gentleman could "dress in the height of fashion without rendering himself a subject for the pencil of Dighton, or Cruickshank."[5]

King John presented Planché with the first opportunity to put his theories into practice; it was followed by subsequent engagements to supervise Kemble's productions of *As You Like It, Hamlet, Cymbeline,* and *Henry IV, Part I,* the last with new scenery painted by John Henderson Grieve and his sons. Planché's contributions to accurate historical costume were offered for the enlightenment of the public in a series of volumes with critical and explanatory notes, published by John Miller in the 1820s, with figures designed and executed on stone by J. K. Meadows.

Planché's interest in archaeological studies led in 1829 to his election as a Fellow of the Society of Antiquarians. He was equally prolific as an author of scholarly articles and books as he was as a playwright; his major works on the history of dress are the *History of British Costume from the Earliest Period to the Close of the Eighteenth Century,* published in 1834, and the two-volume

Cyclopaedia of Costume; or, A Dictionary of Dress, Including Notices of Contemporaneous Fashions on the Continent, and Preceded by a General History of the Costumes of the Principal Countries of Europe, with Numerous Illustrations, published in 1875-79, plus an extensive list of articles for a variety of journals. When still a young boy, E. W. Godwin learned his first lesson, and became interested in the history of costume, from one of Planché's articles printed in the shilling series known as "Knight's Monthly Volume for All Readers."[6]

In 1831, Planché joined Mme. Vestris at the Olympic Theatre, with the title of "Superintendent of Decorative Departments," and remained with her, as provider of plays and production adviser, during her management at Covent Garden, from 1839 to 1842, and during the glorious seasons at the Lyceum. Throughout those years of collaboration, Planché found in Mme. Vestris an understanding manager, who had concerns similar to his own and who allowed him to continue in the path of reforming stage costume. William A. Armstrong, in an article published in *Theatre Notebook* in 1956, explored the possibility that Madame's interest in costuming may well have developed as a consequence of her sojourn in Paris, between 1816 and 1819, where she became familiar with the theories of the actor Talma.[7] François-Joseph Talma (1763–1826), the greatest French tragedian of the Revolutionary and Empire periods, was also a reformer of stage costumes. In his essay *Reflections of the Actor's Art,* Talma urged costumiers to study the art of the past in order to attain historical accuracy. He summed up his position: "Truth in the dresses ... contributes greatly to theatrical illusion, and transports the spectator to the age and country in which the persons represented lived. This fidelity, too, furnishes the actor with the means of given a peculiar physiognomy to each of his characters."[8]

Although the years at the Olympic were spent mainly in the production of burlettas and light pieces, Planché managed to introduce an important reform, outside the realm of historical research, in his "mythological, allegorical burletta" *Olympic Revels; or, Prometheus and Pandora,* first seen on January 3, 1831. He had long believed that the traditional English burlesque costumes, with their exaggerated features and outrageous colors, were too grotesque. He theorized that funny lines did not necessarily have to be delivered by actors in ridiculous dress to make an impact and that the juxtaposition of normal dress and farcical dialogue would emphasize, rather than detract from, the comic effect. To his credit, he persuaded Mme. Vestris to experiment with his theories in *Olympic Revels.* Decades later he declared:

> The extraordinary success of this experiment—for it may justly be so termed—was due not only to the admirable singing and piquant performance of that gifted lady [Mme. Vestris], but also to the charm and novelty imparted to it by the elegance and accuracy of the costumes; it having been previously the practice to dress a burlesque in the most *outré* and ridiculous fashion. My suggestion to try the effect of persons picturesquely attired speaking absurd doggerel fortunately took the fancy of the fair lessee, and the alteration was highly appreciated by the public; but many old actors could never get over

Mme. Vestris as Mistress Ford in *The Merry Wives of Windsor*. This portrait, dated 1826, shows the actress in costume for the role in an earlier production, not the one she presented at Covent Garden. Her fashionable 1820s dress does not comply with the principles of historical accuracy. Courtesy of the Board of Trustees of the Victoria and Albert Museum.

their early impressions. Liston thought to the last that Prometheus, instead of the Phrygian cap, tunic, and trousers, should have been dressed like a great lubberly boy in a red jacket and nankeens, with a pinafore all besmeared with lollipop![9]

Occasionally, Planché furnished some pieces that afforded him and the actress an opportunity to display their flair for spectacle, and their interest in historically accurate costumes, at a higher artistic level. One was *The Court Beauties* in 1835, a play that dramatized the rivalry between two Restoration painters: Sir Peter Lely and Sir Godfrey Kneller. Through the intervention of a friend, Madame obtained permission for her designers to study Lely's portraits at Hampton Court in order to re-create, as a *tableau vivant*, the gallery of beauties of the court of Charles II. In the final scene the curtain rose to reveal eight ladies, posing within gilded frames, in costumes identical to those painted by the seventeenth-century artists. Madame appeared not as a beauty but as the Merry Monarch's favorite page, leading a brace of buckhounds (the small hounds used to hunt deer) borrowed from the royal kennels at Windsor.

Sometimes, however, Madame's interest in historically accurate costumes would be overshadowed by her desire to appear in rich but inappropriate attire, particularly when playing female roles. Westland Marston, in his book *Our Recent Actors*, remarked: "She was such a votary of elegance in dress, that she would display it even in rustic or humble characters. That a silk skirt, a lace-edged petticoat, a silk stocking, a shoe of satin or patent leather, would never have been worn by some of the characters she personated, was of no more concern to her on the ground of consistency than were their rich attires to Marie Antoinette and the ladies of her court, when they masqueraded as shepherdesses and milkmaids in the grounds of the Petit Trianon."[10]

When Mme. Vestris secured the lease of Covent Garden, she undertook the production of more serious drama and some of Shakespeare's plays; from that repertoire she presented *Love's Labour's Lost* (fall 1839), *The Merry Wives of Windsor* (spring 1840), and *A Midsummer Night's Dream* (fall 1840). Madame's production of *A Midsummer Night's Dream* marked the first time London theatregoers had seen the play in its original form since the closing of the playhouses in 1642. It also marked the beginning of the trend, which would continued until the end of the century, of presenting Shakespeare's comedy in what was alleged to be "historically accurate" dress, that of Athens in the fifth century BC. A drama critic, who acknowledged the play had "at length been put on the stage in a style which must satisfy the most fastidious voluptuary in scenic art," nevertheless had some reservations about the results of consulting historical sources. He said: "The costumes for the most part rest upon authority ... yet authority might be found for dresses falling in more graceful lines than those worn by Demetrius and Lysander, and the Amazonian garb put on Hyppolita, whatever Etruscan vase may say to the contrary, might advantageously, and at least with equal correctness, be exchanged for a more becoming as well as a more modest costume. The fairies are clad ... in virgin white, and immaculate silk stockings. For the benefit of our lady readers, we may explain that the porringers or straw baskets which hang at the back of Demetrius and others, are *petasi* or hats."[11] Another reviewer, more sensitive to Madame's intentions, paid her homage for inventing fairyland on stage; she had invested it "with a dreamy spirit" and had populated it with elfins "costumed with the fantastic splendour which tells a tale of power, riches, and romance." [12] *A Midsummer Night's Dream* gave Mme. Vestris the opportunity to display not only her concern for costumes but also, once more, her well-turned legs in the role of Oberon.

In April 1842, Madame appeared as Prince Paragon in another one of Planché's fairy spectacles: *The White Cat*. This "feline extravaganza," as it was termed in the *New Monthly Belle Assemblée*, showed Mme. Vestris as "*the* prince of story-books, who is all perfection and misfortune till the end of his adventures, which invariably wind up with the concentrated essence of happiness."[13] The same publication praised the great beauty of this and previous productions under Vestris's stewardship and conceded that a new era had dawned on the stage from the moment she had undertaken the role of manager.

The virginal fairies and storybook princes moved with Madame and Planché to the Lyceum in 1848, to inhabit the spectacular scenery created by William Beverley. When reviewers exhausted their praises for Beverley's scenery in *The Golden Branch*, they proceeded to admire the "succession of exquisite *tableaux* ... perfectly resembling the works of Watteau," with shepherds and shepherdesses all dressed in lovely French Regency costumes. [14] In the Christmas extravaganza of 1848, *The King of the Peacocks*, Mme. Vestris played Argus, the "Brilliant-Eyed King" of a realm where all the subjects were dressed in brightly colored medieval costumes. The actress appeared "more magnificently attired than a Persian prince ever was, for nobody but herself could have ever suggested so much gay and glittering ornament without spoiling the general effect. Prince Esterhazy's celebrated jacket of diamonds [was] nothing compared to her coat."[15]

When Madame was not playing "breeches" parts herself, the tradition was preserved by casting younger female members of her company in male roles. In the Easter piece of 1849, *The Seven Champions of Christendom*, all seven heroes were played by women. However, in the heart of some admirers, the undeniable charms of those actresses could not make up for Mme. Vestris's absence. The *Times* lamented, "So admirably has she played in a long series of such productions, that we feel there is something wanting when she does not stand personally before us in one of her graceful fantastic dresses, although we still see the guiding spirit in the general elegance and splendour." The same reviewer remarked that the costumes for the corps de ballet were chosen with the "most tasteful regard for harmony with the scene.... The cool garments of the water nymphs, and the rich fantastic dresses of the dancers ... [were] striking instances of this feeling of propriety."[16]

Princes and potentates were a source of inspiration for Madame's attire when she played kings. In the Christmas extravaganza of 1850, *King Charming*, her costume was an exact replica of that worn by the Nepalese ambassador to London, who had been very conspicuous in society during that

MADAM VESTRIS AS KING CHARMING.

Mme. Vestris in costume as King Charming. Lithograph by J. Brandard (Harvard Theatre Collection).

season. The ensemble showed a combination of "pale pink satin tunic embroidered with pearls, Turkish trousers, a turban hat, one mass of pearls, hung with pendant diamonds surmounted by a spray of bird-of-paradise feathers."[17] For the last extravaganza Planché wrote for his friend, *Once upon a Time There Were Two Kings*, he confessed to having "servilely copied from authorities of the period in which the original story was written, viz., the close of the 17th century, exhibiting the 'comical-tragical' and 'pastoral-comic' habits invented ... by artists of the Augustean age of Louis Quatorze."[18]

When the final curtain fell on Mme. Vestris's reign at the Lyceum, Planché did not abandon the magical world he had shared with the actress. In 1855 he published *Fairy Tales*, a translation from the Countess D'Aulnoy, with biographical and historical notes; three years later *Four and Twenty Fairy Tales*, his second volume of translated stories, appeared in print. For the rest of his long life (he died at the age of 84 on May 30, 1880), he continued to dedicate his efforts to the study of history and was able to witness how his advocacy of historically correct dress was embraced by some actor-managers of his time.

It is not surprising that Planché's most loyal disciple was Charles Kean, whose ambition to turn the stage into "a true and perfect mirror of history and manners" included costumes as well as scenery.[19] Kean chose *King John*, the same play that had initiated the trend toward faithful reconstruction of historical costume in 1823, as his first attempt to attain this goal.

It is interesting to note that after 30 years of more or less continuous presentations of historically accurate costumes, Kean was still apprehensive about the reception his efforts would receive. Shortly before the opening of *King John*, Kean expressed his fears in a letter to a Mr. Baldwin: "When I tell you that I have expended over a thousand pounds upon the getting up you may imagine how anxious I am as to the *results*. P.S. Everything in the play is taken from authorities. You will find us strictly correct in the most minute details."[20]

The unanimous praise for the splendor, beauty, and correctness of his production must have reassured Kean that his funds and exertions had been well spent. Even Queen Victoria noted in her journal, "The dresses were magnificent and strictly correct."[21]

The success attained by *King John* encouraged Kean to proceed with his plan to educate while entertaining, and he chose the "Scottish Play" for his next revival. His elaborate preface to the acting edition of *Macbeth*, which had originally been one of his flyleaves, left no doubts regarding the scrupulous research he had conducted to ensure unimpeachable accuracy in costumes and decorations. For the benefit of his audience, he explained that, in the absence of available material from the time of the tragedy, he had decided to base the costumes on "materials from the nations to whom Scotland was constantly opposed in war." He continued:

The continual inroads of the Norsemen and the invasion of Canut, in 1031, … may have taught, at least to the higher classes, the necessity of adopting the superior weapons and better defensive armour of their enemies; for those reasons I have introduced the tunic, mantle, cross gartering, and ringed byrnie of the Danes and Anglo-Saxons, between whom it does not appear any material difference existed; retaining, however, the peculiarity of the "striped and chequered garb," which seems to be generally admitted as belonging to the Scotch long anterior to the history of this play; together with the eagle feather in the helmet, which according to Gaelic tradition, was the distinguishing mark of a chieftain. Party coloured woolens and cloths appear to have been commonly worn among the Celtic tribes from a very early period.

Diodorus Sciculus and Pliny allude to this peculiarity in their account of the dress of the Belgic Gauls; Strabo, Pliny, and Xiphilin, record the dress of Boadicea, Queen of the Iceni, as being woven chequer-wise, of many colours, comprising purple, light and dark red, violet and blue.

…Harold Hardrada, King of Norway, is described by Snorre, as wearing in the battle with Harold II, King of England, AD 1066, a blue tunic and a splendid helmet. The Norwegians, not having expected battle that day, are said to have been without their coats of mail. This mail appears to have been composed of iron rings or bosses sewn upon cloth of leather, like that of the Anglo-Saxons.[22]

This is a very short excerpt from an endless description of every detail and source consulted in the design of dresses, scenery, and property. However, all that painstaking research did not deter Kean from following that long-established tradition of "helping" Shakespeare by adding some touches never envisioned by the poet, such as an offstage chorus of 50 singers and four soloists for the witches' scene, as well as an ensemble of eight old men in druidical costumes, aloft in a minstrels' gallery, playing the harp during the banquet scene. Neither did it dissuade Ellen Kean, who played Lady Macbeth, from wearing a crinoline, or at least several petticoats, under her alleged eleventh-century costume.

The promptbook preserved in the Folger Shakespeare Library includes notes, attributed to Kean, regarding the actual look of the costumes. Macbeth's first costume included a chocolate-brown shirt with tight sleeves, a coat of mail, gray leggings bound around the legs with straps of buff leather, buff-leather shoes, a steel helmet with two eagle feathers, and a party colored mantle fastened with a fibula on the right shoulder. He carried a small circular shield, strengthened by rings of brass and a spear with a flame-headed point. For a second outfit, he had a red shirt, blue mantle and leggings, ankle-length black embroidered shoes, a gold turret-shaped crown, and a royal staff. Lady Macbeth had three costumes. first was a light-blue dress with multi-colored stripes below knee level, partially covered by a party colored mantle fastened with a fibula on the right shoulder and a coronet of gold over a kerchief. Later on she appeared in a dress of similar style but made of richer fabric embroidered with gold, and finally she wore a white gown with a light-gray

Charles Kean and Ellen Kean as Macbeth and Lady Macbeth in the "Dagger Scene." Photograph by Martin Laroche. Courtesy of the Board of Trustees of the Victoria and Albert Museum.

mantle. The cast was dressed in modified versions of the same basic style, made of textured woolens vaguely reminiscent of Scottish plaid; the variety of colors and materials indicated social rank. Much metal was used for armor, weapons, and the conical Norman helmets inspired by the tapestry of Bayeux and by other illustrations of the period.[23]

Macbeth was hailed as the most magnificent staging of Shakespeare ever, but Kean would upstage himself and amaze the public even further with *Sardanapalus*, his next production, in June 1853. The sources of his research have been mentioned in reference to the scenery; the splendid Nineveh—re-created for the stage by Lloyds, Gordon, and Dayes—was the background for hundreds of soldiers, dancing girls, courtiers, and slaves, all dressed in the most perfect reproductions of Assyrian costume that money and scholarship could buy. The *Art Journal* singled out the wardrobe as "the great feature of the play," since every fringe and every piece of jewelry, even the earrings, was "as truthful as the Assyrian marbles themselves." The dazzled critic continued: "By colouring the features and dressing the hair of every character in accordance with the antique type, so extraordinary a resemblance has been produced that we seem to recognise even the peculiar features of the antique Assyrian race in their modern representatives. ... It is impossible that accuracy can be carried farther than it is in this gorgeous spectacle. ... An evening at the Princess's will be most instructively spent."[24]

Kean may have taken the last sentences as a challenge to prove that accuracy and spectacle could always "be carried farther." The revival of *Richard III*, on February 20, 1854, provided the manager with a wonderful opportunity to show his expertise in fifteenth-century dress. Once again it is possible to obtain a detailed description of the costumes for this production from the extant promptbook at the Folger Library. Taking as an example just the garments worn by Richard, it would not be difficult to imagine the splendor of the stage picture. The Duke of Gloucester, later Richard III, went through six costume changes. He appeared first in a royal-blue damask doublet with hanging sleeves embroidered in gold and trimmed with sable; he had a gold belt for his sword and dagger, high black-leather boots, gold spurs, gold-embroidered white gloves, and a crimson velvet hat with red and white feathers. He was seen next in the same costume, but the boots were exchanged for poulaines (footwear with exaggeratedly long, pointed toes) over white hose, with a garter on the left knee. The third costume was a cloth of gold floor-length undergarment, covered by a purple robe of state trimmed with miniver; his shoes were of gold-embroidered crimson velvet, and he carried his crown and scepter. From that, he changed first to a dark velvet gown and later to a short open robe, with no color indicated in the promptbook. He died at Bosworth field, vainly calling for a horse, in a suit of armor inlaid in gold over which he wore a surcoat with the royal crest; his hair, cut square on the forehead, was long and bushy around the head. In act 4, scene 4, where Shakespeare indicates "enter King Richard and train, marching with drums and trumpets," Kean provided a retinue of 60 persons, not only drummers and trumpeters wearing tabards with the arms of England but also knights in complete suites of armor, officers of the Royal Guard, pages, spearmen, and banner-bearing soldiers.[25]

However, neither striking costumes nor magnificent scenery could rescue

Charles Kean as Cardinal Wolsey in *Henry VIII*. Photograph by Martin Laroche. Courtesy of the Board of Trustees of the Victoria and Albert Museum.

the production from failure, attributable to having used Colley Cibber's text instead of Shakespeare's.

That lack of public support did not deter Kean from offering another dazzling series of historical illustrations in his *Henry VIII*, the perfect vehicle to achieve his dream of turning the stage into a "true and perfect mirror of history." If the playgoers had had the time to read the flyleaves before taking their seats, they would have been apprised of Kean's reasons for reviving this piece. He explained in his introduction: "The whole life of Henry VIII (especially during the time when that pompous prelate, Cardinal Wolsey was in favour), abounded with processions, princely shows of grandeur, and magnificence. This pageantry Shakespeare has vivified with the inspiration of his genius, and has thus produced, as Coleridge says, 'a sort of historical masque or show play.'"[26] What Kean did not explain to his audience, because he did not know it himself, was how far his wife had gone to ensure historical accuracy. The actor played Cardinal Wolsey in fittingly splendid garb. Although it is difficult to realize—when viewing a black-and-white photograph taken when the technology was in its infancy—how magnificent that costume was, an eyewitness relates that it was made of silk and that the exquisite, deep band of lace, almost three feet wide, had been created by old nuns in a convent. Mrs. Kean, while on holiday in Rome, had bribed a well-connected acquaintance to procure an audience with the Pope in order to gain entrance to the Vatican. Once inside, the crafty lady succeeded in borrowing a cardinal's robe, from which she took measurements, pattern, and even some threads from the hem as a color sample. Those items were used to design Wolsey's costume, but Mrs. Kean never told her husband how she had obtained the information; his passion for authenticity may not have been strong enough to condone such conduct.[27]

Henry VIII was the most successful of Kean's revivals. It played for 100 consecutive performances in that season and for another 69 when it was brought back in subsequent years.

In 1856 Kean revived *The Winter's Tale* and *A Midsummer Night's Dream*, though neither play seems congenial to historical reconstruction. The first is riddled with anachronistic episodes: a visit to the Oracle of Delphi by two sixteenth-century gentlemen; the mention of Apollo and the emperor of Russia almost in the same breath; a bear chasing a character on the shores of Bohemia. The latter play, although set in an Athens ruled by a Duke Theseus, also introduces the rather un-Greek world of Titania and Oberon, besides the very Elizabethan "mechanicals." Nevertheless, Kean succeeded in finding justification and authorities to support his re-creation of the life, customs, and costumes of classical antiquity as a background for both productions.

It has already been related how Kean used the Delphi episode to justify his historical choice for *The Winter's Tale*. Following the same principle for the costumes, he dressed the cast in Greek garb and introduced ceremonies and dance scenes conducive to spectacular displays. A Pyrrhic dance, performed by 36 young ladies in complete Greek armor, was praised most enthusiastically. The character for the allegory of Time, traditionally represented as an old man carrying an hourglass and a scythe, was here seen as a classical figure in Greek attire. In one of the reviews it is difficult to determine whether the author was more impressed by the costumes or by the living fauna onstage, since they are both mentioned in the same sentence: "The costumes are very skillfully chosen, and the introduction of camels, sheep, and goats, add a picturesque beauty to the scenic panorama."[28] The pictorial composition of the whole production was also recognized and admired by the press.

In *A Midsummer Night's Dream* Kean took the audience on a grand tour of fifth-century Athens as it would have appeared to its own inhabitants at the time of its greatest glory. Nevertheless, he had to concede that no research, no matter how arduous, could possibly indicate the sort of raiment that Titania, Oberon, and their elfin subjects donned to cavort in the woods; consequently, he dressed the fairies in romantic tutus, gave them wings, and crowned them with garlands of flowers. Most of the reviews mentioned the great unity of all visual elements and the impossibility of praising one scene above another, since each scene seemed to flow and magically blend into the next one. The *Times* described not so much the costumes as the general impression made by Titania's dream sequence:

> In every one of his details Mr. Charles Kean has taken care to spiritualize his stage as much as possible. Now the strong ... rays thrown on his fairy groups give them a lustre that is not of this world; now an artful diminution of light makes them seem as though they would melt away altogether. Now heavy masses of rock and foliage produce a supernatural gloom that might be associated with the darker objects of superstition; now these break away to discover some bright moonlit lake or verdant plain. ... Titania slumbers not on a substantial bank, but on a waving bough, above pendant bluebells. Puck darts through the air with lightning-like rapidity that seems beyond the reach of ordinary machinery; the fairies that throng the palace of Theseus at the conclusion of the piece, and display their lamps of illuminated flowers at every corner seem, in their perpetual passing and repassing, to be too numerous to assemble within walls raised by human hands, and one is tempted to account for the presence of them all by assuming there is something ethereal ... in their nature.[29]

Perhaps the most telling confession of the appeal this romantic world had for the mid–Victorian public was expressed by the critic for *The Era*: "As we behold the fair Titania, reclining on the bank ... and as her lovely attendants flit about in their elfin robes to the sweetly melodious music of Mendelssohn, we imagine ourselves in the realm of faerydom [sic] and regret the rude shock which dispels the dream and calls us back to everyday existence."[30]

For the next three years, until his retirement in 1859, Kean continued to display his indefatigable energy and devotion to research in all the productions he presented at the Princess's. In *Richard II*, the multitudes who lined the London street for the triumphal return of Bolingbroke were dressed in costumes taken from contemporary illustrations and from the works of Meyrick, Fairholt, and Shaw. For *The Tempest*, Kean found inspiration once again in ancient art and mythology to justify the host of dancing niads, dryads,

Ellen Kean as the queen in the "Garden Scene" from *Richard II*. Photograph by Martin Laroche. Courtesy of the Board of Trustees of the Victoria and Albert Museum.

fawns, and satyrs who, covered with flowers and carrying baskets of fruit on their heads, gathered for the banquet scene. The betrothal masque had built-in opportunities: Juno entered in a chariot drawn by peacocks whose tails emitted brilliant light, and the entire stage was filled with hovering spirits dressed in robes of red, bright blue, and changing opal colors. For *King Lear*, the actor-manager drew his research from eighth-century Anglo-Saxon Britain. *The Merchant of Venice* reproduced late-sixteenth-century Venetian

Charles Kean as Richard II, wearing crown and robes based on the Jerusalem Chamber portrait in Westminster Abbey. Courtesy of the Board of Trustees of the Victoria and Albert Museum.

dress as printed in Vecellio's volume *Degli Habiti Antichi e Moderni di diverse Parti del Mondo*; for *Henry V*, the sources were illuminated manuscripts and eyewitness accounts relating to the heroic deeds of the monarch.

Thus far it has been evident that Kean's presentations were the product of his own attachment to spectacular historical reproduction with didactic overtones. The success of his seasons at the Princess's, and the almost universal approval of his efforts, indicate that the public shared his aesthetic views or, at least, enjoyed the elaboration and the artistic excellence of the productions. However, one question remains unanswered: who really *designed* the costumes? Whereas all the published reviews credit the artists responsible for the scenery, no mention is ever made of a costume designer. The comments always attribute the beauty and accuracy of the wardrobe to Kean himself, but there is not even a hint that, as would be expected in a modern show, he produced drawings that were subsequently made into garments in a costume shop. The experts he consulted were scholars, not designers, and no proof has been found of Mrs. Kean's involvement in determining the look of the costumes, except for her secretive investigations at the Vatican. How, then, were cutters, seamstresses, and tailors able to reproduce such a variety of periods with great fidelity? Possibly, the precious illuminated manuscripts and other materials consulted at museums were copied and delivered to a shop; some names were occasionally mentioned in the programs as "builders" of the dresses. All of these facts clearly indicate that, in spite of Planché's heritage, the notion of commissioning one person to be in charge of creating the costumes was still not a commonly accepted one. It would take another 30 years, and a great deal of struggle, for actor-managers to admit that the presence of a costume designer would benefit the visual unity of their presentations.

The harmony produced by integrated visual elements and made possible by a single person controlling every minute detail had been E. W. Godwin's lifelong artistic ambition and his most advanced and controversial theory. Moreover, he introduced a new dimension to the concept of costume design, a dimension taken for granted today but sorely missing from the stages of his time. In Godwin's estimation, the means to achieve the total integration of costumes into a theatrical presentation were not limited to their historical fidelity or suitability for a specific character because, regardless of how accurate a costume may have been, the effect could be, and usually was, ruined by an actor's lack of understanding of the manners and conventions of a certain period. Godwin repeatedly addressed this problem in his series of articles "The Architecture and Costumes of Shakespeare's Plays." Writing on the subject of *The Merchant of Venice*, Godwin remarked, "The manners of the period were characterised by courtesy combined with stately dignified action ... but modern actors and actresses rarely hold the mirror high enough to reflect the mien, deportment, or bearing of the men and women of a past age." He declared that actors incapable of reproducing the "air and look" of the Renaissance were "not fitted to play in the comedies of the greatest dramatist of that period." He explained, "Correctness of costume, and properties, and furniture is all very well, but if, through it all, we see nineteenth-century action, modern style, the modern Robertsonian society, or the special graces which are the delight of our time, but which would have been looked on as antics, or at least as bad form, in the courts of Philip and Elizabeth, then the picture must be discordant, and the dramatic representation woefully incomplete."[31] Godwin wanted to see performers as "living illustrators of the manners of the past" and "interpreters of its mighty dramatist."[32] His remarks on the failure to produce that effect most certainly could not have made him very popular among contemporary actors. Besides information on sources for research, the article on *Much Ado About Nothing* contains the following comment:

> In ordinary, every-day life, the people who represent on stage the fine dame, the noble duke, or the foreign potentate, are so little accustomed to art, or anything like good style of living, that it is with difficulty they can appear unconscious of their stage surroundings. ... even in modern comedies we see the weak actress dominated by the sheer material force of millinery, and in the revival of old plays, when fairly genuine costumes and scenery approaching reality are produced, the mass of actors and actresses look imbecile. We give them the benefit of the doubt, and assume that they are inside their clothes, but certainly they do not wear them. The human form becomes at last a human peg, with four movable peglets fixed in it, and a costume is thus too frequently brought into ridicule by the ignorant, and made a scapegoat for the incapable player.[33]

Managers, as well as actors, continued to be the cause of Godwin's dismay and scathing denunciations. The haphazard way in which some plays were mounted, the lack of communication among contributors to a production, and the absence of a single strong mind to coordinate visual elements and interpretation were all part of the regrettable conditions prevalent on the stage. In his article on *Twelfth Night*, Godwin elaborated on the dangers inherent in these common practices:

> Stage management ... is one of the colours on which the dramatic picture depends; scenery is another; costumes another; and the choicest tints, the high lights, the jewels of the pictures are to be found ... should be found ... in the expression of the actor's voice, face, and figure. But the whole batch of colours and tints must be as one in their treatment if we want to see a play rendered fitly. For one man to design the interior of Olivia's hose with no control or understanding as to the stage management; another to arrange the business of the action in total ignorance of the inner arrangements of an Italian mansion ... for one to paint the walls knowing nothing of the colours of the costumes; another to design the dresses utterly indifferent to the colours of his background; these are the happy-go-lucky processes usually employed on the English stage, and any success that may result from the adoption of such ways and means must necessarily be of the nature of a fluke.[34]

While the articles in the series "The Architecture and Costumes of Shakespeare's Plays" were being published, Godwin had what he thought would be his first chance to put his ideas into practice when engaged by the Bancrofts as "archaeologist" for their revival of *The Merchant of Venice.*

However well-intentioned the managers may have been in hiring Godwin as historical adviser, the concept of visual unity was still alien to them; his instructions were followed only in matters of scenery, as acknowledged in the program and also in the Bancroft's memoirs.[35] As for the costumes, when the *Times* attributed their design to him, Godwin was prompt to disavow responsibility for them. Five days after the opening, the newspaper printed a correction to that previous statement: "Mr. Godwin thinks it right in fairness to the person that designed the costumes, and in fairness to himself, to say that he is in no way responsible for any of the dresses, as his opinion was neither asked nor given on this subject."[36] Actually, Godwin had designed the dress worn by Ellen Terry as Portia in the casket scene (it can be seen in Ellen Terry's cottage in Smallhythe, Kent), but if there was another person in charge of costumes for the rest of the cast, the name does not appear in the program.

Godwin's subsequent involvement in John Coleman's revival of *Henry V* did not dispel his misgivings about managers' appalling disregard for visual integrity and historical accuracy. Besides the dummy horses previously mentioned, the production was plagued with inconsistencies and blatant errors he found himself unable to correct. With his great flair for creating controversy, Godwin wrote an article with the revealing title of "*Henry V*: A Theatrical Experience." Although he avoided, as much as his temper would allow him, placing all the blame for the mishaps on Coleman's shoulders, Godwin's scholarship and aesthetic sense were affronted by the sheer bad taste that permeated the revival. He began the article by stating: "The process of preparing drawings for the scenery, costumes and properties required in the stage production of any historical work of Shakespeare must per force be pleasurable howsoever laborious. The process of endeavouring to find how your drawings and directions are being carried out is not so pleasurable." The unpleasant experience that followed the creation of the designs had its roots in the refusal of the entire staff and cast to heed his instructions:

> Among English artists, tradefolks, and mechanics there are probably none so profoundly intelligent as those who are chiefly concerned in theatre matters. And as sure consequence of this profundity of intelligence, the beings so blessed are naturally enough apt to resent interference from an outsider. This feeling permeates the stage from one end to the other. It is not merely the costumier and the wardrobe women who look at the antiquary whom the manager consults as an intruder to be resisted; even the scene painter, whose knowledge of medieval art is of course boundless, and the well known actor and actress, whose ideas of historical personages are no less boundless, will scarcely even listen to any mere antiquary.[37]

The tailors and dressmakers had distorted Godwin's designs beyond recognition: the chain-mail shirts were so thin that skin was visible under them;

the skirts were so long, hanging almost to the knees, that they "bobbed about like open-worked ballet dresses." To compound the horrors, "the Marquis of Exeter had kittens instead of the lions of England on his surcoat."[38] Godwin realized that the question of why he was not aware of all these problems at the proper time was a legitimate one, and he responded by stating that he had "spoken but in vain." He had not seen anything but some banners, some old properties, and half-dressed supernumeraries until opening night, due to "the traditional stage atmosphere of jealousy and mystery." He had expected "secret surprises" as the curtain rose and was not, by any means, disappointed.[39]

Godwin's first collaboration with Wilson Barrett, on W. G. Wills's *Juana*, slightly improved his chances to influence the visual unity of a production. The sources of his research have been mentioned in reference to the scenery; on his own copy of the play, he scribbled the color scheme for the costumes:

> Juana: pale blue—white and gold.
> Clara: yellow—tawny white.
> Katrina: pale grey and blue—white apron.
> Carlos: white and gold—pale grey
> Pedro: grey or green—pale red.[40]

Godwin's painstaking research was wasted, however, on the leading lady. Mme. Modjeska was an actress notorious for venting her feelings against the management by refusing to wear her costumes whenever her wishes were ignored (in this instance she objected to a young actor). A newspaper article informed its readers: "The lady will not even consent to tell the distracted designer what century she has selected for the fashion of her dresses, and the scheme of colours runs a fair chance of being annihilated by some totally unforeseen effect. This is soothing to the Polish heart."[41] Whether Mme. Modjeska took pity on the designer, which is doubtful, or whether Barrett somehow managed to appease his leading lady, Godwin was pleased to see that the actress had not departed too much from his designs except for "the *double* puffed sleeves" in her first dress. Nevertheless, the rest of the cast made Godwin ask once again, "What can you do when you find at the last moment a dress made from a design by another hand, when one exclaims against this and another rebels against that?" It was evident to him that "the idea of *control* in the matter of stage costume" had not yet entered the actor's mind, but this insubordination was no more than previous experiences had led him to expect.[42]

Driven by his interest in costume history, as well as by his frustration with the ignorance and insensitivity of actors and managers, Godwin decided in 1882 to gather a group of scholars with the purpose of establishing a society dedicated to the study of fashion through the ages. His colleagues in this enterprise were E. Maunde Thompson, F.S. A., Keeper of Manuscripts at the British Museum; R. R. Holmes, F.S.A., Librarian to the Queen; G. H.

Boughton, A.R.A.; J. D. Linton; L. Fagan; the playwright W. G. Wills; Herbert Beerbohm Tree; and Herman Vezin. The last two were some of the few actors who understood and respected Godwin's erudition. The list of foreign members was most impressive: the staffs of the Bibliothèque Nationale, Paris; Austrian Museum, Vienna; Ufizzi Museum, Florence; Musée Royal, Brussels; Museo Nazionale, Naples; and the Royal Museum of Berlin, among others.

The new Costume Society, as it was called, had its headquarters at 7 Great College Street, Westminster. The first meeting of the officers of the society, at which Godwin was elected Honorary Secretary, took place on July 27, 1882.

The functions of the organization were listed in the prospectus:

> I; to illustrate with guaranteed accuracy the History of Art and Costume by issuing publications of any nature or form which may be found convenient, and
> II; to form a collection of drawings, fac-similes, tracings, photographs, descriptions, and other records of costume taken directly from sources contemporary with the costumes illustrated.[43]

The accuracy of the illustrations was to be guaranteed by the signatures of experts, and the illustrations were to appear in collections of ten or more plates four times a year. Godwin had very clear ideas on the proper way to present these illustrations; since the Costume Society had been established with the purpose of furthering research and teaching, he wanted to avoid the printing of "pretty pictures." He declared, "Etched effects are all very well for an illustrated magazine but our chief aim should be an accuracy that conveys itself and etching in shadows and tones often conceals the facts of the make."[44] He insisted as well on having garments drawn in their entirety, with fragments given only when necessary to clarify details of a full-length figure.

The announcement of the birth of this new society was greeted with enthusiasm by some members of the press. *The Standard* praised the idea and expressed the hope that the novel enterprise would be beneficial in improving the public's awareness on the subject of clothes:

> Reasons of taste have long been annoyed by the persistence with which certain persons dress badly; wearing, that is to say, the wrong thing at the wrong time, and the right thing never. … But what may be permitted to ordinary individuals cannot be tolerated on the part of painters, sculptors, and stage-managers. SMITH, JONES, and BROWN live, dress absurdly, die, and are forgotten. But the men whose lot it is to influence the public mind have heavier responsibilities; and the evil they do lives after them. It is indeed of considerable importance that accuracy of costume should be observed in pictures, in statuary, and in theatrical representations., and for this reason encouragement is due to the "Costume Society."[45]

Godwin addressed the audience gathered at the Grosvenor Gallery for the first public meeting of the Society on October 28, 1882. In his lecture he paid homage to Fairholt and Planché as pioneers in the study of costume history, although he declared that the style of their illustrations was not very useful to artists and antiquarians. He reiterated also his determination to publish only faithful copies of original sources certified by experts.[46]

The Costume Society was not universally welcomed; some feared that the effect of excessive submission to archaeology on the stage would be at the expense of sentiment, feeling, and true dramatic value. In response to a violent attack on the society in the *Times*, Tree felt compelled to write an article, published in *The Theatre*, defending his views and those of his fellow members. To the statement that it did not disturb Shakespeare's audience to find "Brutus and Cassius wearing the same kind of clothes as Bacon and Raleigh," Tree responded with a question: "Why not go further, and argue that Othello might appear in a white tie and patent leather boots; and if played by a white man, why truckle to the vicious taste of the nineteenth-century audience by taking the trouble to black his face, in deference to the hard, bald, dry, unsympathetic regard for archaeological accuracy[?]" the actor ended his piece by declaring: "That archaeological correctness should ever take precedence of dramatic effect would indeed be highly lamentable. But in such event it may be confidently hoped that some avenging scourge will arise, whose mighty army shall scatter the ranks of the usurping Realists, and rear above their mangled corpses a victorious banner, emblazoned with the Rules and Regulations of the Royal Society of British Anachronists."[47]

Despite Godwin's efforts to promote the Society, the designer and his colleagues could not keep their brainchild alive for more than two years. The manuscript of the minutes notes the last meeting of the Costume Society on July 24, 1884.[48]

The failure of that enterprise did not deter Godwin from trying once more to exert his influence on the visual elements of Barrett's *Claudian*. Some reviews suggest that he was consulted not only for the design of sets and costumes but for the composition of the stage pictures as well. The motley, cosmopolitan crowd that paraded in front of Walter Hann's set for the opening scene received a great deal of attention and praise. An article in *The Queen* was dedicated solely to the costumes. After citing all the sources that Godwin had consulted to ensure accuracy, the writer described the costumes:

> It is a notable spectacle displayed, rich in colour and effect—swart Nubian girls, draped in gaily striped tunics, with heavy gold rings in their ears and around their wrists; Scythian girls in narrow robes and veiled heads; Greek maidens in clinging chitons of sea-green, delicate pink, or cream colour, stand or crouch waiting to be sold, guarded by the slave-dealer, a crafty looking individual, in short brown wool tunic and blue mantle. Rich citizens come and go—their long under-tunics, with embroidered hems, are of varied colour;

their mantles sweep the ground; their feet are covered with high boots, or with sandalled shoes of purple, red or gold, enriched with embroideries, gold, cameos, and jewels. A high-born city lady goes past, one slave carries above her a crimson silk parasol, another fans her with a feathered screen. She is dressed in costly saffron silk; the hem of her trailing chiton is jewelled with emeralds and diamonds; her mantle is fringed and studded with gold and precious stones; gems flash round her neck, her arms, in her ears, and gleam in her filleted hair.

...To judge from the scenes depicted by Mr. Godwin, the rage for jewelry had spread to the common folk at Constantinople. Rustics, attired in woolen tunics and mantles of admirable tones, and untanned leather shoes, appear there bedecked with necklets and rings of cornelian, bronze, iron, silver, and sometimes gold.[49]

Roman soldiers in full armor, wild-looking Gauls in hairy skins, and Scythian guards with shields and swords were all part of this crowd. Barrett, as the noble Claudian Audiates, entered surrounded by patrician companions and attended by a black boy dressed in a tiger skin. During the preparations for *Claudian*, Barrett had rebelled against the "tyranny" of the designer by refusing to wear the senatorial tunic ornamented with the *latus clavus*, the purple band running down the center front, because he found it to be too garish. He wore instead a short, gold-embroidered tunic with a gold girdle at the waist, a flaming-red mantle woven with gold, high brodequins of golden leather, and a profusion of gold bracelets on his bare arms; his auburn locks were bound in a filet of diamonds. On reading some statements that Godwin made before the production opened, one wonders how many other members of the cast added their own touches to the original designs. Godwin had hoped that his careful research would eliminate the offensive fashion of showing classical dress, "worried with pins, and puckered into artificial folds," and would instead encourage "simple garments worn in the artistic, unaffected, and simply beautiful way that distinguished the wearers of them in Byzantium."[50] The description of the costumes indicates, however, that simplicity was by no means prevalent on the stage.

Godwin's desire for reform was not limited to theatrical costumes. He frequently found fashionable dress equally offensive to his aesthetic principles, and he believed that the study of dress "ought to be as much the business of the architect as the study of animal and vegetable life." To design noble buildings, "you must have an eye to your boots."[51] In his estimation, lack of beauty could even prove to be a hazard to one's well-being: "Health can never be perfect for you as long as your eye is troubled with ugliness."[52] He firmly believed that art should be an ever-present reality affecting all human endeavors: "No art is possible to us unless we take a broad comprehensive view of the power and purpose of art ... unless we can feel it to be a reality to ourselves. We must be drenched through and through with it, not merely put it on now and then. We must have art in every manifestation of

Wilson Barrett in costume for *Claudian*. From the author's archives.

SKETCHES FROM "CLAUDIAN" AT THE PRINCESS'S THEATRE.

Engravings by Bernard Partridge of the costumes worn by Wilson Barrett and Mary Eastlake as Claudian and Almida in *Claudian*. **Courtesy of the Theatre Museum.**

life ... if we want to have [it] present with us as a growing developing, living, joyous reality."[53]

While Godwin continued to collaborate with Barrett until the actor-manager departed from the Princess's Theatre, he also found other opportunities more conducive to creating beauty and achieving absolute artistic control. In the summer of 1885, a year before he produced, designed, and directed *Helena in Troas* at the Hengler Circus, he had been commissioned by Lady Archibald Campbell, founder of the "Pastoral Players," to design and direct an open-air revival of *As You Like It* on the grounds of Coombe House, a hydropathic establishment near Malden. When it opened, the natural and artistic beauty of the presentation was very much commended, not only by Oscar Wilde, whose friendship and admiration for Godwin were well-known, but also by the popular press. Wilde stated, "the brown and green of the costumes harmonized exquisitely with the ferns through which they wandered, the trees beneath which they sat, and the lovely English landscape that surrounded the Pastoral Players."[54] The *Daily Telegraph* also praised the harmony of costumes and natural environment in its review:

> The absence of all artificial light, the exchange of the glare of the gas for the softness of the woodland scenery; the birds, the trees, the flowers, and the sun substituted for the paste-board, tinsel, canvas, and artificiality.
> ...That which is most notable is the subdued harmony of the colouring. No gaudy tints, no fine new costumes, no wealth of silks and satins, but just such faded greens, purples, reds, and stuffs as suit a background of such assertive green and brilliant freshness. ... There is nothing tawdry or vulgar or theatrical about the scene. It is artistic and it is natural.[55]

Godwin's last year of life was marked by frantic activity, and the summer of 1886 found him submerged in a multitude of projects. After opening *Clito* on July 23 and *Helena in Troas* two days later, he was in charge of yet another open-air production for the Pastoral Players, *Fair Rosamund*, at Wimbledon Common, in addition to supervising the rehearsals for a private presentation of *The Cenci* at the Shelley Society and a revival of Tom Taylor's *The Fool's Revenge* at the Opera Comique. In his last endeavors Godwin came within reach of fulfilling his ambition to demonstrate the importance of a unified stage picture, but only by performing all the functions associated with the duties of producer, director, and designer himself.

Though it was still generally agreed that the actor-manager, and not the designers, had the prerogative to define the direction and establish the style of a presentation, the visual unity that Henry Irving achieved in his productions, without ever relinquishing his final authority, was perhaps the first instance of *real* collaboration between an actor-manager and the designers he employed. All of the trends and traditions that had evolved since the early decades of the nineteenth century came together in Irving's seasons at the

Members of the "Pastoral Players" in costumes designed by E. W. Godwin for *As You Like It* at the Coombe House. The figure in the monk's robe is thought to be Godwin himself. Courtesy of the Board of Trustees of the Victoria and Albert Museum.

Lyceum. He was not only the intense, romantic actor who mesmerized the audience but also the heir to the romantic passion for spectacle, archaeological research, and pictorial illusion in the service of the drama. Ellen Terry, who had made her first appearance onstage at the age of nine as Mamillius in Kean's revival of *The Winter's Tale*, brought to their partnership her firsthand experience of Charles Kean's staging. Furthermore, her taste and ideas regarding the function of costume had been strongly influenced by her early friendship with Godwin in Bristol, even before their subsequent six-year liaison. In 1911 Terry wrote an article for the *Windsor Magazine* in which she related how when she had first gone to Bristol for a stock season in 1862, she had been "still a mere child, ignorant and untutored." There she had met "Mr. Godwin, who was already dreaming of using his unequalled knowledge of the manners and customs, dress, dwellings and furniture of other times—all that is included in the term 'archaeology,' in fact—in the service of the theatre." She noted, "From that time ... I date my interest in colour, texture, effects of light on colour, the meaning of dress, and a certain taste for beauty which I have never lost." And she added a sentence that fully describes the philosophy she shared with Godwin and Irving: "Archaeology is not a pedantic method, but a method of scenic illusion. Costume is a means of displaying character without description, and of producing dramatic situations and dramatic effects."[56]

Shortly after Ellen Terry joined Irving at the Lyceum, she asked Godwin, on Irving's behalf, to design the third-century costumes and provide historical advice for Tennyson's play *The Cup*, which opened on January 3, 1881. How much of that advice was followed is difficult to determine; Irving conducted his own research and made decisions that departed from strict accuracy in order to introduce picturesque effects. He rejected the white robes usually associated with priestesses and votaries and instead adopted colors and embroideries of Indian and Persian origin for the 100 women who appeared as the Vestals. The dress worn by Terry as Camma was the product of experimenting until the proper fabric was found; she eventually chose a loosely woven cloth of gold, imported from India by Liberty's, and used it on the wrong side to achieve the desired effect.

Throughout his years at the helm of the Lyceum, Irving saw the function of costumes in the same manner as he saw the design of scenery and lighting. All visual elements were necessary to create the pictorial effects he envisioned, and the unity of the composition was achieved, under his guidance, with the collaboration of designers who understood and shared his aesthetic views. In addition, more and more often during his management, designers were given credit as "costume designers" and not merely as "archaeologists" or "historical advisers."

One of those designers was Alice Comyns Carr, wife of the critic and playwright Joseph Comyns Carr and a friend of Ellen Terry, with whom she

Ellen Terry, as Ellaline, in the "steamed dress" designed by Alice Comyns Carr. Courtesy of the Board of Trustees of the Victoria and Albert Museum.

shared a taste for simple and unconventional dress. The designer's memoirs give a glimpse of the freedom Ellen Terry enjoyed in choosing her own costumes, even if Irving had the final word on the matter. Until Alice Comyns Carr was trusted with the designs, most of Ellen Terry's costumes had been made by Patience Harris, sister of Augustus Harris, the manager of Drury Lane. Terry had not been pleased with the elaborate gowns that Harris created, and for her role at Ellaline in *The Amber Heart* she decided to wear a simple muslin frock similar to one Comyns Carr had made for herself. What attracted the actress to that garment was the crinkly effect achieved by twisting the fabric into a ball and cooking it in a potato steamer. Both women knew that Harris would reject the idea of "cooking" the fabric as outrageous. With great determination the actress said, "I don't care whether Pattie likes it or not ... if a potato steamer is necessary to make a frock like that, then I'm going to have a lot of my dresses 'steamed.'"[57] Evidently Harris did not like it: Comyns Carr was invited to design all of Ellen Terry's stage clothes from that time forward.

When the preparations for *Faust* were under way, both Comyns Carr and her husband accompanied Irving and Terry on their research trip to Germany. While Irving explored the narrow streets of Nuremberg, the actress and her designer pored over books to find the right type of dress for Margaret, a role that actresses had traditionally played in a trailing white or blue robe. Though unconventional, their choice of a full gathered skirt, a plain bodice laced across the chest, and bell sleeves was considered more appropriate for a fifteenth-century burgher's daughter.

Not much mention was made of Comyns Carr in the reviews of *Faust*, perhaps because the overwhelming impression caused by the supernatural scenes and spectacular scenery painted by Telbin and Craven left little space to elaborate on the costumes. But an article titled "Pictorial Successes of Mr. Irving's 'Faust,'" published in *Century Magazine*, not only described the costumes but also acknowledges their importance in creating the powerful pictorial compositions that Irving intended to accomplish.[58] Irving's medieval red costume for Mephistopheles—with tight breeches, hose, and doublet, a golden girdle around his waist, a sinister cape, and a long cock feather in his cap—was always the focal point of a scene, whether he moved among the crowds in Nuremberg or around the eerie witches. The throngs of supernumeraries in Saint Lorenz Platz displayed the variety of dress expected from a cross section of society: wealthy ladies in brocades and peasant women in full skirts and colorful aprons; soldiers in armor and humble peasants in hose and jerkins; little girls in broad-brimmed hats and beggars in rags; monks in brown habits and nuns in white veils.

The most famous dress Alice Comyns Carr designed for Ellen Terry, if not one of the most famous dresses in the history of costume design, was the one immortalized by John Singer Sargent in his portrait of the actress as

Ellen Terry as Margaret in *Faust* wearing the costume designed by Alice Comyns Carr. Courtesy of the Board of Trustees of the Victoria and Albert Museum.

Henry Irving as Mephistopheles in *Faust*. Wood engraving by Bernard Partridge. Courtesy of the Board of Trustees of the Victoria and Albert Museum.

Ellen Terry as Lady Macbeth in the "beetle dress" designed by Alice Comyns Carr. Courtesy of the Board of Trustees of the Victoria and Albert Museum.

Lady Macbeth. Comyns Carr's intention was to design a costume for the first scene that would look as much like soft chain mail as possible and at the same time give the appearance of the scales of a serpent. To create that illusion, she crocheted soft green yarn twisted with blue tinsel into a straight, thirteenth-century gown with flowing sleeves. When the gown was finished, it hung beautifully but did not have the glittery look the designer had envisioned; the problem was solved by sewing *real* green beetle-wings over the entire dress and adding a narrow border of jeweled trim to the hem. A heather-color velvet cloak with large embroidered griffins and a veil held in place by a circlet of rubies completed the ensemble. When Sargent finished the portrait, now in the Tate Gallery, he told Comyns Carr, "You and I ought to have signed that together, Alice, for I could not have done it if you had not invented the dress."[59]

Alice Comyns Carr had also designed a blood-red mantle for Lady Macbeth's entrance after the murder of the king, but to her surprise, it was Irving who appeared wrapped in the striking cloak on opening night, due, as she put it, to "Henry Irving's dislike for being anywhere but in the center of the picture."[60]

All other characters' costumes had been accurately designed by Charles Cattermole, R.A., a painter of historical subjects. There were 408 Anglo-Saxon costumes in *Macbeth*, including 165 soldiers, 40 lords and ladies, and 16 ladies-in-waiting, plus 80 costumes for "The flight of the Witches" and extensive changes for the leading players.

In 1892, Alice Comyns Carr shared her responsibilities with another Royal Academician, John Seymour Lucas, who specialized in painting seventeenth- and eighteenth-century British scenes. Their combined talents resulted in the wardrobe for *Henry VIII*, one of the most elaborately dressed revivals ever offered at the Lyceum. Irving set before his audience a series of historical tableaux and processions that surpassed even Kean's production in pageantry and lavish splendor.

Like Godwin's costumes for *Claudian*, the sumptuous fashions of the Tudor court received special attention and lengthy commentary. A female correspondent supplied the *Morning Advertiser* with a very detailed description of the exquisite gowns worn by Ellen Terry as Queen Katherine. In the first act Katherine appeared before the king wearing "a soft, heavy, grey brocade gown," shot through with "lines of steel," which gave "almost the effect of armour." She continued:

> Over this appliques in raised work are placed. The bodice has a very long point, very stiffly boned, cut square over the bosom, and long open sleeves ... the undersleeves are studded with jewels in all colours. For head-gear Miss Terry adopts the quaint coif cap of the period, fitting down closely in square lapels over the ears, and hiding the hair completely. The coif is of black velvet, with bands of narrow gold, ornamented with jewels, and completed by

folded bandeaux of gold gauze, laid over the forehead. Some very rare embroidery of lilies and roses, worked on green velvet, is worthy of notice as having been done by the students of the Chiswick School of Embroidery.[61]

Not only the queen's costumes but those of the entire cast were the result of exhaustive research and of attention to the most minute details. The exact patterns and textures of antique fabrics were specially woven for the occasion, every piece of jewelry was made to harmonize with the dresses, and Irving's own costume for the role of Cardinal Wolsey was reproduced from a genuine robe of the period lent by the painter Rudolph Lehmann.

Alice Comyns Carr and Charles Cattermole followed their success in *Henry VIII* with an equally spectacular wardrobe for Lord Tennyson's *Becket*. Ellen Terry, as the Fair Rosamund of legend, had never looked younger of more bewitching. Her first costume was made of gold cloth, covered by a transparent black mantle studded with gold; her blond hair was plaited into a coil at the back of her head and held by a golden net. Her appearance in the forest scene was compared to a painting by Sir Edward Burne-Jones; her slender figure was draped in a grayish-green satin veiled by a transparent overdress of a similar color, while her hair cascaded over her shoulders in the style so dear to the Pre-Raphaelites. She also wore a shimmery, spangle-covered gown of faded-pink satin for her encounter with Queen Eleanor and a severe white dress covered by a hooded black cloak for her final scene. Irving's costumes for the role of Becket showed the process of change in the character's personality, from a purple-and-red-shot silk tunic covered with jewels at the beginning of the play to a simple, neutral-color costume covered by a black cape toward the end. Needless to say, just as many silks, velvets, jewels, and embroideries were lavished on all other players.

Romance and legend could not have found a better interpreter than Sir Edward Burne-Jones when he was commissioned to design sets and costumes for *King Arthur* in 1895. The painter's stage creations had the same dramatic and mystical quality he displayed in his canvases; the period costumes belonged to some lost, magical time that only an artist's imagination could have discovered. The play opened with the Spirit of the Lake rising from the misty waters, "clothed in some shimmering stuff which [seemed] to have caught all the hues of the everchanging sea."[62] Strangely beautiful fabrics in exquisite color schemes were a feast for the eye throughout the performance.

A good example of how costumes had become a symbolic, expressive visual element, meant to enrich the understanding of the plot instead of being purely decorative, may be found in one description of "The Queen's Maying" scene. Guinevere wore "the selfsame green and golden robe in which she appeared in vision form to her liege lord and master." The writer continued,

Opposite: John Singer Sargent's portrait of Ellen Terry as Lady Macbeth. Courtesy of The Tate Gallery.

No. 190   MISS ELLEN TERRY   WINDOW & GROVE

Ellen Terry as Queen Katherine in *Henry VIII*, in a costume designed by Alice
Comyns Carr. Courtesy of the Board of Trustees of the Victoria and Albert
Museum.

Ellen Terry as Queen Guinevere in *King Arthur* (University of Bristol Theatre Collection).

"It struck me as being a master-touch of ironical fate that this should be so, that the passionate love-scene with Lancelot should be enacted in the garment in which Guinevere had been revealed to the King as his fate; and as, in the midst of a world of May-blossom, she holds out her arms to her lover, the vision seems enacted over again."[63] The "vision" was Ellen Terry dressed in a bright-green flowing gown, covered with spangles and embroidered around the hem with a flame-pattern motif of gold, the short bodice studded with fake emeralds and the high waist delineated by a sash of golden gauze. The May-blossoms cascading down her fair hair completed the ideal picture of Pre-Raphaelite beauty.

In designing the armor, Burne-Jones deployed his profuse imagination at its best. With complete disregard for history, or practicality, he added some strangely shaped ornaments to the elbows and shoulders of the costumes and dressed Irving in a black suit of mail with a visored helmet. When asked the reasons for these choices, the painter responded, "To puzzle the archaeologists!"[64]

Sir Lawrence Alma-Tadema's knowledge and vision of the classical antiquity assisted Irving's pursuits in *Cymbeline* and *Coriolanus*. As historical adviser for both productions, the painter guided designers and costumiers to achieve the desired effect. He had made careful studies of Roman sculpture to understand the proper way to wear a toga, the weight of the fabric used, and all the variations possible in it draping, until he was as familiar with the garment as he was with the architecture, decorations, and customs of the ancient world.

Wearing a magnificent red toga embroidered in gold, Irving, as Corioilanus, made his triumphant entrance to the Senate in a chariot drawn by two white horses and followed by a procession of soldiers in full armor. The dignified dignitaries who gathered to greet him wore their senatorial robes with the purple *latus clavus* running down the center front; the assembly was made even more festive by the appearance of young girls waving palm leaves and children scattering flowers. Even to critics familiar with the high standards of Lyceum productions, this scene was extremely impressive.[65]

The most fitting conclusion to this account of Irving's world of pictorial beauty may be left to his longtime leading lady. In the last paragraph of her article "Stage Decoration," Ellen Terry wrote, "The final word must be that the future is opened to the younger men and women, who if they are in earnest, if they *mean it*, can place the theatre, with its plays, acting, scenery, and costumes, amongst the fine arts, and this they will do if only they are fine artists."[66]

Theatregoers who frequented Herbert Beerbohm Tree's beautiful playhouse at the turn of the century had the good fortune to enjoy the extraordinary work of one of these fine artists Terry called on to serve the theatre. Between 1899 and 1916, the collaboration of Beerbohm Tree and Percy Anderson, one

Henry Irving as King Arthur. Drawing by Bernard Partridge. Courtesy of the Board of Trustees of the Victoria and Albert Museum.

of his costume designers, preserved the romantic tradition of spectacular and historically accurate productions.

Percy Anderson began his career in the theatre at a time when costume design was finally being recognized as a "fine art" and when few London managers would have attempted to present a play without the benefit of a well-known artist to design, or at least supervise, the stage costumes. He put aside his early ambitions as a portrait and subject painter when, after having accepted his first commission to design costumes for a friend's opera, he realized that "one may worship art at so many different shrines" and that this particular branch of the painter's profession was one that "Leonardo da Vinci himself was not afraid to work at."[67] Anderson's decision to follow in Leonardo's footsteps was welcomed by the press. His very first professional engagement, Gilbert and Sullivan's *The Yeomen of the Guard* in October 1888, brought him praise for the "tasteful and historically appropriate" costumes.[68] For the next 40 years, until his death in 1928, Percy Anderson's designs never failed to elicit admiration for their originality, attention to detail, and historical accuracy.

Anderson's concern for detail and historical research, in addition to his creative ability, may have attracted Beerbohm Tree, with whom the designer collaborated in 12 productions over the course of 17 years. Tree, as a founding member of the first Costume Society of England, had demonstrated his interest in appropriate stage costumes and had responded to criticism against archaeological correctness by stating that it "should clearly be the ambition of the actor to approach as nearly as possible in every respect the character he is supposed to represent."[69]

Although their initial joint venture at Her Majesty's Theatre took place in 1899, with the revival of Shakespeare's *King John*, it was not until their second project together that the manger and designer found a common language to express their predilection for fanciful, as well as historically accurate, costumes. One of the first productions of the new century was Tree's presentation of *A Midsummer Night's Dream*. The critic of *The Stage* urged all lovers of the beautiful, "all to whom the double gift of fantasy—wonder and humour—is dear," to thank Tree for this offering.[70]

Whereas the originality of Percy Anderson's imagination was highly praised by reviewers, it was the poetic quality of his color scheme that made the greatest impression. This talent for creating a harmonious palette had its origin in Anderson's study of, and reverence for, nature. As he described it: "Nature, whom many are pleased to belittle these days, is always with us to give us ideas. Any artist who has been in the East or among the islands of Greece, and seen the sun setting behind purple mountains amid a glory of crimson and saffron, and who has watched a pale green moon rise at the same time on the opposite side of the horizon in a sky tinted with shades of the most delicate violet, sapphire, and topaz, can never be at a loss for ideas; and in England the simple facts of town and country scenery—poppies in a wheat field, or sulphur-coloured chimney pots on a slate roof—suggest innumerable possibilities to him who cares to look for them."[71]

Percy Anderson's renderings for *A Midsummer Night's Dream*, preserved in the Theatre Collection of the University of Bristol, indicate how the designer created a palette derived both from the study of color in nature and from the study of historical sources. Theseus's first costume is a floor-length tunic of light green-gray, in a fabric patterned with small geometric designs in gold; gold trim was used to edge the sleeves and hem. He wears a metal chest plate with lambrequins and a flowing himation the same color as the tunic. His headdress is a combination of a silver Phrygian cap and a gold crown with upstanding wings. His second costume is a dark-red tunic with a wide purple band reaching from mid-thigh to mid-calf; the red section is covered with a gold star pattern, and the purple band is trimmed horizontally with gold Greek keys and palmettes. His himation matches the red of the tunic. He has also a gold wreath with streamers, a staff, and short soft boots adorned with gold. Hippolyta's act 1 costume is a white chiton covered with a bright-orange himation trimmed with gold Greek keys. Her second dress is a lavender-blue Doric chiton, with peplum of lambrequins in the same color edged with a wide gold band; she also wear s a very elaborate chest plate, a floor-length cape matching her chiton, a gold crown, and wide bracelets, one of them in the shape of a snake.

Titania, played by Maude Tree, is a vision of Pre-Raphaelite loveliness and melancholy on a Prussian-blue background. She has a mane of dark-blond hair crowned by deep-red petals. Her white, sleeveless gown is translucent and shimmery; two panels of the same material hang from the shoulders at the sides of her body. She also dons gray-red wings and sandals. The Queen of the Fairies' consort, Oberon, is rendered to represent the sun, in a gold robe embroidered with jewels and with pale-green wings; onstage, the sun-crown on his head glittered with the effect of tiny, cunningly wired electric lights.

The first costume for Helena is a Wedgwood-blue Doric chiton with a slightly darker himation; her second costume is a white chiton and himation trimmed with gold. Hermia appears first in peach, rose, and gold and later in a combination of ocher and yellow. The Greek-inspired headdresses for both young women match their gowns. Demetrius echoes Helena's color scheme in a darker blue trimmed with gold; he also has armor, helmet, and knee-high boots. The costume sketches also show Peaseblossom in tights, ombré from green to gray, and a lavender leotard with flower petals inserted at waist and chest level; the leotard continued over the neck and head to create a hood. Cobweb wore off-white tights and leotard with a cobweb design from neck to waist, a matching hood, and chiffon panels attached to the wrists, elbows, and shoulders. All the fairies had dainty wings, which were rigged with electric lights similar to those in Oberon's crown.

Percy Anderson's costume rendering for Titania in *A Midsummer Night's Dream*
(University of Bristol Theatre Collection).

Percy Anderson's costume rendering for Cobweb in *A Midsummer Night's Dream* (University of Bristol Theatre Collection).

Herbert Beerbohm Tree as Herod, in a costume designed by Percy Anderson (University of Bristol Theatre Collection).

The reviews were unanimous in praising Anderson's fertile imagination, the poetic color schemes, and the exquisite adornments he had created for the occasion. *The Athenaeum* declared, "Mr. Tree has not only gone beyond precedent and record, he has reached what may, until science brings about new possibilities, be regarded as the limits of the conceivable ... stage illusion and stage splendour being capable of nothing further."[72]

Maud Jeffries as Marianne in *Herod*, wearing a costume designed by Percy Ande
son (University of Bristol Theatre Collection.

Within the next ten months, Tree and Anderson collaborated on another two productions: *Rip Van Winkle* in June and *Herod* in October. *Herod*, a historical tragedy in three acts by Stephen Phillips, required 250 costumes. The play gave both Tree and Anderson the opportunity to display their passion for exotic spectacle, even though the strict archaeological accuracy of the wardrobe may be questionable by present standards of research. Nevertheless, the production was hailed for its splendor "combined with taste." *The Stage* noted, "The scholar will applaud as much as the lover of colour."[73]

Tree played the leading role, wearing the semibarbaric garb of a Middle-Eastern potentate until the last scene of the play, when he appeared in a long tattered robe of dull-green color, with a leather belt around his waist. The part of Marianne was played by the American actress Maud Jeffries, who had acquired great experience in "costume characters" as Wilson Barrett's leading lady. Although her delivery of the verse was not as good as her handling of the costumes, she was much admired in her gold-glinting robes as "a picture of a beauty that the eyes, once seeing, cannot easily efface from memory."[74]

In 1901 Tree produced *Twelfth Night* and Clyde Fitch's *The Last of the Dandies*, with costumes designed by Percy Anderson. One of the novel ideas introduced in *Twelfth Night*, besides dividing the play into three acts instead of five, was to set the action in Illyria, where, of course, it originally takes place. This locale gave Anderson a chance to use the firsthand research he had collected during his frequent visits to Greece; the great variety of Greek and Albanian folk dress that was found in almost every village in the eastern Mediterranean had not changed for centuries and could be used, without trepidation, as historically accurate.[75] The press admired the lavish ethnic costumes and found their semi-Oriental look perfectly acceptable due to the proximity of ancient Illyria to Turkey and the Balkan region. Malvolio, played by Tree, appeared not in ethnic costume but in late-sixteenth-century dress, with a large white neck ruff, exaggerated pumpkin-breeches, slashed doublet, and a wisp of a mustache and beard; his cross-garters were green over pale-yellow stockings. The color scheme for Maud Jeffries as Olivia was black for her mourning scene and red for the subsequent ones.

The Last of the Dandies, presented on October 24, 1901, offered the possibility for a complete change of style from previous productions. The plot revolved around the adventures and misadventures of Count D'Orsay, the "last of the dandies," and included such real-life characters as Benjamin Disraeli and Sir Edward Bulwer-Lytton. This story line called for the presentation of a series of vignettes depicting the early Victorian era, and once again, both manager and designer succeeded in re-creating the period with all the correctness and artistic taste they had displayed in earlier collaborations. A reviewer remarked, "The pompous artificiallity [sic], the airs, graces, and curious costumes that, to our present view, verge on the ridiculous, are presented

Chorus of maidens in *Herod*, in costumes designed by Percy Anderson (University of Bristol Theatre Collection.

with the artistic fidelity and minute finish that are characteristic of Mr. Tree's management."[76]

    Ulysses, a new drama in prologue and three acts by Stephen Phillips, followed *The Last of the Dandies* in February 1902. The dramatis personae were divided into three categories: the Mortals, led by the wandering hero of the *Odyssey*; the Immortals, gods and goddesses of the Olympic pantheon; and

Phantoms in Hades, a motley group that included Agamemnon, Phaedra, and Eurydice.

Percy Anderson worked relentlessly for over six months to create the costumes. His sources for historical research were examples of archaic Greek pottery found in the British Museum; the color scheme was inspired by one of the murals recently discovered during the excavations at Knossos. That wall painting, with its very limited color range of blue, terra-cotta, and yellow, as well as black and white, became the foundation for the basic palette, with the single exception of a bright-green tunic for Eurymachus. Since the archaeological artifacts were rather scanty, Anderson had to supplement his reference materials by doing an exhaustive search of literary sources that would provide information on the preclassical world. This search led to the occasional use of Tyrian purple, a color known by the early Greeks, in some of the robes of the Immortals.[77] The scene designers—William Telbin, Joseph Harker, and Hawes Craven—also used the available research from the newly excavated ruins of Crete to create a background of "barbaric gorgeousness" in which the "archaic costumes of richly harmonized hues" were shown in all their splendor.[78]

In the early summer of 1902, when the final curtain came down on *Ulysses* after a run of six months, Tree celebrated the fifth anniversary of his playhouse, now renamed His Majesty's, with a revival of *The Merry Wives of Windsor*. It starred two of the most revered ladies of the English stage: Ellen Terry and Madge Kendal in the roles of Mrs. Ford and Mrs. Page. Tree played Falstaff and Mrs. Tree played Ann Page. All were dressed by Percy Anderson.

Of the two productions costumed by Anderson for Tree during 1903—an adaptation of Tolstoy's *Resurrection* and Shakespeare's *Richard II*—it was no doubt the second one that gave the designer, once again, the opportunity to display his flair for historical dress. Tree, following the tradition established by Charles Kean at the Princess's Theatre, distributed among the audience a leaflet with explanatory and instructive notes on the subject of research. In this publication he acknowledged the contributions of Percy Anderson and the aid received from G. Ambrose Lee, of the Heralds' College, who had helped in directing the heraldry and ceremonial. Their cooperation had made the revival "as accurate as possible in all matters of archaeological detail."[79]

One reviewer, awed by the amount of thought and labor required to mount such as elaborate offering and by the multitude of supernumeraries employed, nevertheless noticed a slight mishap on opening night. Oscar Asche's horse sank under him in the "Lists at Coventry" scene. Otherwise, the reviewer considered the production to be a smashing success.[80]

In 1904 Tree and Anderson collaborated in the revival of *The Tempest*. In his role as Caliban, the actor-manager appeared as a hybrid monster, with claw-like nails and hairy skin, plus "long, lank hair, a ragged moustache and beard, [and] tusky teeth," which enabled him to produce the effect of a snarl.

Percy Anderson's rendering for Lady Blessington's costume in *The Last of the Dandies* (University of Bristol Theatre Collection).

The other monsters of the island belonged to no geographical location or era; their origin was thought to be either the "palaeozoological period" or, perhaps, "some ancient Egyptian monolith."[81]

For the next seven years, until 1911, Anderson and Tree seem to have parted company. Anderson's career continued to be as active as ever; his work was in great demand both in London and in New York, where his designs

had been commissioned by Harrison Fiske and Charles Frohman.[82] In London, he designed several Shakespearean revivals as well as the premieres of George Bernard Shaw's *Caesar and Cleopatra* and Franz Lehár's *The Merry Widow*, among innumerable other projects.

When Anderson and Tree renewed their collaboration, in 1911, it was to produce a Royal Gala Performance to celebrate the coronation of King George V. The program selected to entertain Their Majesties on the evening of June 28 was not so much a series of plays as of displays: the "letter scene" from *The Merry Wives of Windsor*, starring Ellen Terry and Madge Kendal; the "Forum scene" from *Julius Caesar*, with Tree as Marc Antony; Richard Sheridan's *The Critic* with Gerald du Murier, Laurence Irving, Gertie Millar, Lilie Elsie, Violet Vanbrugh, and Marie Tempest; and to close the event, Inigo Jones's masque *The Vision of Delight*, with the participation of every actor and actress of any importance on the London stage. It was for that masque, originally presented for a Christmas entertainment at the court of James I in 1617, that Percy Anderson had designed costumes. His delicate sense of color was eminently present in *Vision of Delights*; a critic remarked, "To convey the effect of the dresses in the dim mystery of the woods you must invent new colours—split-rose and dawn-aflame, cave blue and foam of the morning, moon-flake and glimmering-wave."[83]

Before the year was over, the Tree-Anderson partnership had produced two more spectacular successes: *Macbeth* in September and *Orpheus in the Underground* in December.

In his "Note by the Producer" for *Macbeth*, Tree indicated that he had neither tried "to lay stress upon the historical aspect of the period" nor "insisted upon archaeological detail of scenery and costume." Nevertheless, the source of inspiration for the costumes seems to have been the early Middle Ages in northern Europe. Macbeth and Macduff were described as having "huge, fiercely-flowing mustachioes, length, indeed being the characteristic of the chevelure employed generally."[84] The unifying color scheme for the "chevelure" of all Scots was reddish, auburn, or flaxen hair. The armor, weapons, and shields also belonged to that period of history. Lady Macbeth appeared in the sleepwalking scene wearing a loose, dark robe instead of the traditional nightgown; for her other scenes, she wore a queenly dark-red gown. The witches, in flaxen hair and gray robes, were seen as described in the text—"hovering through the fog and filthy air"—borne aloft in rigging cables hidden by great masses of mist blown across the stage. It is interesting to note that two of the witches were played by men: A. E. George and Ross Shore. The third one was Frances Dillon.

The production chosen for the Christmas season of 1911 was an appropriate selection for a festive time. On December 20, Sir Herbert presented

Opposite: **Production photograph of *Orpheus in the Underground* University of Bristol Theatre Collection.**

Orpheus in the Underground, an adaptation by Alfred Noyes and Frederick Norton of Jacques Offenbach's *Orphée aux enfers*. Percy Anderson not only designed the costumes but also received credit for having suggested the scenery. The costumes for this Second Empire extravaganza were described in *The Era* as "deliciously droll."[85] Although they appear to have given the designer a chance to show the whimsical, witty side of his creative personality, he could not refrain from adding subtle touches of historical inspiration. The gods and goddesses each seemed to "recall some well known canvas of the great days when painters thought deeply of the pagan deities and Olympus was an appanage of the most brilliant courts. ... Venus suggested Rubens, and some of the other gods and goddesses seemed to have come straight from the Louvre or the National Gallery."[86]

Orpheus in the Underground was the last production developed by Tree and Anderson together, but the designer was associated with yet another spectacular project, *Chu-Chin-Chow*, presented at His Majesty's Theatre under the direction of Oscar Asche during Tree's absence from London. *Chu-Chin-Chow*, a musical tale of the East based on the story of Ali Baba and the Forty Thieves, opened on August 31, 1916, while the Battle of the Somme was raging in the fields of France. It was described by its producer as an Oriental review but was meant to be, above all else, an escape into a world of fantasy and beauty, an escape from the frightful reality of war. Percy Anderson created an extraordinary wardrobe, with "spiral costumes, conchoidal costumes, elliptical costumes," costumes that seemed "to realize the wildest dreams of [the] most recent artistic decadents," and a great deal of décolletage too.[87]

Some suggestive contortions performed by black female slaves in a bazaar seemed to have been a bit too risqué for one reviewer's sense of propriety. *The Stage* remarked that the wild dance was reminiscent of "*the dance du ventre.*" The writer noted, "The negresses in their excitement let themselves go with an abandon a little disturbing to occidental taste." He hoped that the choreography would be "moderated" after opening night; he objected to the excessively realistic scene. "The slaves are assumed to have only a Monna-Vanna-like covering, which, turning their back to the audience, they draw apart for the benefit of the slave-buyers sitting up stage and facing the audience. The detail may be true enough, but this sort of truth is inexpedient on the stage."[88]

Chu-Chin-Chow was the last production designed by Percy Anderson at His Majesty's during Tree's tenure as proprietor and manager. After Tree's death in 1917, Anderson continued his prolific career. His work was in great demand for plays that required historical or fanciful dress, and he was also responsible for all the revivals of Gilbert and Sullivan's operas during the 1920s. *Chu-Chin-Chow* was given another run at His Majesty's in December 1928, two months after the designer's death. It is possible that in the "Jazz

Decade" no critic objected to the racy choreography or the excessively realistic slave market.

Percy Anderson emerged in the theatre scene at a time when costume designers were becoming a new breed of professionals, only recently accepted as legitimate and significant contributors to stage presentations. His long and successful career in the twentieth century established him as an unquestionable artist in the field. Furthermore, in his collaborations with Tree, he proved to be an heir to the omnipresent romantic tradition that refused to surrender its hold on the imagination of managers and the public for over a century.

Yet, as one surveys successful shows at the end of the twentieth century, a question comes to mind: is Romanticism really dead? Would Mme. Vestris, Kean, Irving, Tree, and all their designers feel totally alienated if they could return to attend a performance of the current "feline extravaganza" *Cats*, or of *The Phantom of the Opera*, or of *Beauty and the Beast*? Certainly, they would be dazzled by the technology, but just as certainly, they would recognize the impulse that made those productions possible. If, as Thomas Hardy believed, "Romanticism will exist in human nature as long as human nature exists," it will be left to future historians to discover the form of Romanticism that is "the mood of our age."

Appendix A

On the Painting of Fairy Scenes and Other Stage Illusions

The prominence acquired by scenic artists in the early nineteenth century was due not only to their extraordinary skills, and to the public's desire for pictorial scenery, but also to the introduction of gaslight in 1817, which made it possible for the sets to be appreciated under better conditions. The flickering candles and oil lamps that had previously been used could not be properly balanced or controlled, and they concentrated the light in certain areas of the stage at the expense of others. The changes introduced by Philippe De Loutherbourgh at Drury Lane allowed him to devise the romantic effects of light and shadow, effects so admired by his contemporaries. However, the arrival of gas increased the ability to control the intensity of the lighting and resulted in a much wider range of possibilities to create atmospheric effects while, at the same time, allowing every corner of the acting space to be seen in equal clarity. For the scene painters, the new system afforded a completely different approach to their art and their capacity to create the ever-growing stage illusions demanded by the audience. William Beverley, whose fairylands and stunning transformation scenes would not have been possible without gas lighting, said, "To excel nowdays, the devotee of the double-tie brush needs to unite pictorial and constructive talents with mechanical ingenuity, and to possess a perfect knowledge of the possibilities of lighting."[1] The use of limelight, when combined with gas, opened new horizons for scenic artists in the realm of fairyland.

In some playhouses there was an added attraction, although this was not exactly the kind of show that Victorian fathers would attend with their wives and daughters. Percy Fitzgerald complained that the limelight had begotten a new series of spectacles, "the attraction of which, under the names of '*pièces à femme,*' *féeries*, burlesque, etc., consisted of making bands of nude or seminude women do duty as scenery." Under the candles and oil lamps, the human figure had looked dull and earthy, but "under the dazzling blaze of the new illumination, it became a show worthy of the pagan Eleusina."[2]

Victorian scenic artists practiced their craft in shops that would look familiar to modern painters. The main feature of the space was the gigantic paint frame, which could be raised and lowered through the specially designed opening on the floor by means of a system of winches and counterweights. An alternative was the fixed frame with a bridge, or cradle, in front of the canvas; the painter operated the cradle himself in order to move it up and down. This vertical method of scene painting was peculiar to the British theatre. On the Continent, large backdrops were painted flat on the floor with long-handled brushes. The amount of space allowed to step back from the drop was (and usually still is) rather limited, a condition that impaired the painters ability to judge the effect of the whole picture until the drop is taken off the frame and hung in the theatre.

The large proportions of the backdrops and the limitations to viewing them in their entirety were often intriguing, and sometimes baffling, to the easel painters invited to design scenery for Henry Irving's productions. Keeley Halsewelle, when commissioned to contribute his artistic talent for *Macbeth*, fled in terror at the sight of acres of white cloth he had volunteered to paint. Edward Burne-Jones, on the other hand, derived great pleasure from studying the difference between scene-painting techniques and those used for his own branch of art; it amused him to borrow Hawes Craven's large brushes, during the preparations for *King Arthur*, and try his hand at executing some corner of the scenery. He was also amazed at Craven's expertise in foreseeing the final effect of the huge backdrops when the painter could work on only one small section of the paint frame at a time.[3]

The scenic artists had to have an extraordinarily clear idea of the effect they wanted to produce and how the colors they had used would perform and change under the colored light on the stage. After decades of admiring the pictorial scenery and its contributions to the success of some theatre managements, critics began to understand and respect the craft, and the art, of scene painting. In 1885 G. Sheridan Le Fanu wrote, "The scenic artist has great difficulties to overcome, difficulties so great, that it seems a Herculean task to master them; his colour must be of that quality which seems natural and telling by gaslight; the form of his work must be very exact, for the large scale of his paintings would show any bad defect in drawing immediately, which might be overlooked in a smaller work; his perspective must be drawn with a view to the stage, and not the ordinary science of the architectural draughtsman."[4]

Some Victorian theatres had their own paint shops; others contracted the scenery to outside studies. When as much scenery was required as in Charles Kean's productions, both arrangements could take place simultaneously. In 1851, Thomas Grieve and William Telbin, in association with John Absolon, built their own studio on Macklin Street, a side street off Drury Lane, despite the fact that Kean had added a paint room to the Princess's

Theatre at about the same time. Until the mid–1980s, the Grieve-Telbin building, which may have been the first one to be designed from scratch as a paint shop, survived with most of its equipment intact. Behind the warehouse-like facade, there was a low-ceilinged ground floor, probably used for offices and carpenter's shop. The huge paint room itself, lit by a skylight, was on the floor above and had the capacity to hang, lower, and raise drops in three out of the four walls.[5]

The pigments used in scene painting were available as powder or in solid blocks that had to be ground and mixed with the water-based, gelatin glue binding medium before being applied to the white-primed surface. Frederick Lloyds, the creator of many spectacular sets for Charles Kean, wrote a manual in 1875, *Practical Guide to Scene Painting and Painting in Distemper*, which constitutes the best remaining evidence of the methods used by the great Victorian painters. Lloyds recommended the use of distemper painting above all other media due to the speed and ease with which the colors could be laid in, its rapid drying time, and its lack of a disagreeable smell, as well as its ability to bind to any material, whether silk, cotton, canvas, wood, or paper. His advice on the techniques of painting "fairy scenes" seems to be an apt example of the craftsmanship displayed by scenic artists in the creation of their magical worlds.

> The great thing in painting fairy scenes is ... to use as pure colours and tints as possible, because, when you come to put brilliant coloured foils on the scene, in front of which there are already the brightest and most brilliant coloured dresses, it will be sure to look dirty, if the colours employed are not the purest. Pure grey, and plenty of it, would serve well, for instance, to set off your rich colours. Fairy scenes ... should be painted in the lightest possible manner, so as to have, especially in the middle and extreme distances, that airy, dreamy, indefinite look about them, so well exemplified in the beautiful pictures of Turner. Study closely those wonderful creations of his, trying to catch the spirit of them, and you can scarcely go wrong. ... in most fairy scenes, especially transformation ones, there will be a plentiful display of [metal] ornament, whether yellow, white, or copper coloured, the last one having a lovely effect. In putting on foils, they should, when possible, be, made to stand out from the canvas so as to catch the light. This can be done by first sticking some cotton wadding on, and then pasting the foil over that with glue paste.
>
> ...Avoid painting with dark colours where foil is used, for, when the foil catches the light, a very light colour lying close to it, will by contrast, appear dark; while on the other hand, the foil itself will appear dark when it does not catch the light, producing heaviness, should your colour happen to be dark. Choose the lighter coloured foils as a rule, for the darker coloured ones will look heavy and coarse and some of them even black.
>
> In sticking on the strips of foil in fairy scenes, do not rub them flat down, but let parts of them stand up. [A diagram shows a sort of accordion effect: the strip is glued down flat for a couple of inches while the next section is

raised away from the background, followed by another glued-down section.] You will thus obtain a rich as well [as] sparkling effect.

Matte gold and silver have a charming soft effect, and large quantities of it may be used without vulgarity. An agreeable effect is produced by staining on these with lake, blue or green; and when they are used for the insides of shells, a delicate staining in of the prismatic colours ... can be done with oil colours in tubes, mixed with a little varnish and turpentine.

When coral is required for a fairy scene, it is a good plan to paint carefully a branch of coral on a sheet of zinc with orange red and strong size, used hot, then to send it to the zinc-worker's with instructions to cut away all but the painted part. From this single one he can also cut out any number of coral patterns that may be required. ... The corals can be painted any colour in what is called "flatting," that is, dry white lead and colours mixed with Japan gold size and turpentine. The colours that have the most charming effect are crimson, pink, orange, violet, and white. Take afterwards some strips of foil and glue—paste them in the centre of all stems, leaving a little of the colour on each side. ... An admirable imitation of coral can be made with branches from thorn bushes, of which the thinner ends are to be cut off from the stumpy and knotty parts. The latter must then be dried and painted as above, very thin strips of foil being afterwards wound round some so as nearly [to] cover them...

A good subject for a fairy scene is the representation of the effects produced by moonlight on the surface of a lake. With a sharp knife, so as to get a clean edge, cut a perfectly round hole in the cloth. Then take a piece of clear tracing cloth, which needs no preparation, and with thin glue (not paste), glue it over the round hole you made, keeping it smooth and free from wrinkles. ... To imitate the stars, use spangles of various sizes. The largest are the most effective; but they must be bent a little in order not to show too flat a surface. They must be fixed to the cloth in the following manner:—Take some dark blue cotton and pass it through the hole in the spangle. Tie the spangle round and leave about 1½ inch at both ends of the cotton; glue over about half of each end and then press them against the cloth with a flat piece of wood till they stick on firmly. The spangle will, of course, hang loose, and being in consequence always on the twitter, it will keep on sparkling.

For the lake, tarlatan water rows may be advantageously used in place of solid ones. They produce a more transparent effect and the reflection of the moon will be seen through all the rows. The best way to create tarlatan water rows will be as follows:—For the back or highest row take a piece of tarlatan, 3 feet 6 inches in depth, and as long as the full width of your stage. Then take another piece 3-feet deep and of the same length, and take it on with needle and threat to the former piece, and 6 inches below the top of it as before. To the bottom of all three pieces sew a piece of glazed calico of nearly the same colour as the tarlatan, and 1 foot 6 inches deep, so that the total depth of the row will be 5 feet. Stretch a piece of wire line or strong whipcord from a hook in the wall at one side of the stage to an upright roller, which is contained in a box having a handle to it that turns the roller. This box must be screwed by means of foot irons to the stage, and have an angle brace also. Then, by means of the handle to the roller, a strain can be put to the wire or cord that will keep it as near the straight line as possible. ... A few white streaks should be painted on the water rows with flake white and a little strong size....

The water rows, the cuts in the cloth, and the spangle cloth used in moonlight scenes may also be employed when the effects caused by a sunset have to be shown. But in this case the spangle cloth must be lighted either with the aid of red glasses on the gas row, or with a limelight shinning through an amber or red glass. [Limelights served the same purpose as our modern follow spots; unlike gaslight, limelights could be narrowly focused on a tight, single place.] For the sun, use fine Persian amber silk, and let both sun and moon be lighted by a limelight, or if that is not convenient, by a ring of glass and a reflector.

Various pretty effects may be contrived with the help of spangles. To represent a fountain ... string a number of spangles on some fine Dutch twine, knot each of them at a distance of an inch or two ... from one another, and use them to represent the water. ... Used in the same way, spangles could be very effective in representing a dropping well or a grotto under the sea, where they could be hung from all the borders and spread all about the scene....

Transparent cloths must, of course, be painted entirely in transparent colours, and by means of successive glazings, either in oil or size colour. Oil colour is to be preferred when the transparent cloths are not more than about 20 feet square; but beyond that size, they had best be painted in size colour, which is a rather difficult process to manage, as the colour sets faster than the cloth can be painted, and, in the case of the sky, it is not easy to make it look smooth. The best plan ... is to mix the size a little stronger than half-and-half, letting it cool into a jelly; and then, when required for use, to put an equal quantity of cold water to it, mixing the two with a large sash tool thoroughly together by twirling it rapidly round and round. The size will thus become a thin jelly, and, when mixed with your colour, will work almost like oil paint. ... When painting in oil, mix with the colour about equal parts of coachmakers' varnish and turpentine, adding a little boiled oil.

...The best colours to use will be scarlet lake, crimson lake, raw sienna, Indian yellow, yellow lake and Prussian blue, all of which, except the last one, must have sugar of lead mixed with them, or they will never dry hard. The above colours are for the sky; and for the landscape portion of the cloth the glazing colours will all be useful. The same colours will also do for cloths painted in size colour, but they will not then want sugar of lead mixed with them. Use your colours moderately thin, and constantly bear in mind that you can always make your painting darker, but never lighter, when once it is dry.[6]

Lloyds also elaborated on the best ways to achieve transitions from moon-light to daybreak, sunrise, and bright daylight, in rapid succession:

Paint the face of your cloth with very thin size colour ... and very lightly as it will be lighted from the front only with all the blue mediums over the gas battens, the wings or side lights down, green glass on the footlights, and gas lengths at the sides with green glasses on them. With this amount of light the slightest stain of colour on the sky will be sufficient. Commence with a slight tinge of yellow lake and scarlet lake at the bottom of your sky; then work up to crimson lake, and afterwards add a little blue, continuing to add blue till it is all blue from about one-third up the sky to the top. The warm tints must be so faintly laid in that the blue colour from the mediums may be able entirely to overpower them, producing all the effects of moonlight on the sky. Now paint the landscape portion of the cloth, from distance to foreground, in a manner suitable for a night view, and so light that the subdued and coloured light in front may not cause your scene to look black. [Next come instructions on how to rig the drop to be rolled up and down, since the next painting steps are accomplished on the back side of the cloth.]

...Now paint the sky,—on the back of the cloth, ...—beginning at the top with Prussian blue, and then working down the sky with crimson lake, continually added to the above till the colour is all lake; then with the scarlet lake with a little yellow lake in it, finishing at the bottom with Indian yellow and a little scarlet lake and a little scarlet lake with the yellow lake. Next throw in such clouds as you think will be effective, taking care that the edges of them are lighted up with a warm colour, lighter than the sky. Let the distant hill and part of the landscape be lighted in the same way and paint the shades and shadows with a cool purple tint. Strengthen up the whole subject, and, in parts, block out the transparencies altogether, so that the lights may tell out more strongly and warmly. Now you can lay in freely, and where you want the lights to tell out well, you can wipe them out with a piece of calico or cloth of any kind, before the colour hardens. ... The next thing to do will be to prime a piece of canvas, about three-fourths the depth of the cloth, so as to exclude the light; and to the bottom of that have a piece of crimson silk, about four or five feet deep, sewed on softening the edge of the silk into the primed cloth with priming. Then have a piece of yellow silk, about four feet deep, sewed to the crimson silk, into which you must soften the edges of it with some crimson lake colour. These silks should have been varnished before being joined to the canvas.

To work the effect, have the above cloth and silks hung close behind the transparent cloth, a part of the crimson silk only appearing above the horizon. Behind this, again, let there be two or three rows of gas, which must be turned quite down at first. When the day is supposed to break, gradually turn up the gas in the lowest row, and there will appear a faint glow of crimson light, which will, of course, grow stronger as the gas in the bottom row is turned on to full.

The gas last alluded to being full on, let the cloth with the silks be slowly raised. While the yellow begins to appear, the crimson is rising higher and higher in the sky, the gas behind must all be gradually turned up to the full, the mediums in front being worked round from blue to red, and then to yellow, in unison with the change at the back, and the green lights at the wings being gradually turned down and the white lights partly up. The cloth and the silks will by this time have worked up out of sight, and the whole of the painting at the back of the cloth will be seen, in consequence of the strong light at the back of it, to help which the white lights in front have been kept subdued. If lime-lights are used, the glasses will then change from blue to crimson, and next to yellow, in unison with the other changes of colour. By reversing the movement, the same painting and arrangements will serve to represent the change from sunset to moonlight.

For a stormy sky a transparent cloth produces a fine scenic effect, when well managed. Huge dark masses of clouds can be painted in, and, as these are in reality lighted up from the back of the cloth, lighting may be shown to flash from behind them, at one moment all being dark and black, at another all in a blaze.

For a fire scene a transparent cloth is most valuable. On the front of the cloth, the building which is to figure in the scene is to be painted in sound condition with transparent colours, while, on the back, it must be represented in a state of conflagration, and partly in ruins. Where parts of the building are required to tell out strongly against the flames and light, block them out with strong opaque colour. At the back of the transparent cloth have three opaque cloths hung on separate lines, one in the centre, and one of the other two on each side. Let them overlap each other, so as to cover the whole of the front cloth, the edges being cut very deeply with a very rough and broken line. When the first is supposed to break out, raise the middle one; the gas rows at the back will then cause a light and the flames painted on the back to begin to appear. Now have a small quantity of red fire lighted at intervals, behind the transparent cloth at the back. Then light more red fire, but at shorter intervals, and move the cloths entirely away, keeping the red fire flashing all over the back of the cloth till the end of the scene.[7]

Lloyd's *Practical Guide* included many other instructions: how to disclose a vision behind transparent drops, how to paint floor cloths, and how to best manage lightning and thunder.

Gauze drops had frequently been used in Shakespearean revivals to create dramatic effects for the supernatural scenes. Samuel Phelps made use of them in his *Macbeth* at Sadler's Wells in 1844, in the third scene of the first act. "Where the venom which is afterwards to rankle with fateful purpose in Macbeth's mind, is first instilled, the observant spectator might have noticed what appeared to be a long narrow strip of dark sand lying before the three witches. This was in reality a carefully folded gauze curtain made in gradually increasing thickness and drawn slowly upwards towards the close of the scene by fine cords which were rendered invisible by the dimness of the light. The movement at first was barely perceptible, but soon the figures of the witches seemed to be gradually melting into thin air, until at last they vanished altogether from sight without stirring hand or foot."[8] Charles Kean also used gauze drops for his production of *Macbeth*, and for *A Midsummer Night's Dream* he introduced green gauze curtains in front of the fairy scenes to shed a misty tone and to differentiate the imaginary beings from the real ones. Irving used gauze and steam passing through it to create the transition scene from the witch's kitchen to the Saint Lorenz Platz set.

A decade after Lloyds's treatise was published, technological developments had advanced the possibilities of stage illusion even further. To the painted fire effects could be added the white smoke produced by burning lycopodium, which, when lit by a red-colored limelight, perfectly reproduced the glowing tints of a conflagration. Steam could be used, in addition to gauze drops, to duplicate clouds in motion or, as was done in Irving's *Faust*, to emphasize a supernatural appearance. In *Faust*, one-inch pipes were connected to a gas-heated boiler generating steam at 60 pounds per square inch of pressure; the pipes widened to four inches close to the stage floor and extended in funnel-shaped devices, fitted to openings on the stage floor. At the prompter's signal, the steam in the small pipes was allowed to expand into the larger ones, and on the second signal, stagehands pulled open the cocks that controlled the admission of steam to the scene. In the same production, fire spurting from the ground was produced by a funnel-shaped gas pipe, covered with paper, held under a grating on the stage; as the prompter turned up the gas, which was kept lighted, the particles of burning paper gave a realistic impression to the flames.

Electricity was slowly being introduced in the late 1880s. It was used to produce the flashing effects, previously described, when Faust and Valentine crossed their swords in Irving's production. However, Percy Fitzgerald had misgivings about its application: "The pure electric light, though it has been a good deal displayed in pantomimes, seems to be cold in its effects, and it is not likely to grow in favour."[9] What would he say if he could come back with the Victorian managers and designers?

Since the wave of romantic dreams had made ghosts and other apparitions fashionable early in the nineteenth century, one of the most popular effects was achieved by the use of traps. The common, run-of-the-mill trap was simply made of a platform that could be operated by a system of counterweights through an opening on the stage floor while a stagehand stood by with a rope to prevent it from moving too fast. However, the English praised themselves for excelling at daring new ways of dealing with stage mechanisms, and they invented what was called the *trappe anglaise*, as opposed to the unimaginative French trap. The English trap consisted of a number of elastic belts of steel, fitting together like the teeth of two combs; the trap was covered with painted canvas to match the scenery where it was placed. When the actor playing some terrifying creature was meant to disappear through a wall, he flung himself against the trap; the teeth of the steel combs let him through and closed immediately behind him, leaving no opening. There was usually a stagehand behind the contraption, waiting to catch the player on his way out. Performers could also make sudden and scary entrances through the stage floor in a variation of the English trap called the "star trap," consisting of a circular opening in the shape of a star. From under the stage floor through the opening, the actor would be propelled upward at great speed and had to jump out of his base in order not to be thrown off balance by the jolt. Obviously, this operation called for a great deal of nerve and recklessness. The "Vampire trap," specially developed in 1820 for the disappearance of the "creature" in J. R. Planché's play by that title, was formed of rubber doors, or leaves, that allowed the actors to vanish through and that closed as soon as he had done so. This kind of trap could be set either in a flat or on the stage floor.

In 1852, Charles Kean introduced the sensational "Corsican Effect," or "Ghost Glide," for his production of *The Corsican Brothers* at the Princess's.

The plot called for the ghost of a murdered man to appear to his brother, asking him to mount a vendetta to avenge the death. Although there are no extant drawings of the mechanisms used to achieve the effect, David Anderson has researched and made a model of the Ghost Glide, now in the University of Bristol Theatre Collection. As a source for his reconstruction, Anderson quotes a logbook left by H. R. Eyre, manager of the Theatre Royal, Ipswich, from 1887 to 1890.

> Under an opening 17 feet long and 14½ inches wide, a small 2 foot platform ran on a sloping rail. On this the player stood, entirely hidden under the stage at the beginning of its travel. As it was drawn across, it rose on its rails, until, when it reached the far side of the stage, the "ghost" was in full view. Attached to either side of the trap opening, so as to move with it, were two lengths of jointed flooring which slid along the aperture covering the gap, except where the trap happened to be at any given moment. Furthermore, the circular opening of the trap itself was lined with a fringe of bristles which pressed against the figure as it rose and so prevented any aperture being visible between the player's body and the stage through which it was passing.[10]

The golden age of Victorian scene painting, which had greatly benefited from the introduction of gas, began to suffer a decline with the advent of the harsher light generated by electricity. The Savoy Theatre in London was the first to incorporate electricity, used to illuminate the auditorium and the stage in 1882; by the turn of the century, most playhouses had followed the trend. The two-dimensional painted scenery was no longer sufficient to create the illusions that had so delighted the public in earlier decades, and increasingly, scenic artists were compelled to add a third dimension to their sets, with the purpose of improving their details under stage lights. This practice was sometimes attacked by critics who considered it unworthy of the theatrical tradition. William Telbin, who certainly did not need to apologize for his scene-painting skills, rose to the defense: "We very often hear the remark that in the past the best scene-painters were content with *painting*, and in consequence, because some of us wish to strengthen the effect by *relief*, we are told that scenic art in this country does not occupy the position it did 30 or 40 years ago. That may be so, but the fact that we model our foreground and certain portions of our scenes that are in juxtaposition with the actor is no proof of it. Painting, however good, must suffer under certain conditions. Why the addition of the sculptor's art to the painter's should be evidence of incapacity I do not know."[11] Eventually the controversy died down, and both painted and modeled scenery became acceptable techniques within the same set. However, without the incentive to rely solely on painted effects, in addition to the tendencies toward abstraction and simplified staging, which developed after World War I, the art of scene painting, which had flourished in the nineteenth century, soon joined the vanished fairies and ghosts of the romantic stage.

Appendix B

Brief Biographical Notes

ALMA-TADEMA, Sir Lawrence, R.A., O.M. (1836–1912)

Born in Dronrijp, Holland. Alma-Tadema was educated in Leeuwarden and at the Antwerp Academy, where he developed the interest in archaeology that was to influence his work. He moved to London in 1869; in 1876 he was elected an Associate of the Royal Academy, becoming a full Academician in 1879.

His careful reconstruction of historical architecture and dress led to Henry Irving's commission to design scenery for *Henry VIII, Cymbeline,* and *Coriolanus* at the Lyceum. He also designed sets for Herbert Beerbohm Tree's management of the Haymarket in *Hypatia,* 1897; and for *Julius Caesar* at Her Majesty's in 1898. His designs for *Coriolanus* were seen in Irving's production in 1901. He was knighted in 1899 and received the Order of Merit in 1907. Alma-Tadema died in Weisbaden, Germany, and was buried at St. Paul's Cathedral.

ANDERSON, Percy (1851–1928)

Anderson's fame was based mainly on his accurate and imaginative costume designs, although he also created or suggested ideas for scenery in some productions. In the late 1880s and through the 1890s, he designed costumes for Gilbert and Sullivan's *Ruddigore, Yeoman of the Guard, The Gondoliers,* and *Utopia* at the Savoy. Between 1899 and 1916, Anderson designed costumes for most of the plays presented by Herbert Beerbohm Tree at Her Majesty's, as well as some of the scenery for *Orpheus in the Underground.* From the list of his credits it is possible to assume that he designed for every theatre and every manager in London, plus some in the United States, where his costumes were seen in Harrison Fiske's productions of *Becky Sharp* (1899) and *Mary of Magdala* (1902) and in Charles Frohman's *A Gentleman of France* and *Quality Street,* both in 1901. Throughout the 1920s he again designed costumes for the revivals of Gilbert and Sullivan's pieces, as well as for another production of *Chu-Chin-Chow* at the Regent Theatre in 1928.

Anderson exhibited his paintings at the New Watercolour Society in the

1880s and also did portraits of many distinguished people. He is represented at the Louvre by a portrait of the actor Coquelin; his painting of Joseph Conrad is at the National Portrait Gallery; and his portrait of Sir Claude Phillips is at the British Museum.

BEVERLEY, William Roxby (c 1810–1889)

Born in Richmond, Surrey; his father, Roxby, was a lessee of theatres in Scarborough and Filey; his brother Harry managed the Royal Coburg Theatre in London (c. 1839). Beverley received early instruction in landscape painting from Clarkson Stanfield. He acted and painted scenery under his father's management of the Theatre Royal, Manchester (c 1830), and acquired further scene-painting experience at the Royal Coburg under his brother's management. He also worked as principal scenic artist at the Theatre Royal, Manchester, where he won considerable local fame. From 1847 to 1855, he produced spectacular scenery for Mme. Vestris's management at the Lyceum. Beverley achieved unprecedented success as the designer of J R. Planché's extravaganzas and the creator of the "Transformation Scene." For the next three decades his sets were seen at Drury Lane in the Christmas pantomimes as well as in Shakespearean revivals and contemporary drama, among them *Antony and Cleopatra* in 1873 and Dion Boucicault's *The Shaughraun* in 1875. His innumerable contributions to the stage include *Lady Audley's Secret* at the Saint James's in 1863, *Henry IV, Part One* for the Shakespeare Tercentenary at Drury Lane in 1864, and *La Favorita* at Covent Garden and *The Dodge of Venice* at Drury Lane in 1867. He was forced to retire in 1887 due to failing eyesight.

BROWN, Ford Madox (1819–1893)

Born in Calais; son of an English naval purser. Brown studied in Bruges, Ghent, and Antwerp. His reputation derived from the historical and romantic canvases associated with the style of the Pre-Raphaelite Brotherhood. He exhibited watercolors and oil paintings at the Royal Academy and British Institution. Brown provided advice on the period and overall visual effect and designed three scenes for Henry Irving's production of *King Lear* at the Lyceum in 1892.

BURNE-JONES, Sir Edward Coley, A.R.A. (1833–1898)

Born in Birmingham. Burne-Jones was educated at Exeter College, Oxford, where he met William Morris. In 1856, he worked with Dante Gabriel Rossetti for "La Mort d'Arthur" wall painting in the Oxford Debating Society's room. Leader of the second phase of the Pre-Raphaelite movement, Burne-

Jones exhibited at the Grosvenor Gallery, the Old Watercolor Society, and the National Gallery. His designs for stained-glass windows and tapestries were produced by Morris and Co. Burne-Jones was created baronet in 1894 and was awarded the French Legion of Honor, among many other European honors. He provided the designs for the scenery and costumes seen in Henry Irving's production of *King Arthur* at the Lyceum in 1895.

CAPON, William (1765–1827)

Born in Norwich; son of a portrait painter. Capon was an architectural historian and scenic artist famous for historically accurate medieval scenes. He worked for J. P. Kemble at Drury Lane and Covent Garden from 1794 to 1815.

CRAVEN, Henry Hawes (1837–1910)

Born in Kirkgate, Leeds; son of James Green, a pantomimist, and Elizabeth Craven, an actress. Craven studied drawing at the Marlborough House School of Design on the advice of Dearlove, a scene painter at the Strand Theatre. After his early training, he apprenticed with John Gray, scene painter of the Britania Theatre, Hoxton, in 1853. Craven accompanied Gray as his assistant at the Olympic Theatre under the management of Alfred Wigam. Craven was offered the post of second painter in 1855 and painted scenery for Wilkie Collin's play *The Frozen Deep* and an act drop for Collin's *The Light-house* from original ideas by Clarkson Stanfield. He joined William Beverley at Drury Lane and Frederick Gye at the new Covent Garden Theatre where he worked on designs for the major operas *The Hugenots, Robert the Devil, Der Freischutz, Norma, Dinorah, Marta,* and many others. Between 1862 and 1864, he worked at the Theatre Royal, Dublin. On his return to London, Craven designed for Covent Garden, the Adelphi, and the Lyceum under Charles Fletcher's management. He continued at the Lyceum with Bateman, and on Bateman's death, he was engaged by Henry Irving.

It was under Irving that he achieved his most notable successes, including scenery for *The Bells* in 1871, *Hamlet, The Merchant of Venice, The Belle's Stratagem, Much Ado About Nothing, Charles I, Cymbeline, Richard III, The Corsican Brothers, The Cup, Romeo and Juliet, Faust, Macbeth, King Lear, Henry VIII, Becket, King Arthur,* and *Coriolanus.*

He was also a painter of river and coastal scenes, exhibiting watercolors at the Society of British Artists between 1867 and 1875. Besides his work for Irving at the Lyceum, his designs were seen at the Savoy, the English Royal Opera House, Her Majesty's, Daly's, Adelphi's, and Garrick Theatres.

CUTHBERT, Henry John (1810–1888)

Cuthbert was one of the scenic artists for Charles Kean's Shakespearean revivals at the Princess's Theatre. He worked on several productions, notably *Macbeth, Pizarro, The Winter's Tale, Much Ado About Nothing,* and *King Lear.* In 1861 Cuthbert joined Charles Fechter at the Princess's, where he collaborated with the scenic artists J. Dayes and James Gates on a season of melodramas. He also designed scenery for *La Fille de Madame Angot* at Drury Lane in 1880.

DAYES, J. (dates unknown)

Dayes worked for Charles Kean at the Princess's in, among others, *King John, The Corsican Brothers,* and *Sardanapalus* where, with Frederick Lloyds and William Gordon, he reconstructed the city of Nineveh and provided the design for "A Chamber in the Royal Palace." After Kean's retirement, he painted scenery at the Princess's with Henry Cuthbert and James Gates for the season of melodramas produced by Charles Fechter.

DE LOUTHERBOURGH, Philippe Jacques (1740–1812)

Born in Strasbourg; son of chief painter to the Prince of Hanaudarmstadt. De Loutherbourgh was a scenic artist and painter of battles, sea, and landscapes in the romantic style. During David Garrick's and Richard Sheridan's management at Drury Lane, 1766–82, he designed scenery for Christmas pantomimes as well as serious drama. He initiated the first reforms to the system of wings and borders by introducing cut flats placed at an angle and transparent gauze drops to achieve dramatic lighting effects.

FENTON, Charles (1821–1877)

Son of James Gill Fenton, prompter at Drury Lane and later stage manager for Edmund Kean; brother of Frederick Gill Fenton, scenic artist. In 1831 Fenton began to play small parts in pantomimes at Drury Lane; afterward he became underprompter and acquired some experience in the property and paint rooms. From 1844 to 1859 he was at Sadler's Wells under Phelps and Greenwood's management, assisting his brother Frederick in the paint room and playing Shakespearean roles as well as Harlequin in the pantomimes. In 1855 he joined Charles Kean's team of designers at the Princess's, where he painted the Palace of Bridwell scene in *Henry VIII.* From 1863 to 1873 he worked at the Strand Theatre both as actor and scene painter. He also acted in David James and Thomas Thorne's company at the Vaudeville Theatre until illness forced him to retire from the stage in 1874.

GODWIN, Edward William (1833–1886)

Born in Bristol. Trained as an architect, Godwin won the competition to design the Northampton town hall in 1861. Fellow of the Society of Antiquarians. He wrote 30 articles on "The Architecture and Costumes of Shakespeare's Plays," published in *The Architect* almost weekly from October 1874 to June 1875. His interest in history, archaeology, and drama led to his early involvement in the theatre. Godwin was adviser to William Harford and George Gordon, scene painters to the Bancrofts, for the scenery of *The Merchant of Venice* at the Prince of Wales Theatre in 1875. He was engaged as historical consultant by John Coleman for a revival of *Henry V* at the Queen's Theatre in 1876 and received full credit for designing Isabell Bateman's costumes in *Othello* at Sadler's Wells in 1880. The following year he designed Ellen Terry's costumes for Irving's production of *The Cup* and the sets and costumes for *Juana* for Wilson Barrett at the Court Theatre and *The Queen and the Cardinal* at the Haymarket. Other productions included *The Cynic* at the Royal Globe in 1882, *Storm Beaten* at the Royal Adelphi, *Claudian, Hamlet, Junius,* and *Clito* for Bartlett at the Princess's, and *Romeo and Juliet* for Benson at the Olympic in 1884. Godwin designed and directed the open-air productions of *As You Like It, The Faithful Shepherdess,* and *Fair Rosamond* for Lady Archibald Campbell's Pastoral Players; he designed sets and costumes, directed, and produced *Helena in Troas* at the Hengler's Circus in 1886. He was also a designer of furniture and wallpaper inspired by the ideas of the Aesthetic Movement. Godwin was the father of Edith and Edward Gordon Craig.

GORDON, William (1801–1874)

Gordon worked as a scenic artist for Charles Kean at the Princess's Theatre from 1850 to 1858. He designed and painted scenery for *King John, The Corsican Brothers, Macbeth, Sardanapalus, Richard III, Faust and Marguerite, The Courier of Lyons, Louis XI, Henry VIII, The Winter's Tale, Pizarro, A Midsummer Night's Dream, Richard II, The Tempest, King Lear,* and *Much Ado About Nothing.*

He was also a painter of coastal scenes, exhibiting at the Society of British Artists from 1833 to 1836 and presenting one painting at the British Institution in 1858.

GRIEVE, John Henderson (1770–1845)

Grieve was the father of scenic artists Thomas and William Grieve and grandfather of Thomas Walford Grieve, also a scene painter. From 1794 to 1845, he and his sons made Covent Garden famous for the spectacular scenery and effects they created. He introduced the panorama to the theatre for the Christmas pantomime *Harlequin and Cinderella* in 1820. Grieve designed *Artaxerxes, Loves Labours Lost, A Midsummer Nights Dream,* and *Romeo and Juliet* for

Mme Vestris's management at Covent Garden from 1839 to 1840. He also designed and painted scenery for the Astley's Amphitheatre, Theatre Royal, Bath, the King's Theatre, Drury Lane, and Her Majesty's.

GRIEVE, Thomas (1799–1882)

Born in Lambeth; son of scenic artist John Henderson Grieve. He joined his father as an assistant painter at Covent Garden in 1817; continued to work with his father and his younger brother, William, both at Drury Lane and Covent Garden until 1845. In 1853 he joined Charles Kean's team of designers at the Princess's Theatre, where he collaborated in the scenery of *Macbeth, Sardanapalus, Henry VIII, A Midsummer Night's Dream, The Winter's Tale, Richard II, The Tempest, The Merchant of Venice, King Lear,* and *Henry V.* During this period he was also responsible for producing several panoramas and dioramas, including "The Route of the Overland Mail" at the Gallery of Illustration with John Absolon and William Telbin, "The Campaigns of Wellington," "The Ocean Mail," and "The Crimean War." Among his innumerable designs were *The Magic Flute* and *La Favorita* at Covent Garden in 1851, *The Corsican Brothers* and *Rouge et Noir* for Fechter at the Lyceum in 1866, and *The Merry Wives of Windsor* and *Gulliver* at Covent Garden in 1874 and 1879.

Grieve also exhibited occasionally at the Royal Academy. He continued an active career in the theatre until his death at the age of 82.

GRIEVE, William (1800–1844)

Younger son of John Henderson Grieve. At the age of 18, he joined his father and his brother, Thomas, as an apprentice at Covent Garden. Grieve was principal scenic artist at the King's Theatre (later Her Majesty's) from 1833 to 1844. He was the first designer to be called before the curtain by the audience's insistent applause, in *Robert le Diable* in 1832. Like the other members of his family, he was famous for his romantic, moonlit scenic landscapes. He exhibited watercolors and oil paintings at the Royal Academy from 1826 to 1839.

HALL, Stafford (1858–1922)

Hall worked in London, Leeds, and Liverpool during the later half of the nineteenth century. He painted scenery for Wilson Barrett's production of *Claudian* in 1883 at the Princess's Theatre, *Ali Baba* and *Cinderella* at the Court Theatre, Liverpool, and an act drop for Barrett at the Grand Theatre, Leeds.

HANN, Walter (1837–1922)

Hann's early work was seen at the Surrey Theatre under W. J. Callcott in 1853 and at Her Majesty's Theatre for the Royal Italian Opera in 1856. His first complete production was *Ambition* for John Coleman at the Adelphi Theatre, Sheffield, in 1857. Hann collaborated with Frederick Lloyds at the St. James's in 1863; from 1865 to 1868 he painted scenery at the Princess's Theatre for the original productions of *Arrah-Na-Pogue, Streets of London, After Dark,* and *The Hugenots* for George Vining. He designed J. R. Planché's "super-extravaganza" *Babil and Bijou* at Covent Garden in 1872 and *Rienzi* at Her Majesty's in 1878, and he collaborated with Henry Irving at the Lyceum beginning in 1879. Hann worked on all of the Bancrofts' productions at the Haymarket from 1880 to 1885 and all of Wilson Barrett's presentations at the Princess's from 1881 to 1886. He also designed for George Alexander at the St. James's and, with Joseph Harker and Hawes Craven, for Herbert Beerbohm Tree's management at Her Majesty's.

Hann was a noted landscape painter as well; he exhibited works at the Society of British Artists between 1879 and 1882 and at the Royal Academy between 1883 and 1904.

HARFORD, William (1842–1919)

in collaboration with George Gordon, Harford designed scenery for the Bancrofts' productions of *The Merchant of Venice* in 1875, *Peril* in 1876, and *Diplomacy* in 1878. Other stage designs included *Romeo and Juliet* for Forbes Robertson at Drury Lane in 1895, *The Grand Duke* in 1896, *His Majesty of the Court of Vignolia* and *The Grand Duchess of Gerolstein* in 1897 at the Savoy, and *Trelawney of the Wells* at the Court Theatre in 1898. In his later years he contributed scenery for productions at the Vaudeville, Duke of York, and Comedy Theatres.

Between 1874 and 1878 he exhibited watercolor landscapes of Jersey, Northumberland, and the West Country at the Royal Academy.

HARKER, Joseph Cunningham (1855–1927)

Born in Levenshulme, Manchester. Harker was educated at Manchester and Edinburgh. He began his theatrical career working on *Hamlet* at the Theatre Royal Glasgow in 1881, becoming staff scenic artist for a while. He moved, in a similar capacity, to the Gaiety Theatre, Dublin, where he met and began his long association with Henry Irving. His first designs at the Lyceum were for *Macbeth* in 1888; subsequently he contributed scenery for *Ravenswood, Henry VIII, Becket, King Arthur, Madame Sans-Gene, The Medicine Man,* and *Robespierre.* He collaborated with the most notable scenic artists as well as the leading managers of the period: Herbert Beerbohm Tree, Augustus Harris, George Alexander, Oscar Asche, and Arthur Collins. He produced spectacular scenes for *Kismeth* at the Garrick in 1911 and *Joseph and His Brethren* and *Chu-Chin-Chow* at His Majesty's in 1913 and 1916 respectively. Harker remained extremely active as a scene designer well into the twentieth century, and he wrote extensively on the subject, including a book of reminiscences, *Studio and Stage* (1924). Four of his five sons worked as scenic artists-designers; the fifth son became an author and actor.

James, Charles Stanfield (1833–1868)

Son of Charles James James, scene painter. He was one of the principal assistants to William R. Beverley at Drury Lane, and for five years he worked for Frederick Fenton under Phelps and Greenwood's management of Sadler's Wells. Marie Wilton, later Mrs. Bancroft, engaged him for her seasons at the Prince of Wales Theatre, where he designed *Society* in 1865, *Ours* in 1866, and *Caste* in 1867. James exhibited watercolors both at the Society of British Artists and at the Royal Academy between 1854 and 1862. He retired in 1867 due to illness.

Lloyds, Frederick (1818–1894)

Lloyds was engaged by Charles Kean at the Princess's Theatre from 1848 to 1858. He designed four scenes for *King John*, the "carnival" in *Merchant of Venice* and the Hall of Nimrod for *Sardanapalus*, two scenes for *Richard III*, two for *Faust and Marguerite*, and a cafe in Paris for *The Courier of Lyons* in 1854; three fairy scenes for *A Midsummer Night's Dream*, a garden in the Palace of Leontes in *The Winter's Tale*, and the French tent for *King Lear* in 1858. He was responsible for the designs of Charles Reade's production of *Never Too Late to Mend* at the Princess's in 1865, where he converted the whole stage into a treadmill.

In 1875, Lloyds wrote his *Practical Guide to Scene Painting and Painting in Distemper*, a "how-to" book that includes detailed instructions on materials, techniques, perspective drawing, and a "Method of Painting a large quantity of flowers in a rapid and effective manner." He exhibited at the Royal Academy, the British Institution, and the Society of British Artists and also painted a portrait of Charles Kean.

Lucas, John Seymour, R.A., R.I. (1849–1923)

Lucas was a painter of portraits and historical subjects, mostly genre scenes set in seventeenth- and eighteenth-century England. He exhibited at the Royal Academy, the Royal Society of British Artists, and the New Watercolour

Society. He designed or supervised costumes for several of Henry Irving's productions. In 1914 he was commissioned to paint a large fresco of "The Flight of the Five Members in 1642" for the House of Commons.

STANFIELD, Clarkson, R.A. (1793–1867)

Stanfield began his theatrical career as a child actor in his father's traveling company. He joined the navy for two years as a collier in 1812. His early work as a scene painter was seen at the East London Theatre, Wellclose Square, in 1816 and at other minor theatres. In the 1820s he was engaged at Drury Lane, where he became famous for his moving panoramas and dioramas, among them the ones he designed for *The Flying Chest, The Queen Bee,* and *The Destruction of Algiers.* His many set designs included *The Knights of the Arrow, Harlequin and Little Thumb, St. George and the Dragon, Sardanapalus,* and the ballet *The Sleeping Beauty.* For William Macready he designed *Henry V* at Covent Garden in 1839, *Acis and Galatea* in 1842, and *As You Like It* and *Comus* in 1843 at Drury Lane. Although he retired from the theatre to concentrate on his easel painting, Stanfield designed scenery in the 1840s and 1850s for the amateur theatricals of his friend Charles Dickens at Tavistock House.

From 1827 to 1867 Stanfield exhibited his land and seascapes at the Royal Academy, the British Institution, and the Society of British Artists. He was elected an Associate Member of the Royal Academy in 1832 and was made a full member three years later.

TELBIN, Henry (1840–1865)

Telbin worked with his father for several years. Assisting in the panorama in honor of the Prince of Wales, he designed the view of "Beyrout, The Landing Place." His body of work was very limited due to his early death at the age of 25 as the result of an accident in the Alps.

TELBIN, William (1813–1873)

Father of Henry and William Lewis, also scenic artists. Telbin began his career in provincial theatres; his first important commission was *King John* for William Macready in 1842. In 1856 he joined Charles Kean and his designers at the Princess's Theatre, where he contributed scenes for *The Winter's Tale, The Tempest,* and *The Merchant of Venice.* In 1861 he designed *Othello* and a highly acclaimed *Hamlet* for Charles Fechter at the Princess's. During the 1850s and 1860s he also created panoramas and dioramas. One of them, in collaboration with Thomas Grieve, was titled *The Route of the Overland Mail from Southampton to Calcutta* for the Gallery of Illustration in

1852; another was commissioned by J. B. Buckstone for the Haymarket Theatre to commemorate the tour of Syria and Palestine by the Prince of Wales in 1861.

He exhibited easel paintings at the British Institution, the Royal Academy, and the Society of British Artists.

TELBIN, William Lewis (1846–1931)

The second son of William Telbin, Telbin worked for many years at the Theatre Royal Manchester before joining his father in London.

He designed scenery for many managements, most notably for Henry Irving in the 1880s. His work at the Lyceum included *The Cup, Romeo and Juliet, Much Ado About Nothing, Faust, Macbeth,* and *Becket.* He also designed, among others, *Puss in Boots* at Drury Lane in 1887, *Ivanhoe* at the English Opera House, *Maid Marian* at the Prince of Wales, and *Orfeo* at the Empire in 1891. He also collaborated with Hawes Craven and Joseph Harker in productions at the Savoy and Daly's Theatres.

Telbin exhibited watercolors at the Society of British Artists.

Notes

Introduction

1. Cited by Jaques Barzun in *Classic, Romantic, and Modern* (Boston: Little, Brown & Co., 1961), 167.

Chapter 1

1. Godfrey Turner, "Scenery, Dress, and Decoration," *Theatre* (March 1884).
2. Quoted in Richard Southern, *The Victorian Theatre: A Pictorial Survey* (New York: Theatre Art Books, 1970), 28.
3. Richard Southern, *Changeable Scenery* (London: Faber & Faber, 1952), 380.
4. *Saturday Review* (March 9, 1891).
5. W. J. Lawrence, "A Century of Scene-Painting," *Gentleman's Magazine* 264 (January-June 1888):286.
6. James Laver, *Drama: Its Costume and Decor* (London: Studio Publications, 1951), 193.
7. Lawrence, "A Century of Scene-Painting," 287.
8. Quoted in ibid., 289.
9. Sybil Rosenfeld, *A Short History of Scene Design in Great Britain* (Totowa, N.J.: Rowman & Littlefield, 1973), 91.
10. Quoted in Lawrence, "A Century of Scene-Painting," 291.
11. Kenneth Clark, *The Gothic Revival*, 3d ed. (London: John Murray, 1962), 68–69.
12. *The Georgian Playhouse* (catalogue of an exhibition held at the Hayward Gallery, London, August to October 1975), plate 227.
13. Sybil Rosenfeld, "Scene Designs by William Capon," *Theatre Notebook* 10 (1956): 119. See also Lawrence, "A Century of Scene-Painting."
14. James Boaden, *Memoirs of the Life of John Philip Kemble*, 2 vols. (London: Longman, 1825), 1:101.
15. Cited by Paul Ranger in *Gothic Drama in the London Patent Theatres, 1750–1820* (London: Society for Theatre Research, 1991), 63.
16. Rosenfeld, "Scene Designs by William Capon," 121.
17. Quoted by George C. D. Odell in *Shakespeare from Betterton to Irving*, 2 vols. (London: Constable & Co., 1921), 2:219.
18. Rosenfeld, *Short History*, 110.

19. George Vandenhoff, *Dramatic Reminiscences* (London: Thomas W. Cooper, 1860), 59–61.

Chapter 2

1. Squire Bancroft and Marie Bancroft, *Recollections of Sixty Years* (New York: E. P. Dutton, 1909), 29.

2. *Era* (December 31, 1848).

3. Albert Edward Wilson, *The Lyceum* (London: Denis Yates, 1952), 67.

4. George Vandenhoff, *Leaves from an Actor's Note-Book* (London: D. Appleton & Co., 1860), 5.

5. Ibid., 4.

6. *New Monthly Magazine* 85 (1849): 261–62. Planché was not alone in his familiarity with the fairies' way of life; T. Crofton Croker, in his *Fairy Legends and Traditions of the South of Ireland*, made a study "On the Nature of Elves" and also included a survey of their form, dress, habitation, food, mode of life, and connections to mankind.

7. James Robinson Planché, *The Extravaganzas of J. R. Planché, Esq.*, 5 vols., ed. T. F. D. Croker and S. Tucker (London: Samuel French, 1874), 1:207.

8. Planché, *Extravaganzas* 3:183.

9. *Era* (December 26, 1847).

10. Planché, *Extravaganzas* 3:184.

11. *Era* (April 30, 1848).

12. Ibid.

13. Planché, *Extravaganzas* 3:225–26.

14. Busybody, "Enthusiasts Interviewed," *Times* (March 1, 1885).

15. Planché, *Extravaganzas* 3:314.

16. Ibid.

17. Ibid. 3:359.

18. *Era* (April 15, 1849).

19. *Illustrated London News* (April 14, 1849).

20. *Era* (December 30, 1849).

21. *Theatrical Journal* 11, no. 525 (January 3, 1850).

22. Planché, *Extravaganzas* 4:7–9.

23. James Robinson Planché, *The Recollections and Reflections of J. R. Planché*, 2 vols. (London: Tinsley Brothers, 1872), 2:52.

24. *Era* (December 29, 1850).

25. Ibid.

26. *Illustrated London News* (April 26, 1851).

27. *Era* (April 27, 1851).

28. Planché, *Extravaganzas* 4:171–72.

29. *Era* (December 28, 1851).

30. George Rowell, *Queen Victoria Goes to the Theatre* (London: Paul Elek, 1978), 75.

31. Planché, *Extravaganzas* 4:213.

32. *Era* (January 2, 1853).

33. Ibid.

34. *New Monthly Belle Assemblée* 16 (May 1842).

35. Busybody, "Enthusiasts Interviewed," *Times* (March 1, 1885).
36. Ibid.
37. Percy Fitzgerald, *The World behind the Scenes* (London: Chatto & Windus, 1881), 256. The paint room at Covent Garden, 70 feet long and 50 feet high, had been built according to Beverley's specifications.
38. *New Monthly Magazine* 86 (1849): 122.

Chapter 3

1. Arnold Hauser, *A Social History of Art*, 5 vols. (New York: Vintage Books, 1951), 3:168.
2. William Shakespeare, *Richard II* (London: John K. Chapman, 1857), acting edition with preface and historical notes by C. Kean.
3. Ibid.
4. *Times* (May 21, 1855).
5. George C. D. Odell, *Annals of the New York Stage*, 5 vols. (New York: Columbia University Press, 1928), 5:173–77.
6. John William Cole, *The Life and Theatrical Times of Charles Kean*, 2 vols. (London: Richard Bentley, 1859), 2:26.
7. *Times* (February 10, 1852).
8. *Leader* (February 14, 1852).
9. *Illustrated London News* (October 23, 1858).
10. Cole, *Charles Kean* 2:52.
11. William Shakespeare, *Macbeth* (London: John K. Chapman, 1853), acting edition with preface and historical notes by C. Kean.
12. *Illustrated London News* (February 19, 1853).
13. *Times* (February 15, 1853).
14. Ibid.
15. Cole, *Charles Kean* 2:57. Layard's discoveries did for Assyria what Howard Carter's did for Egypt in the 1920s: they rendered the ancient cultures an object of interest not only to scholars but also to the general public. In both cases the artifacts found in the excavations influenced fashion. As the reviewer of *Sardanapalus* stated in the June 14 issue of the *Times*, the objects were "all the rage even with the softer sex." The newspaper added, "The fashion of the Royal Crown of Niniveh is as familiar as the pattern of the last new Parisian bonnet."
16. Cole, *Charles Kean* 2:57.
17. *Lloyd's Weekly Newspaper* (June 12, 1853). The *Times* remarked, "*Sardanapalus* in itself has no great powers of attraction, but it is an admirable peg where on to hang those Assyrian antiquities of which Lord Byron never dreamed" (June 14, 1853).
18. Cole, *Charles Kean* 2:101.
19. *Illustrated London News* (February 25, 1854).
20. The panorama began at the Palace of Bridwell and continued with views of Fleet Ditch, Blackfriars, St. Paul's, London Bridge, the Tower, Limehouse, and the celebrated man-of-war the *Great Harry*; it ended at Greenwich, where the infant princess had been christened on September 10, 1533.
21. *Illustrated London News* (May 19, 1855).
22. Godfrey Turner, "Show and Its Value," *Theatre* 3 (May 1884): 231–32.

23. Ibid.

24. *Illustrated London News* (May 19, 1855).

25. *Art Journal* 1 (1855): 240.

26. William Shakespeare, *Winter's Tale* (London: John K. Chapman, 1856), acting edition with preface and historical notes by C. Kean.

27. Ibid.

28. Not only Kean, but the critics as well, showed a complusion to educate the public with scholarly tidbits. *The Era*, in its May 4, 1856, issue, remarked: "There is some doubt whether the 'Pyrricha' was not originally a feigned combat on horseback or cavalry exercise, but we have the authority of Xenophon for describing it as a dance introduced into Greece by the noble Pyrrhus, the son of Achilles, in which the dancers were armed, and exhibited to the sound of the flute all the evolutions of military discipline. This, of course, is the view adopted at the Princess's, and a most exciting and animated spectacle is the result."

29. Cole, *Charles Kean* 2:172.

30. *Illustrated London News* (May 3, 1856). This comment is contrary to Kean's intentions expressed in the flyleaf, where he declared his hope that the introduction of painting, music, and architecture would "be considered less an exhibition of pageantry appealing to the eye, than the illustration of history addressed to the understanding."

31. *Era* (May 4, 1856).

32. Cole, *Charles Kean* 2:188.

33. William Shakespeare, *A Midsummer Night's Dream* (London: John K. Chapman, 1856), acting edition with preface and historical notes by C. Kean. It is interesting to note that both for *The Winter's Tale* and for *A Midsummer Night's Dream*, Kean chose a period in the history of Syracuse and Athens when both cities were at the zenith of their glory; this fact would suggest that perhaps, in a rather subliminal fashion, the actor was indulging in a subtle form of Victorian propaganda by equating the ancient lands with contemporary England.

34. *Illustrated London News* (May 3, 1856).

35. Robert Thorne, in his article "The Princess's Theatre, Oxford Street," *Theatrephile* vol. 2, no. 8 (1987), indicates that at the time of its opening, in September 1840, the new playhouse was thought to be "somewhere between the English Opera House and the Haymarket" in size. Both Cole and critics often remarked that the small size of the stage made Kean's direction of crowd scenes even more admirable. The theatre could seat 1,500. When Kean leased the Princess's, Greive and Telbin built their own scene-painting shop on Macklin Street, Covent Garden, but the manager added a scene room in 1851 and a painting room in 1853. In 1857, Kean proceeded with interior renovations; he commissioned Charles Kuckuck, "decorator to the King of Hanover," to paint medallions in the front of the boxes illustrating his Shakespearean revivals, while in the panels between the boxes were added full-length portraits of the English kings from the dramatist's history plays. As their contribution to the renovations, Greive and Telbin painted a new curtain, "with a statue of Shakespeare partially shown by an opening in crimson tapestry." The Royal Princess's Theatre was demolished on Friday, June 12, 1931.

36. *Art Journal* 3 (1857): 256. Several reviews also commented on the realistic playing of the crowd. "It seems a real mob—nay, a real people," said the *Times* (March 16), while *The Era* (March 15) stated, "We no longer look on actors."

37. Flyleaf attached to the playbill of *The Tempest*.

38. Frederick J. Marker, "The First Night of Charles Kean's *The Tempest*—From the Notebook of Hans Christian Andersen," *Theatre Notebook* 25 (Autumn 1970): 20–23. Marker cities Herman Charles Merivale's *Bar, Stage, and Platform* (1902) to clarify the flying effect: "Ariel and the angels float in the apparent air by a mechanical contrivance all his [Kean's] own. Kneeling on a solid perch hidden by gauze in the back, which glided up and down a groove, and was covered by long trains or petticoats, they were a puzzle always to the audience."

39. Ibid.

40. Ibid.

41. Shakespeare, *King Lear* (London: John K. Chapman, 1858), acting edition with preface and historical notes by C. Kean.

42. Cole, *Charles Kean* 2:333.

43. *Illustrated London News* (April 2, 1859).

44. *Times* (March 31, 1859).

45. "Termination of Mr. Charles Kean's Management," *Theatrical Journal* (August 31, 1859), 276–77.

46. Marker, "The First Night," 23.

47. See Muriel St. Clare Byrne, "Charles K ean and the Meiningen Myth," *Theatre Research* 6, no. 3 (1964): 137–53, for Kean's innovations in stage practice two decades before the Duke of Saxe-Meiningen's company toured Europe.

48. *Saturday Review* (September 17, 1859).

Chapter 4

1. Squire Bancroft and Marie Bancroft, *Mr. and Mrs. Bancroft, on and off the Stage*. 2 vols. (London: Richard Bentley, 1888): 1:203.

2. Ibid. 1:398. Mme. Vestris had also set a precedent with her careful production of *The School for Scandal* at Covent Garden in 1839. The *John Bull* critic remarked, "Each appartment is elegant and substantial, not merely in accordance with the station of the occupier; but in what may be presumed to have been his or her taste" (October 13, 1839).

3. Edward Craig, "E. W. Godwin and the Theatre," *Theatre Notebook* 31, no. 2 (1977): 30.

4. Kathleen M. D. Barker, "The Terrys and Godwin in Bristol," *Theatre Notebook* 8, no. 22 (1967): 34.

5. *Bristol Western Daily Press* (October 5, 1864), cited by Kathleen Barker in "The Terrys and Godwin in Bristol," 40.

6. *Mask* 1, no. 7 (September 1908): 129. Godwin's articles, "The Architecture and Costumes of Shakespeare's Plays," were reprinted by his son, Edward Gordon Craig, in *The Mask* between August 1908 and April 1912.

7. E. W. Godwin, "Henry V: An Archaeological Experience," *Architect* (September 9, 1876), 142.

8. E. W. Godwin, "The Merchant of Venice," *Architect* (March 27, 1875), 182–84.

9. *Building News* (April 23, 1875), 471. For the controversy that surrounds Godwin's contributions to *The Merchant of Venice*, see William E. Kleb, "E. W. Godwin and the Bancrofts," *Theatre Notebook* 30, no. 3 (1976): 122–32. Although Kleb dismisses the theatrical "tradition" of attributing to Godwin any influence in that

production as the misguided efforts of Gordon Craig and others, Godwin himself wrote: "I had already seen my suggestion, as to the real size of architecture being employed on stage, carried out by Messrs. Gordon and Hardford in the first scene of *Merchant of Venice*. ... For even within the narrow limits of the old Prince of Wales's stage *we* [italics added] managed to build two arches of the lower arcade of the ducal palace" (*Dramatic Review* [February 22, 1885], 53).

10. *Mask* 1, nos. 3 & 4 (May-June 1908): 75.

11. Ellen Terry, *The Story of My Life* (London: Hutchinson & Co., 1908), 106.

12. Program of *The Merchant of Venice*, Godwin Collection, Theatre Museum, London.

13. E. W. Godwin, "*Henry V*: A Theatrical Experience," *Architect* (September 30, 1876), 192–94.

14. Letter from E. W. Godwin to John Coleman, September 1876, Godwin Collection, Theatre Museum, London.

15. E. W. Godwin, "Archaeology on the Stage," *Dramatic Review* (February 22, 1885).

16. *Dramatic Review* (March 28, 1885).

17. John Coleman, "On Stage Management," *Dramatic Review* (March 14, 1885).

18. E. W. Godwin, "Archaeology on the Stage," *The Dramatic Review* (February 8, 1885), 19.

19. James Thomas, *The Art of the Actor-Manager: Wilson Barrett and the Victorian Stage* (Ann Arbor: UMI Research Press, 1984), 12.

20. *Era* (October 11, 1884).

21. E. W. Godwin's copy of the program, Godwin Collection, Theatre Museum, London. Godwin annotated the program with his rating of the scenery: "1 & 2 good, 3 poor, 4 fair."

22. W. G. Wills, *Juana* (London: Ballantyne Press, 1881), printed for private circulation only. Copy in Godwin Collection, Theatre Museum, London.

23. Letter from Godwin to Barrett with pen-and-ink sketches, November 1883, Godwin Collection, Theatre Museum, London.

24. Ibid. The letter included a very detailed list of the sources Godwin consulted. It was published as a pamphlet, together with the pen-and-ink drawings, under the title "A few notes on the Architecture and Costumes of *Claudian*" and was also reprinted in *Architect* (December 7, 1883), 268–70.

25. *Times* (December 7, 1883). In his article "The Stage as a School of Art and Archaeology," Henry Herman quotes a letter from the famous art critic John Ruskin to Wilson Barrett, dated February 16, 1884, as saying: "With scenic painting like this, the Princess's Theatre might do more for art-teaching than all the galleries and professors of Christendom" (*Magazine of Art* [1888]: 332–37).

26. *British Architect* (December 14, 1883), 277.

27. *Daily News* (December 7, 1883).

28. *British Architect* (June 17, 1881), 303.

29. *Times* (January 4, 1884).

30. *Modern Society* (December 15, 1883), 47. William Beverley, the scenic artist, found the earthquake in *Claudian* only fair. He could remember a better one in a play titled *The Earthquake* at the Adelphi, where the whole stage was cut away and made into a giant trap. The scenery broke and tumbled, sinking into the trap with all the people on it. *Sunday Times*, March 1, 1885, 2.

31. "*Hamlet* at the Princess's: An Interview with E. W. Godwin, F.S.A.," *Life*

(October 16, 1884), 312. In the article on *Hamlet* (*Architect*, October 31, 1874), God-win declared that Shakespeare, "could he be consulted on the subject," would have certainly wanted to "present through his play *the history* in all the perfection of truth-ful accessories and surroundings," because the playwright had paid so much attention to actual historical facts in the early eleventh century.

32. Ibid.

33. Ibid.

34. *Times* (October 17, 1884). In his interview with *Life* magazine, Godwin had stated that King Claudius would be "a really gorgeous attraction," although perhaps licentious and a "murderous" figure so that there would be "some apparent excuse for Gertrude's rapid second nuptials."

35. *Life* (October 16, 1884).

36. *Times* (October 17, 1884).

37. *Topical Times* (October 18, 1884).

38. *Chronicle* (October 17, 1884).

39. Godwin's copy of the opening-night program, Godwin Collection, Theatre Museum, London.

40. *Athenaeum* (October 18, 1884), 505.

41. Godwin Collection, Theatre Museum, London. The *Morning Post* (October 17, 1884) had similar reservations in its review: "A deeper tone and more solemn speech are requisite in the case of the Ghost."

42. Unidentified newspaper clipping, Godwin Collection, Theatre Museum, London.

43. *Dramatic Review* (February 22, 1885).

44. "Greek Plays in London," *Stage* (May 14, 1886), 16.

45. *Times* (January 3, 1845).

46. Oscar Wilde, *Essays, Criticisms, and Reviews* (London: Privately printed, 1901), 69.

47. *Dramatic Review* (May 22, 1886).

48. Ibid.

49. *Daily News* (December 7, 1883).

50. *Illustrated London News* (May 22, 1886).

51. Barzun, *Classic, Romantic, and Modern*, 58–60.

52. Godwin, "Archaeology on the Stage" (February 8, 1885).

53. Ibid.

54. E. W. Godwin, "Archaeology on the Stage," *Dramatic Review* (October 10, 1885).

55. John Semar, "A Note on the Work of E. W. Godwin," *Mask* 3 (1910–11): 53–56. Gordon Craig often used names he invented for himself (e.g., John Semar) to sign his writings.

Chapter 5

1. Laurence Irving, *Henry Irving: The Actor and His World* (London: Faber & Faber, 1951), 221.

2. *Pall Mall Gazette* (September 13, 1886).

3. Indeed, some vestiges of the famed management were discovered when the theatre underwent renovations in 1878. As the ceiling was being stripped, ornate imi-tation lacework, painted on a pink background, was revealed. The veteran actor Walter

Lacy, present at the time of this discovery, exclaimed: "This is a portion of the work done to please Madame Vestris! Why! My boy, the whole place was hung with imitation lace; it was a fairy-like oriental ecstasy!" Alfred Darbyshire, *The Art of the Victorian Stage* (1907; reprint; New York: Benjamin Blom, 1969), 96.

4. Cited by Alan Hughes in *Henry Irving, Shakespearean* (Cambridge: University Press, 1981), 8.

5. George Rowell, *Theatre in the Age of Irving* (Totowa, N.J.: Rowman and Littlefield, 1981), 2.

6. Darbyshire, *Victorian Stage*, 105.

7. *Theatre* (April 1, 1882), 231.

8. *Pall Mall Gazette* (September 13, 1886).

9. Bram Stoker, "Irving and Stage Lighting," *Nineteenth Century and After* 69 (May 1911): 903–12. See also Alan Hughes, "Henry Irving's Artistic Use of Stage Lighting," *Theatre Notebook* 33, no. 3 (1979): 100–109.

10. "Theatrical Mechanisms at the Lyceum Theatre," *Engineer* (April 2, 1886), 260.

11. Irving, *Henry Irving*, 466.

12. Ibid., 467. "Lycopodic brimstone" refers to the higly inflamable vegetable sulfur contained in the spore cases of *Lycopodium*, especially *L. Clavatum* and *L. Selago*, used to achieve fire and smoke onstage.

13. "Theatrical Mechanisms," 260. On opening night, George Alexander, who played Valentine, was almost electrocuted by the 90-volt intermittent current this contraption generated when he inadvertently touched a portion of uninsulated sword hilt, but he survived the experience and later became a famous actor-manager.

14. *Era* (December 26, 1885).

15. *Stage* (December 25, 1885).

16. *Era* (December 26, 1885).

17. Bram Stoker, *Personal Reminiscences of Henry Irving*, 2 vols. (Westport, Conn.: Greenwood Press, 1970) 1:184. For a complete reconstruction of Irving's *Faust*, see Michael R. Booth *Victorian Spectacular Theatre, 1850–1910* (London: Routledge & Keagan Paul, 1981), 93–126.

18. From reviews in *Stage* (January 4, 1889) and *Era* (January 5, 1889).

19. Cited by Irving, *Henry Irving*, 504.

20. "Mr. Irving on the English Stage," *Daily Telegraph* (November 29, 1888).

21. *Daily Telegraph* (January 6, 1892).

22. *Echo* (November 11, 1892).

23. G. B. Burgin, "The Lyceum Rehearsals," *Idler* (1893), 123–41.

24. *Era* (February 11, 1892).

25. Irving, *Henry Irving*, 567.

26. Joseph Harker, *Studio and Stage* (London: Nisbet & Co., 1924), 97.

27. *Era* (September 26, 1896).

28. *Stage* (September 24, 1896).

29. Irving, *Henry Irving*, 624–26.

30. William Gaunt, *Victorian Olympus* (London: Jonathan Cape, 1952), 173, tells a story attributed to a Lyceum stagehand. Since the production was billed as presented by *Sir* Henry Irving, with incidental music by *Sir* Alexander Mackenzie, and scenes designed by *Sir* Lawrence Alma-Tadema, the technician declared, "Three blooming knights, and that's about as long as it'll run!"

31. "Rome in the Theatre: A Talk with Sir Lawrence Alma-Tadema," *Daily News* (April 16, 1901).

32. Ibid.

33. Sybil Rosenfeld, *Alma-Tadema's Designs for Henry Irving's Coriolanus* (Heidelberg: Quelle & Meyer, 1974), 87. I am very grateful for Miss Rosenfeld's help, particularly for her present to me of her last copy of this article.

34. *Stage* (April 18, 1901).

35. William Archer, *Henry Irving: Actor and Manager* (London: Field & Tuer, 1883), 96–98.

Chapter 6

1. *Times* (September 9, 1916).

2. Irving, *Henry Irving*, 482.

3. Herbert Beerbohm Tree, "The Staging of Shakespeare: A Defense of the Public Taste," *Fortnightly Review*, n.s., 68 (July 1900): 52–65.

4. G. B. Shaw, "Tree's Production of *Julius Caesar*," *Saturday Review* (January 29, 1898).

5. Max Beerbohm, *Herbert Beerbohm Tree* [1920], 2d ed. (New York: Benjamin Bloom, 1969), 108.

6. *Stage* (January 18, 1900).

7. *Stage* (February 6, 1902).

8. *Era* (September 12, 1903).

9. *Era* (September 17, 1904).

10. Tree, "The Staging of Shakespeare," 61.

11. *Stage* (September 7, 1911).

Chapter 7

1. *Apology for the Life of George Anne Bellamy*, quoted by Diana de Marly, *Costume on the Stage, 1600–1940* (London: B. T. Batsford, 1982), 33.

2. Cole, *Charles Kean* 1:107.

3. Archives of the Royal Opera House Covent Garden.

4. *Album* 3, no. 4 (August 1823): 298–304.

5. Ibid.

6. E. W. Godwin, "The Cyclopaedia of Costume," *Architect* (October 16, 1875), 208.

7. William A. Armstrong, "Madama Vestris: A Centenary Appreciation," *Theatre Notebook* 2 (1956): 11–19.

8. Ibid.

9. Planché, *Recollections and Reflections* 1:79–80.

10. Westland Marston, *Our Recent Actors*, 2 vols. (London: Sampson & Low, 1888), 2:142.

11. Odell, *Shakespeare from Betterton to Irving* 2:225.

12. Quoted by Charles E. Pearce, *Madame Vestris and Her Times* (London: Stanley Paul & Co., 1923), 258.

13. *New Monthly Belle Assemblée* (May 1842), 16.

14. *Era* (January 2, 1847).

15. *Era* (December 31, 1848).

16. *Times* (April 10, 1849).

17. Henry Turner, "Random Recollections," *Theatre* (November 1, 1885), 263.

18. Planché, *Extravaganzas* 4:327.

19. William Shakespeare, *Henry VIII* (London: John K. Chapman, 1853), acting edition with preface and historical notes by C. Kean.

20. Letter from C. Kean to Mr. Baldwin, February 4, 1852, Folger Shakespeare Library, Y.c. 332 (1).

21. *Queen Victoria's Journal*, RA (QVJ), February 6, 1852, Royal Archives, Windsor Castle. Quotation by gracious permission of Her Majesty Queen Elizabeth II.

22. William Shakespeare, *Macbeth* (London: John K. Chapman, 1853), acting edition with preface and historical notes by C. Kean. Not all critics were enthusiastic about Kean's contributions to their eduction. G. H. Lewes ridiculed the display of erudition: "[Kean] talks familiarly of Diodorus Siculus, Pliny, Strabo, Xiphlin, and the Eyrbyggia Saga. Xiphlin! He read Xiphlin! What a name to fling to the pit!" *Leader* (February 19, 1853).

23. C. Kean promptbooks, *Macbeth*, Princess's Theatre, 1853, Folger Shakespeare Library.

24. *Art Journal* 5 (1853): 228. *Era* (June 19, 1853) mentioned Sardanapalus, in his gold-fringed robe, with all his earrings and bracelets around his biceps and wrists, as "elegantly and effeminately attired."

25. C. Kean promptbooks, *Richard III*, Princess's Theatre, 1854, Folger Shakespeare Library.

26. William Shakespeare, *King Henry the Eighth* (London: John K. Chapman, 1855), preface to the acting edition.

27. Clara Morris, *Life on the Stage: My Personal Reminiscences and Recollections* (New York: McClure, Phillips, & Co., 1901), 168–69.

28. *Illustrated London News* (May 3, 1856).

29. *Times* (October 16, 1856).

30. *Era* (October 19, 1856).

31. E. W. Godwin, "The Architecture and Costumes of Shakespeare's Plays," *Mask* (July 1908), 91.

32. Godwin, "Architecture and Costumes" (October 1912), 166.

33. Ibid.

34. Godwin, "Architecture and Costumes" (April 1912), 287.

35. Bancroft and Bancroft, *Recollections*, 205.

36. *Times* (April 23, 1875).

37. Godwin, "Henry V," 192–94. This is the first mention I have ever seen that drawings for sets, costumes, and properties were done by a single designer and handed over to technicians and craftsmen for construction.

38. Ibid.

39. Ibid.

40. Wills, *Juana*.

41. *World* (May 4, 1881).

42. *World* (May 11, 1881). After many years of writing articles and letters to the editors disavowing responsibility for the actors' rebellion against his advice, Godwin said: "Now a-days when things promise to go wrong I do not threaten to write to the papers. My work is known fairly well by this time and the blunders of the wilful actress, or the errors of the obstinate actor, never are attributed to me by those to whose

judgment I appeal" (E. W. Godwin, "Archaeology on the Stage, No. VI," *Dramatic Review* [October 10, 1885], 92–93).

43. Prospectus of the Costume Society, Godwin Collection, Theatre Museum, London.

44. Letter from Godwin to L. Fagan, October 2, 1882, Godwin Collection, Theatre Museum, London. When Godwin wrote the review for J. R. Planché's newly published *Cyclopaedia of Costume*, he objected very strongly to the quality of the illustrations in the book, calling them "wretched." They were "bad as woodcuts, bad as drawings, and bad as illustrations of the subject" (*Architect*) [October 16, 1875], 208).

45. *Standard* (September 28, 1882).

46. Manuscript of the Minutes of the Costume Society, Godwin Collection, Theatre Museum, London.

47. Herbert Beerbohm Tree, "The New Costume Society and the Stage," *Theatre* (February 1, 1883), 96–98.

48. Manuscript of the Minutes of the Costume Society, Godwin Collection, Theatre Museum, London.

49. "Dresses in *Claudian*," *Queen, The Lady's Newspaper* (February 23, 1884), 204.

50. Letter from Godwin to Barrett, November 1883, illustrated with pen-and-ink drawings, Godwin Collection, Theatre Museum, London. This letter was published as a pamphlet, to coincide with the production, titled "*Claudian*: A Few Notes on the Architecture and Costume, a Letter to Wilson Barrett, Esq., by E. W. Godwin, Esq., 1883."

51. E. W. Godwin, "A Lecture on Dress," *Mask* (April 1914), 337–52.

52. E. W. Godwin, *Dress and Its Relation to Health and Climate* (London: William Cowes & Sons, 1884), 2.

53. Godwin, "A Lecture on Dress."

54. Quoted by Dudley Harbron, *The Conscious Stone* (London: Latimer House, 1949), 168.

55. "The Pastoral Players," *Daily Telegraph* (June 1, 1885). This review also mentions that the Duke of Saxe-Meiningen, "no mean authority in the art of stage management," attended the performance and congratulated Lady Campbell and Godwin "on what he considered the most original and at the same time the most beautiful of the many tributes to the genius and beauty of Shakespeare and his plays."

56. Ellen Terry, "Stage Decoration," *Windsor Magazine* 35 (December 1911–May 1912): 74.

57. Alice Comyns Carr, *Mrs. Comyns Carr: Personal Reminiscences* (London: Hutchinson & Co, 1925), 80. It is quite possible that Ellen Terry's predilection for that crinkly frock was caused by fond memories of a costume that Godwin had designed for her in her youth, for her first appearance as Titania. She mentioned in her memoirs that the dress, made to look like primitive pleating also by twisting and boiling the fabric, was the "first lovely one she ever wore."

58. Joseph Pennell and Elizabeth Pennell, "Pictorial Successes of Mr. Irving's 'Faust,'" *Century Magazine* 35 (December 1887): 309–12.

59. Comyns Carr, *Reminiscences*, 299.

60. Ibid., 213.

61. *Morning Advertiser* (January 6, 1892).

62. "The Costumes in 'King Arthur,'" *Sketch* (January 25, 1895).

63. Ibid.

64. Bram Stoker, *Personal Reminiscences of Henry Irving* (London: William Heineman, 1907), 165.

65. See reviews in *Era* (April 20), *Daily News* (April 16), *Stage* (April 18), and *Westminster Gazette* (April 15, 1901). A letter from Alma-Tadema to Irving in the Theatre Museum, dated April 26, 1901, scolds the actor for the color of his wreath: "The oak wreath you wear in the triumphal scene is too grass green. Oak leaves are not that colour." Costumes had become important enough in the early twentieth century to justify giving credit to everybody responsible for them. The wardrobe had been designed by Karl, based on Alma-Tadema drawings, and executed by Mrs. Nettleship, E. Terry's costumier, and the costume house was run by L. And H. Nathan.

66. Terry, "Stage Decoration," 90.

67. Percy Anderson, "Costume on the Stage," *Magazine of Art* (1894), 7–12. There is no mention in this article of the name of the opera or the composer.

68. *Times* (October 4, 1888).

69. H. B. Tree, "The New Costume Society and the Stage," *Theatre* (October 1, 1883), 97.

70. *Stage* (January 18, 1900).

71. Anderson, "Costume on the Stage," 7.

72. *Athenaeum* (January 21, 1900), 91–92. For additional reviews see *Times* (January 11), *Era* (January 13), *Stage* (January 18), and *Saturday Review* (January 20).

73. *Stage* (November 8, 1900).

74. Ibid.

75. Gladys Beattie Crozier, "Mr. Percy Anderson: Costume Designer," *Magazine of Art*, n.s., 1 (1903): 280–86.

76. *Stage* (October 31, 1901).

77. Crozier, "Mr. Percy Anderson," 283.

78. *Illustrated London News* (February 8, 1902), 194.

79. *Stage* (September 17, 1903).

80. *Era* (September 12, 1903).

81. *Era* (September 17, 1904).

82. Anderson designed *Becky Sharp* and *Mary of Magdala* for Fiske's management, plus *Quality Street* and *Two Gentlemen of Verona* for Frohman, in addition to three Shakespearean revivals for Augustin Daly. However, since costume designers were not yet given credit for their work in the American theatre, either in programs or in reviews, his name does not appear anywhere. The costumes for those productions were invariably praised, but there is no mention of the artist responsible for them.

83. *World* (July 4, 1911).

84. *Stage* (September 7, 1911).

85. *Era* (December 23, 1911).

86. *World* (December 26, 1911).

87. *Times* (September 1, 1916).

88. *Stage* (September 7, 1916).

Appendix A

1. W. J. Lawrence, "Some Famous Scene Painters," *Magazine of Art* (1889), 41–45.

2. Fitzgerald, *World behind the Scenes* , 41.

3. Comyns Carr, *Reminiscences*, 205–6.

4. G. Sheridan Le Fanu, "Scenic Effect," *Dramatic Review* (April 18, 1885), 182.

5. Robert Thorne, "Thomas Grieve's Scene-painting Shop," *Theatrephile* 1, no. 2 (March 1984): 34. At the time this article was written, negotiations were taking place between the owner and local authorities to restore and preserve the building. William Telbin considered that very few of the recently built theatres had "painting-rooms that anyone who value[d] health and sight would care to paint in." Only the older houses— Covent Garden, Drury Lane, and Her Majesty's—had good spaces to practice his craft. Covent Garden's shop was 90 feet long, 30 feet wide, and 55 feet high, with four stretching frames, the largest of which was 42 feet by 70 feet. "The Painting of Scenery," *Magazine of Art* 12 (1889): 195–201.

6. Frederick Lloyds, *Practical Guide to Scene Painting and Painting in Distemper* (London: N.P., 1875), 71–79.

7. Ibid., 79–83.

8. W. J. Lawrence, "Some Stage Effects: Their Growth and History," *Gentleman's Magazine* 265 (July-December 1888): 94.

9. Percy Fitzgerald, "On Scenic Illusion and Stage Appliances," *Journal of the Society of Arts* 35 (March 18, 1887): 456–63.

10. David Anderson, "Forgotten Theatre Machinery: The Corsican Effect or Ghost Glide," *Theatrephile* 1, no. 4 (September 1984): 76.

11. William Telbin, "Art in the Theatre," *Magazine of Art* 12 (1889): 96.

Select Bibliography

Appleton, William. *Mme. Vestris and the London Stage.* New York: Columbia University Press, 1974.

Archer, William. *Henry Irving: Actor and Manager.* London: Field and Tuer, 1883.

Aria, Mrs. *Costume: Fanciful, Historical, and Theatrical.* Illustrated by Percy Anderson. London: Macmillan & Co., 1906.

Bancroft, Squire, and Marie Bancroft. *Mr. and Mrs. Bancroft, on and off the Stage.* 2 vols. London: Richard Bentley, 1888.

_____. *Recollections of Sixty Years.* New York: E. P. Dutton, 1909.

Barzun, Jacques. *Classic, Romantic, and Modern.* Boston: Little, Brown & Co., 1961.

Beerbohm, Max. *Herbert Beerbohm Tree.* 2d ed. New York: Benjamin Bloom, 1969.

Bingham, Madeleine. *Henry Irving: The Greatest Shakespearean Actor.* New York: Stein & Day, 1978.

Boaden, James. *Memoirs of the Life of John Philip Kemble.* 2 vols. London: Longman, 1825.

Booth, Michael R. *Theatre in the Victorian Age.* Cambridge: Cambridge University Press, 1991.

_____. *Victorian Spectacular Theatre, 1850–1910.* London: Routledge & Keagan Paul, 1981.

Bunn, Alfred. *The Stage: Both before and behind the Curtain.* 3 vols. London: R. Bentley, 1840.

Clark, Kenneth. *The Gothic Revival.* 3d ed. London: John Murray, 1962.

_____. *The Romantic Rebellion.* New York: Harper & Row, 1973.

Clinton-Baddeley, V. C. *The Burlesque Tradition in the English Theatre after 1660.* London: Methuen & Co., 1952.

Cole, John William. *The Life and Theatrical Times of Charles Kean.* 2 vols. London: Richard Bentley, 1859.

Coleman, John. *Players and Playwrights I Have Known.* 2 vols. London: Chatto & Windus, 1888.

Comyns Carr, Alice. *Mrs. Comyns Carr: Personal Reminiscences.* London: Hutchinson & Co., 1925.

Cook, Dutton. *Nights at the Play.* 2 vols. London: Chatto & Windus, 1883.

_____. *On the Stage.* 2 vols. London: Sampson Low, 1883.

Craig, Edward Gordon. *Ellen Terry and Her Secret Self.* London: Sampson Low, Marston & Co., 1931.

Craig, Edward T. *Gordon Craig.* New York: Alfred Knopf, 1968.

Daly, Frederick. *Henry Irving in England and America.* London: Unwin, 1884.

Darbyshire, Alfred. *The Art of the Victorian Stage.* 1907. Reprint. New York: Benjamin Blom, 1969.

De Marly, Diana. *Costume on the Stage, 1600–1940.* London: B. T. Batsford, 1982.

Donaldson, Francis. *The Actor-Managers.* Chicago: Henry Regnery, 1970.

Driver, Tom F. *Romantic Quest and Modern Query.* New York: Dell Publishing Co., 1970.

Fitzgerald, Percy. *Henry Irving: A Record of Twenty Years at the Lyceum.* London: Chatto & Windus, 1895.

_____. *Sir Henry Irving: A Biography.* London: T. Fisher Unwin, 1906.

_____. *The World behind the Scenes.* London: Chatto & Windus, 1881.

Forbes-Robertson, Sir Johnston. *A Player under Three Reigns.* Boston: Little Brown & Co., 1925.

Foulkes, Richard, ed. *Shakespeare and the Victorian Stage.* Cambridge: Cambridge University Press, 1986.

Gaunt, William. *Victorian Olympus.* London: Jonathan Cape, 1952.

Harbron, Dudley. *The Conscious Stone.* London: Latimer House, 1949.

Harker, Joseph. *Studio and Stage.* London: Nisbet & Co., 1924.

Hauser, Arnold. *A Social History of Art.* 5 vols. New York: Vintage Books, 1951.

Hazelton, Nancy J. Doran. *Historical Consciousness in Nineteenth-Century Shakespearean Staging.* Ann Arbor: UMI Research Press, 1987.

Hudson, Lynton. *The English Stage, 1850–1950.* London: Harrap, 1951.

Hughes, Alan. *Henry Irving, Shakespearean.* Cambridge: University Press, 1981.

Irving, Laurence. *Henry Irving: The Actor and His World.* London: Faber & Faber, 1951.

Jackson, Holbrook. *The Eighteen-Nineties: A Review of Art and Ideas at the Close of the Nineteenth Century.* London: Grant Richards, 1922.

Joplin, Louise. *Twenty Years of My Life, 1867–87.* London: John Lane the Bodly Head, 1925.

Knight, G. Wilson. *Shakespearean Production.* London: Faber & Faber, 1964.

Knight, John. *The History of the English Stage during the Reign of Victoria.* London: N.P., 1901.

Laver, James. *Costume in the Theatre.* New York: Hill & Wang, 1964.

_____. *Drama: Its Costume and Decor.* London: Studio Publications, 1951.

Lawrence, W. J. "Contributions towards the History of Scene Painting, together with the Lives of the Most Eminent Scenic Artists." Manuscript in the University of Bristol Theatre Library. 11 vols. 1887–1908.

_____. *Old Theatre Days and Ways.* 2d ed. New York: Benjamin Bloom, 1968.

Lloyds, Frederick. *Practical Guide to Scene Painting and Painting in Distemper.* London: N.P., 1875.

Manvell, Roger. *Ellen Terry.* New York: G. P. Putnam, 1968.

Mathews, Charles. *The Life of Charles Mathews.* Edited by Charles Dickens. 2 vols. London: Macmillan, 1879.

Merchant, William. *Shakespeare and the Artist.* London: Oxford University Press, 1959.

Morley, Henry. *Journal of a London Playgoer from 1851 to 1866.* London: G. Routledge & Sons, 1866.

Morris, Clara. *Life on the Stage: My Personal Reminiscences and Recollections.* New York: McClure, Phillips, & Co., 1901.

Newton, Stella Mary. *Health, Art, and Reason, Dress Reformers of the Nineteenth Century.* London: John Murray, 1974.

Odell, George C. D. *Annals of the New York Stage.* 5 vols. New York: Columbia University Press, 1928.

_____. *Shakespeare from Betterton to Irving.* 2 vols. London: Constable & Co., 1921.

Pearce, Charles E. *Madame Vestris and Her Times.* London: Stanley Paul & Co., 1923.

Pearson, Hesketh. *Beerbohm Tree.* 2d ed. London: Columbus Books, 1988.

Planché. James Robinson. *The Extravaganzas of J. R. Planché, Esq.* 5 vols. Ed. T. F. D. Croker and S. Tucker. London: Samuel French, 1874.

_____. *The Recollections and Reflections of J. R. Planché.* 2 vols. London: Tinsley Brothers, 1872.

Poel, William. *Shakespeare in the Theatre.* London: Sidgwick & Jackson, 1913.

Prideaux, Tom. *Love or Nothing: The Life and Times of Ellen Terry.* New York: Charles Scribner, 1975.

Ranger, Paul. *Gothic Drama in the London Patent Theatres, 1750–1820.* London: Society for Theatre Research, 1991.

Rose, Enid. *Gordon Craig and the Theatre.* London: Sampson Low, Marston & Co., 1931.

Rosenfeld, Sybil. *A Short History of Scene Design in Great Britain.* Totowa, N.J.: Rowman & Littlefield, 1973.

Rowell, George. *Queen Victoria Goes to the Theatre.* London: Paul Eleck, 1978.

_____. *Theatre in the Age of Irving.* Totowa, N.J.: Rowman and Littlefield, 1981.

_____. *Victorian Dramatic Criticism.* London: Methuen & Co., 1971.

_____. *The Victorian Theatre.* London: Oxford University Press, 1956.

Salgado, Gamini. *Eyewitnesses of Shakespeare: First-Hand Accounts of Performances, 1590–1890.* New York: Barnes & Noble, 1975.

Scharf, Sir George. *Recollections of the Scenic Effects at Covent Garden, 1838–1839.* London: J. Pattie, 1839.

Shearson, Erroll. *London's Lost Theatres of the Nineteenth Century.* London: John Hane, 1925.

Southern, Richard. *Changeable Scenery.* London: Faber & Faber, 1952.

_____. *The Seven Ages of the Theatre.* London: Faber & Faber, 1962.

_____. *The Victorian Theatre: A Pictorial Survey.* New York: Theatre Art Books, 1970.

Speaight, Robert. *Shakespeare on the Stage: An Illustrated History.* New York: Little Brown & Co., 1973.

Stoker, Bram. *Personal Reminiscences of Henry Irving.* 2 vols. Westport, Conn.: Greenwood Press, 1970.

Stokes, John. *Resistible Theatres: Enterprise and Experiment in the Late Nineteenth Century.* London: Paul Elek, 1972.

Thomas, James. *The Art of the Actor-Manager: Wilson Barrett and the Victorian Theatre.* Ann Arbor: UMI Research Press, 1984.

Vandenhoff, George. *Dramatic Reminiscences.* London: Thomas W. Cooper, 1860.

_____. *Leaves from an Actor's Note-Book.* London: L. D. Appleton & Co., 1860.

Waitzkin, Leo. *The Witch of Wynch Street.* Cambridge: Harvard University Press, 1933.

Watkinson, Raymond. *Pre-Raphaelite Art and Design.* 2d ed. London: Trefoil Publications, 1990.

Watson, Earnest. *Sheridan to Robertson: A Study of the Nineteenth-Century London Stage.* Cambridge: Harvard University Press, 1926.

William, Michael. *Some London Theatres Past and Present.* London: Sampson Low, 1883.

Wilson, Albert Edward. *The Lyceum.* London: Denis Yates, 1952.

Woodfield, James. *English Theatre in Transition, 1881–1914.* London: Croom Helm, 1984.

Wyndham, Henry S. *Annals of the Covent Garden Theatre.* 2 vols. London: Chatto & Windus, 1906.

Periodicals

Art Journal

Athenaeum

British Architect

Daily News

Daily Telegraph

Dramatic Review

Era

Graphic

Illustrated London News

Illustrated Sporting and Dramatic News

London Times

Magazine of Art

Mask

Morning Advertiser

New Monthly Belle Assemblée

Queen

Saturday Review

Stage

Theatre

Theatrical Journal

Westminster Gazette

World

Index